Interview Puzzles Dissected

Solving and Understanding
Interview Puzzles

Rod Stephens

Interview Puzzles Dissected, Solving and Understanding Interview Puzzles
Published by Rod Stephens, `RodStephens@CSharpHelper.com`
Copyright © 2016–2017 by Rod Stephens
All rights reserved

About the Author

In a previous life, **Rod Stephens** studied mathematics, but during his stay at MIT he discovered the joys of computer algorithms and he hasn't looked back. Since then he's worked on an eclectic assortment of applications in such diverse fields as automated repair dispatching, billing, telephone switch programming, fuel tax collections, scientific visualization, wastewater treatment, concert ticket sales, cartography, optometry, and coaching tools for professional football players. His favorite topics remain algorithms and graphics.

Rod has been a Microsoft Most Valuable Professional (MVP) for more than 13 years. He consults (email him if you want help with an interesting application), maintains his web sites, and occasionally speaks at users' group meetings and conferences.

He has written more than 30 books, some of which have been translated into languages from all over the world, and more than 250 magazine articles. He's even created a few video training courses.

Rod's popular *C# Helper* website www.csharphelper.com contains thousands of example programs that demonstrate tips, tricks, and useful techniques for C# programmers. His *VB Helper* website www.vb-helper.com provides similar material for Visual Basic developers.

You can contact Rod (particularly if you want help on an interesting project) at RodStephens@CSharpHelper.com.

Credits

The pictures used in this book are either in the public domain or are available under various Creative Commons licenses. Figure 0–1 lists the authors and locations where you can find the original images. To save space, I've used TinyURL to shorten the full URLs, some of which are remarkably long.

Image	Author	TinyURL
Cards and chips	History Channel	j323s8s
Revolver	Evgenij Rabchuk	jravwzz
Fire ants	Stephen Ausmus	zw4bvm5
Bridge	Shakeelgilgity	zz3yjn9
Glassware	Tweenk	he5l2fh
Balance	Bernd Schwabe	gmko39t
Jail cell	Bmwrider1	htybvnb
Ship	WikiPedant	hnvc3zj
Wine cellar	Le Grand Portage	hthk3kh
Lockheed Model 10a	John Oxley Library	zhtjl7c
Camels	amira_a	hacdnks
Wolf	U.S. Fish & Wildlife Service	jfgyjc9
Swan	Charlesjsharp	jq5d2us
KK100 building	Popolon	jknxofm
Puzzle pieces	Atlasowa	zzhs3dq
Gray Wolf (cover)	U.S. Fish & Wildlife Service	gms29jr
Swan (cover)	Moritz Praetorius	grenffd
Sand dunes (cover)	David Rosen	hhrj3bt

Figure 0–1: Image sources.

The TinyURL addresses have the format `http://tinyurl.com/`*code* where *code* is the value listed in the third column in Figure 0–1.

Go to those URLs to see additional details, in some cases including methods for contacting the image's original authors. Those pages also provide details about each image's licensing. Go to `creativecommons.org/licenses` for general information about Creative Commons licenses.

To use the images in this book I needed to resize and crop them, and to remove their color. I'm happy to send you my versions if you want them, but the originals are much nicer! Visit the URLs shown in Figure 0–1 to get the originals.

Many of the smaller clip art images are from `openclipart.org` or `pixabay.com`. Most of the remaining images are my drawings or photographs.

If you have any questions about specific images, or if you want copies of my modified versions, email me at `RodStephens@CSharpHelper.com`.

Figure 0-2: A gratuitous picture of Himeji Castle in Japan, just because I think it's cool.

Contents

Introduction

Two events made me decide to write this book.

First, while preparing to interview with some big technical companies including Google, a friend of mine read my book *Essential Algorithms: A Practical Approach to Computer Algorithms* (Rod Stephens, John Wiley & Sons, 2013). That book provides an introduction to many useful and interesting algorithms. It also explains how some of those algorithms may apply to interview puzzles, and it provides exercises to help you prepare to use them in interviews.

After reading it, my friend said that the book made it clear that I hated interview puzzles. That's not quite true. I actually enjoy those sorts of challenges. I do, however, think that interview puzzles usually do a poor job of judging your fitness for particular position in a company. Common experience and recent studies have shown that interview puzzles are good at discovering whether a candidate has seen a particular puzzle before, but they aren't good at learning whether a candidate will make a good employee.

The second incident occurred when I was interviewing for a job teaching children how to write Scratch programs after school and at day camps. The interviewer asked the classic "Counterfeit Coin" puzzle.

> *Suppose you have eight coins, one of which is lighter than the others. How can you use a double pan balance to identify the light coin?*

This is probably the most commonly asked interview puzzle in history. (It's explained in Chapter 9.) I had seen it before, so I easily rattled off the correct answer. The interviewer then said, "So you've seen this before?" When I admitted that I had, she told me that she wasn't a technical person, so she hadn't seen it before and she had needed to bash her way through the problem during her interview.

So what did we each learn from this?

I learned that she isn't technical, which is fine because she's a hiring manager and not an engineer.

She learned that I had seen the problem before and that I had remembered the solution, but that's about all she learned. My answer might indicate that I'm the type of person who likes puzzles, but it didn't really indicate that I'm more or less qualified to teach fifth-graders how to use Scratch to write moon lander games. It didn't show that I know how to explain complicated concepts, figure out what's wrong when someone else's code doesn't work, or make programming interesting and fun.

Perhaps more importantly, what would have been learned if I hadn't solved the puzzle? My interviewer would have learned that I hadn't seen the puzzle before, but little else.

The question still served as a reasonable ice-breaker, but that's probably all it did.

The next part of the interview was with an instructor and was much more directly relevant. During that piece I analyzed an existing Scratch program, explained what it did, modified it to do something new, and thought of some modifications for students to make if the initial problem was too easy for them. That part of the interview was much more useful because it showed that I understood at least a little Scratch and that I could think of ways to extend a program that I had not seen before.

What was the purpose of the puzzle part of the interview? I suspect it was there just because the company thought it should be there. Microsoft, Google, Amazon, and other technical giants use these sorts of puzzles (in fact, probably this exact same puzzle) so there must be some benefit to it, right?

All that made me start thinking about whether interview puzzles were completely useless. Was there some way to save them and make them produce some useful information?

I actually think I've found a way. Interview puzzles can be quite useful, but only if they're used correctly.

HOW TO USE INTERVIEW PUZZLES

Probably the most common reason companies use interview puzzles, aside from "Because everyone else is doing it," is to see if a candidate can solve unexpected problems. Ignoring the fact that most jobs only rarely involve unexpected problems, interview puzzles don't do a very good job of measuring this ability in any case. Usually the puzzle is about a topic that's so far removed from the candidate's everyday experience that it's meaningless.

For example, suppose an interviewer asked you, "How would you treat acute glomerulonephritis?" Even assuming the interviewer could pronounce the question correctly (0.5 probability), a typical programming candidate would have a probability of roughly 0.0 of guessing the right answer. (Chapter 2 gives a brief introduction to probability.) Similarly how many job candidates cross rope bridges in the dark on a regular basis? Or use a double pan balance to weigh golden eggs? Or cross the desert with banana–powered camels?

Still, creativity is important in many jobs. When a situation evolves or the rules change, it's useful to be able to adapt. That observation leads to an approach that can make interview puzzles useful.

Rather than springing a puzzle on a candidate and shouting, "Gotcha!" work through the puzzle in two stages. First present a puzzle and give the candidate a minute or two to work through it. If the candidate is getting bogged down, help. The goal here is to get through the basic puzzle as quickly as possible.

After you get through the basic puzzle, ask follow–up questions and work through variations. Ask the candidate what the underlying principle behind the puzzle is. Why does the puzzle work? Why is it surprising or non–intuitive? What happens if you change the puzzle's parameters and conditions? What if you add more people/coins/camels? What techniques can you use to solve the puzzle? If possible, extend the puzzle in ways that you haven't thought of before and work through them together with the candidate.

This approach gives you a lot more information than a puzzle alone does. It lets you learn about whether the candidate can distill an admittedly silly situation to see if there's an underlying structure that may be useful. It tells you whether the candidate can adapt to changing situations and rules. It also gives you an idea about what is probably the most important thing in any interview: Do you think you can work with this person?

WHAT'S IN THIS BOOK

This book describes more than 180 puzzles that you might encounter during a technical interview. If you're an interviewer, you can use them as a basis for a discussion that may help you better understand a job applicant. If you're a job applicant, they can help you learn general techniques for solving interview questions. They can also help you keep your cool under the pressure of an interview.

For each puzzle, the book contains an explanation of the puzzle and the puzzle's solution. It then dissects the puzzle. It pulls the puzzle apart and explains the key concepts that you can use to solve that puzzle and other similar puzzles. If an interviewer asks you to identify rotten eggs by using double a pan balance or to calculate Russian roulette probabilities, you'll be able to do it even if you haven't seen the exact same puzzle before.

The book also includes dozens of variations and follow–up questions that you can use to further explore the puzzles. Some of the puzzles build on each other, so you can use them to form a thoughtful line of discussion.

Finally the book includes programming exercises. Some of these could be used as programming challenges during an interview. Many of them, however, are too involved to reasonably solve during an interview. They are included so you can experiment with them on your own to gain a deeper understanding of the puzzles. Besides, many of them are interesting and even fun.

Of course the programming challenges don't apply to you if you're not a programming type. For example, the hiring manager who asked me the "Counterfeit Coin" puzzle would gain nothing from the programming exercises. If that's not your thing, just skip them.

WHO THIS BOOK IS FOR

This book is designed for three main audiences: job seekers, interviewers, and people who just enjoy these sorts of puzzles.

The first audience includes people who are preparing to apply for a technical job. If you're part of this audience, this book will prepare you to solve, or at least try to solve, the puzzles that you may encounter during interviews. Even if you're asked a particular puzzle that isn't described in this book, the general analysis and problem–solving techniques described here should help you demonstrate a methodical approach that prospective employers value.

The book's second audience includes those who are preparing to interview job candidates. For this audience the book describes puzzles that can help you understand how a potential employee approaches problem–solving. The book describes puzzles that you can use as a starting point, but even more importantly it explains ways you can elaborate and extend the puzzles to learn how the candidate thinks.

If both the candidate and the interviewer know a bit about puzzles in general, or even about a particular puzzle, they can have a more meaningful interview. The puzzle can provide the candidate with a way to demonstrate logical approaches to problem–solving and the interviewer can look for signs that the candidate can take a logical approach.

A puzzle alone can't determine whether the candidate is the best fit for a particular job, but it can provide one more clue about how the candidate might fit into a new position.

The third audience is self–explanatory. If, like me, you think that this kind of puzzle is fun, this book can help you better understand these puzzles and their variations. The techniques used to solve them will help you solve other, similar puzzles. And who knows? Maybe those techniques can even help you design new puzzles of your own. If you do, post them on the book's web site!

PUZZLE SELECTION

I selected the puzzles described in this book for three reasons.

First and foremost I've included puzzles that you are likely to encounter during a technical interview. These are puzzles that have been used in the past by tech giants such as Apple and Microsoft. Even if those companies no longer use these specific puzzles, other companies sometimes recycle them in their own interviews reasoning, "If it's good enough for them, it's good enough for us."

Second, I've included puzzles that demonstrate useful mathematical and programming concepts. These puzzles let job candidates show that they can recognize and apply those principles in a non–programming context.

Finally, I've included some puzzles just because they're particularly interesting, surprising, or fun. Even if a puzzle doesn't fit into either of the other two categories, it can still be useful for studying a candidate's puzzle–solving approach.

This book doesn't include every possible interview puzzle. There are thousands of such puzzles floating around on the internet. This book does, however, include examples from most of the main categories of common puzzles. If you run across one that isn't in the book, hopefully it'll be similar enough to one of those described here to give you a chance at solving it.

HOW THIS BOOK IS STRUCTURED

Chapter 1, "Basic Background," explains some of the history of interview puzzles so you can understand why companies use them today. It explains some of the motivation for using interview puzzles and how you can get the most out of them as an interviewer or as a job candidate.

Chapter 2, "Probability Primer," provides a brief introduction to simple probability. It explains how you can perform the basic calculations that you need to solve most interview puzzles.

The rest of the book describes the puzzles, their solutions, solving techniques, variations, follow–up questions, and programming exercises. I've grouped the puzzles by their general theme or solving techniques. Many puzzles fall into multiple categories, however, so the categories are more guidelines than hard and fast rules.

GETTING THE MOST OUT OF THE BOOK

To get the most out of a puzzle, you should try to solve it after you read its description and before you move on to the solution, analysis, variations, and follow–up questions. You'll learn a lot more if you work on a problem for a while rather than just jumping to the punchline. Working on the problem will help you know which lines of attack are promising, misleading, or downright frustrating.

If you're a job candidate, knowing which lines of reasoning are useful may help you with other problems. If you're an interviewer, knowing which chains of thought lead to dead ends will help you keep the candidate moving forward so you don't waste precious interview time.

Working on the puzzles before peeking at the solutions is particularly important if you're an interviewer. Many of the puzzles have solutions that seem glaringly obvious in retrospect. If you don't try to solve them, then you won't really have any idea how long it will take a candidate to find the solution. It may take only seconds to read and understand the answer, but it may take an hour to arrive at that answer yourself.

It also may help if you ask a few other people to give a puzzle a try. Just because you found a particular puzzle easy doesn't mean everyone will.

After you've given a puzzle the old college try, read the solution and its analysis. Think about any variations and extensions so you're sure you understand the underlying principles.

Also see if you can think of other solutions, even if they aren't as good as the "correct" solution. Sometimes a "second–best" solution is useful when a slight modification of a problem makes the optimal solution impossible.

INTERVIEWERS

If you're an interviewer, you might find it frustrating that your candidates have read about these puzzles, essentially peeking at the answer sheet. That would be a problem if your goal was to see if a candidate can use first principles to solve obscure puzzles involving pirates, hats, light bulbs, and rope bridges. Fortunately there are few jobs that actually require anyone to do that.

You shouldn't really care whether the candidate can figure out how many days it takes a snail to climb out of a well. (Unless you're trying to hire a malacologist.) Instead you're trying to learn about how the candidate approaches and solves problems. In that case you can learn a lot even if the candidate has seen your puzzle before, but only if you use the correct approach.

Instead of just presenting the puzzle and then listening to the standard answer, follow up by having a discussion about the puzzle. Ask why the solution works. Ask if the candidate can prove that it works. Discuss possible variations and extensions. See if the candidate can generalize the problem so it applies to other domains and problem sizes.

> Being able to generalize problems is a useful programming skill. If you can generalize a programming solution so it handles a larger variety of problems, you may be able to finish your project with less code so write, debug, and maintain.
>
> You need to weigh the benefits of more flexible code with a possible increase in complexity, but it's nice to have a more flexible option available if you need it.

You can only have this more in–depth discussion if the candidate has some knowledge about how the puzzle can be solved. A candidate who comes in without a clue may get stuck, leaving you with little to talk about.

That means having a candidate who's seen the puzzle before may actually be a good thing. In fact, you may want to have a couple of hints ready in case the candidate is completely baffled.

Then, if you've had a nice discussion about problem–solving and you still really want to watch the candidate fumble around with an impossible task, ask an impossible question.

WHAT YOU NEED TO USE THIS BOOK

To read this book and understand the puzzles in this book, you don't need any special equipment. In an interview you probably won't have access to a computer, the internet, a calculator, or any other special equipment, so it wouldn't make sense for this book to require those kinds of special tools.

For many problems you'll find a pencil and some paper useful, and I highly recommend that you bring those to any interview. You'll want them to take notes anyway, if for no other reason than to prove that you're paying attention.

If you want to dig deeper into some of the puzzles, you may want to experiment with them on a computer. For example, you might want to try writing a program that tries random seating arrangements on an airplane or that calculates the number of paths through a grid of streets. Those programs can verify your calculations, and they may give you a deeper (and probably more relevant) understanding of the problem and its solution.

ESSENTIAL ALGORITHMS

I wrote this book partly as a supplement to my previous book, *Essential Algorithms: A Practical Approach to Computer Algorithms* (Rod Stephens, John Wiley & Sons, 2013). That book explains a variety of useful and interesting algorithms, some of which may appear in interviews as programming challenges.

This book (*Interview Puzzles Dissected*) focuses more on interview puzzles and less on general algorithms. A few of the puzzles relate to programming concepts, but many of them don't. They much more oriented toward interviews or just fun puzzle–solving.

If I were interviewing someone for a programming job, I would much rather that they knew the algorithms in *Essential Algorithms* instead of the puzzles in this book, but I think both of them are pretty fun and interesting. Perhaps that tells you too much about the kinds of things I like to do, but I'm hoping you agree, at least enough to enjoy both books.

CONVENTIONS

To make using this book easier, I've adopted a few conventions. Puzzles begin with a title and one or two icons. The four puzzle piece icon is just there to make it easy to spot the puzzles in the book. If it is present the antique car indicates that a puzzle is a classic. That means it is known to be used in interviews, or is likely to be used in interviews, or is just really well–known. The following text shows the general idea.

PUZZLE TITLE

> **Puzzle:** Suppose you're reading this book and ...

Variations and follow–up topics may be highlighted with a shaded background and a different puzzle piece icon as shown in the following.

> **Variation:** Suppose you read a different book and ...

> **Follow–up:** The previous analysis said ...

Particularly important notes are highlighted with a box and a notepad icon.

> **Note:** This is something important and you should pay special attention.

Finally, some puzzles indicate particular problem–solving strategies with a sub-heading and a chess piece icon.

Detailed Strategy

As for styles in the text:

- New terms are *italicized* when they are first introduced.
- Pseudocode, URLs, and email addresses are written in a monofont as in `RodStephens@CSharpHelper.com` or `www.CSharpHelper.com`.

Speaking of URLs ...

IMPORTANT URLS

The following sections describe ways you can use the internet to get more information about this book.

Web Page

This book's main web page is `www.CSharpHelper.com/puzzles.htm`. There you can find links to an overview, table of contents, discussions, and errata.

That page also includes links to some places where you can purchase the book. In addition to letting you buy the book, those pages provide reviews. Please post a review when you have a chance!

Discussion

If there's some aspect of a puzzle that you would like to discuss with others, or if there's some other puzzle that you'd like to discuss, feel free to post it on the page `www.CSharpHelper.com/puzzles_discussions.htm`. You can also post responses to previous comments in their own threads so others can follow the discussion.

Errata

I do my best to ensure that my books contain content of the highest possible quality, but mistakes do sneak through the editing process. Imagine trying to debug a 200,000–word program without a compiler to help you find mistakes. For example, consider these three sentences.

> After lying on the floor for days, my brother finally washed his socks.
> I love cooking my dogs and my family.
> Time flies like a banana.

All of these are syntactically correct, so grammar checkers won't flag them, but they probably aren't saying what I mean. My brother wasn't lying on the floor for days (probably). I love cooking, my dogs, and my family, but I don't combine them in a cannibalistic way. Time may fly, and flies may like a banana, but I don't see how flying time is similar to a banana.

If you find one of these errors or some other mistake in the book, I would be grateful for your feedback. Posting errata may save other readers time and frustration, and will help me provide better information in the future.

To post errata, go to the errata page `www.CSharpHelper.com/puzzles_errata.htm`. First look to see if "your" error has already been reported and, if it has not, add it as a comment on that page. Please include your email address (which won't be posted publically) so I can contact you if I have questions. I'll review your comment and post a follow–up if necessary.

Email

If you have questions, comments, or suggestions while you're working through the book, please feel free to email me at `RodStephens@CSharpHelper.com`. I can't promise to solve all of your puzzles, but I'll do my best to point you in the right direction.

SUMMARY

After reading this book, studying the puzzles, and thinking about the variations and extensions, you should have a deeper understanding of these puzzles and puzzles in general. You will have a good foundation in puzzle–solving techniques and you'll know how to use puzzles to get the most out of interviews.

Now turn to Chapter 1 and learn a bit about the history and motivation behind interview puzzles. Or if you're really eager to get started, skip to Chapter 3 and start solving puzzles!

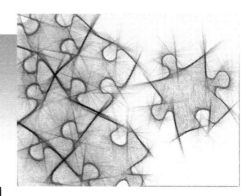

1

Basic Background

This chapter provides some background and general tips for using and solving puzzles in interviews. The following section contains a brief history of puzzles in interviews. Although you probably won't need to answer questions about puzzle history during an interview, knowing a bit about the history of puzzle questions will help you understand why companies use them.

The sections later in this chapter describe the purposes of interview puzzles. They also provide some tips about solving puzzles for job candidates and about using puzzles for interviewers.

HISTORY

Think back for a moment to the computer stone ages when engineers worked by candlelight on pedal–powered computers. In other words, think about the 1950s and 1960s.

In those days computers cost millions of dollars, lived in air–conditioned nests occupying thousands of square feet, and were just about powerful enough to replace an abacus or a slide rule. A single smartphone today is millions of times more powerful than all of the combined computing power on the planet in 1960. Plus it supports text messaging with emojis! ☺

Back in the early days, companies such as IBM needed to hire qualified programmers to operate their warehouse–sized computers. Unfortunately programmers hadn't been invented yet. Universities didn't offer degrees in software engineering, user interface design, or viral marketing. The closest thing they had were degrees in electrical engineering.

With no ready–made programmers available, the obvious solution was to hire likely candidates and then train them to become programmers. That left the companies with a puzzle of their own: How do you find and hire employees who are likely to be good programmers?

At the time no one really knew how to predict whether someone would become a good programmer. Lack of information rarely stops a determined company for long, however, so they decided that a good approach would be to hire people who were clever, adaptable, and fast learners, and then train them in the technical skills they would need. To looks for those traits, the companies devised all sorts of tests to measure a job applicant's ability at mathematical tasks, numeric pattern recognition, geometric manipulation, crossword puzzles, chess, and algebraic word problems. (The last of which has and always will terrorized many math students.)

Some of those tests were grueling, requiring candidates to answer 100 questions or more in less than an hour. (If 10 candidates can answer 100 questions in 23 minutes, how many questions can 17 candidates answer in 13 minutes?)

The whole process reminds me of the methods NASA used to test the first astronauts. They didn't really know what characteristics an astronaut would need to have. At least aside from obvious ones like being physically fit, cool under pressure, photogenic, and willing to tolerate endless poking and probing. So NASA threw every strange test they could think of at the candidates, mostly to see if they could handle the stress.

Similarly in the early programming days, companies subjected job applicants to all sorts of tests including puzzle tests.

Unfortunately those companies eventually discovered that the tests didn't do a very good job of predicting whether a candidate would someday turn into an effective programmer. Being a chess wizard or crossword guru doesn't seem to portend a bright future in algorithm analysis, user interface design, or debugging.

Fast–forward a couple of decades to the 1980s and 1990s. As Microsoft began its explosive growth, it needed to hire giant flocks of people to fill all sorts of fairly technical but non–programming positions such as trainers, technical writers, phone support agents, quality and assurance engineers, managers, and so on.

Asking those people programming questions would have been largely pointless because they were generally not programmers. Microsoft decided that a good approach would be to hire people who were clever, adaptable, and fast learners, and then train them in the technical skills they would need. (Does this sound familiar?) Not exactly knowing how to test for those skills, Microsoft followed the path of the ancients and added puzzle questions to their interviews.

It wasn't long before puzzles crept out of the non–programmer interviews and into programming interviews. Initially they were probably used as conversation starters rather than as part of the actual interview, but soon they were part of the formal process.

Many other large technical companies followed Microsoft's example and eventually Apple, Google, Facebook, PayPal, Boeing, eBay, Walmart, and hundreds if not thousands of other companies added puzzle questions to their interviews. Many of those companies were just trying to keep up with Microsoft. Other smaller companies probably decided that the bigger companies wouldn't use puzzles if it didn't work. (Some may have even used puzzles as a form of sympathetic magic. "Microsoft is successful and uses interview puzzles, so if I use interview puzzles perhaps it will make me successful.")

Unfortunately, as was the case in the 1950s and 1960s, interview puzzles don't seem to be good indicators of whether someone will become an effective technical writer. Recent studies have shown that they really don't help predict success in technical jobs, including programming. All they really seem good for is learning whether someone is good at puzzles, and even then only puzzles that are similar to the ones they've seen before.

In fact, there's even evidence that interview puzzles alienate some perfectly fine job candidates who then decide that they don't want to work for the company after all.

Does all of this mean that interview puzzles are worthless? Should interviewers write off puzzles as useless and go back to traditional methods such as crystal balls and Ouija boards? Should job applicants run screaming for the door at the first mention of golden eggs, goats, or burning ropes?

I've heard some people state in no uncertain terms that interview puzzles are worse than useless and should be outlawed at the federal level. I've heard others just as staunchly defend interview puzzles and claim that they should be given the same importance as advanced degrees and good SAT scores.

As is usually the case when experts take such extreme views, my option lies somewhere in between. Interview puzzles can provide useful information, but only certain kinds of information and only when used properly.

Before you use a puzzle in an interview, you need to know what the puzzle can tell you and how you can get that information. The following section describes some of the things that you can learn from an interview puzzle.

PUZZLE PURPOSES

Let's take as a given that interview puzzles can't accurately measure future success in technical or programming jobs. They can even do some harm by discouraging otherwise fine job candidates.

That's not as big a problem as it sounds because there are other, better ways of assessing a candidate's fitness for a job. For example, why not let the candidate work on a problem that's actually realistic?

If you're looking for a technical writer, review some writing samples (including the résumé) and have the candidate write a few paragraphs about some procedure that you demonstrate during the interview. If you're hiring a user interface specialist, look over the candidate's portfolio and ask what kind of user interface might solve a particular problem related to your industry. If you need a programmer, work through some programming problems. If you're trying to find a good database designer, ask the candidate to design a database to store data about your Pokémon and Warcraft characters.

You should also ask all of the normal interview questions such as:

- What are your greatest strengths?
- What are your greatest weaknesses?
- What do you want to be doing in five years?
- Why did you leave your previous job?
- Did you *really* say that to your previous CEO?

Search online or read a book about giving and taking interviews to learn more about these kinds of generic interview questions.

After you ask the standard questions and the realistic job–specific questions, what is there left for you to learn from puzzle questions? The following sections describe a few of the things that puzzle questions might help you learn.

Thought Process

The most commonly stated reason for using puzzle questions is to study the candidate's thought process. The following list gives some of the things that you might learn by watching the candidate work on a problem.

- Whether the candidate approaches problems in a methodical or haphazard way.
- Whether the candidate works logically from facts or makes wild guesses.
- Whether the candidate seems uncertain or confident in his reasoning.
- Whether the candidate explores different approaches.
- Whether the candidate can relate problems to real–world programming concepts such as dynamic programming or the fencepost problem.
- Whether the candidate sees through extraneous information and figures out what's important.
- Whether the candidate asks for clarification about vague or ambiguous items.

- Whether the candidate can articulate his thoughts.

Unfortunately you won't necessarily learn those things simply by presenting the candidate with a puzzle. You need to do a few other things to make things go smoothly.

First, you need to actually watch the candidate solve the problem. Some interviewers give candidates a puzzle and then leave them alone to work on it for 5 or 10 minutes. If you don't watch candidates at work, how can you know what thought processes they use?

Second, it helps if the candidate vocalizes while working on the problem. If the candidate tells you why he's working in a particular direction, you can get a better idea about how he approaches a problem. You can also give hints if the candidate is heading in the wrong direction, although seeing how someone handles minor setbacks while working on a puzzle can be interesting, too. Just don't let them stray too far afield.

Vocalizing while working is also a useful skill in certain development environments. For example, if you use agile development methods with pair programming, it's important for the pair to be able to talk about what they're doing as they're doing it.

Unfortunately many people find vocalizing while working unnatural and even embarrassing, particularly with a strange interviewer watching. You may need to encourage candidates to explain what they're thinking or even ask questions such as, "Why are you trying that?"

You need to keep the mood light and non–judgmental to keep the candidate comfortable and talking. You could even tell the candidate flat out that you're not really interested in the answer (unless your company actually needs to weigh counterfeit coins in the fewest possible weighings) and that you really just want to see how the candidate attacks a problem.

Note also that you can learn most of these things by giving the candidate a realistic job–related challenge.

Working in a Group

You can also use a puzzle to see how the candidate works in a group, a skill that is quite important in software engineering.

One way to do that is to present a relatively simple puzzle such as a bridge crossing puzzle or a weighing puzzle. Help the candidate move quickly to the solution and then describe one of the trickier variations or extensions. Now work with the candidate to find possible solutions.

An approach that may be even better is to pair the candidate with one of your current employees and let them try to solve a puzzle together. Tell the other employee to be sure to work *with* the candidate and not hog the spotlight or try to make things more difficult for the candidate.

You might need to have several puzzles ready so you can pick one that neither of them has seen before.

This approach not only gives you some insight into how the candidate works with others, but it may also help the candidate feel more like a potential part of the team instead of an outsider.

Willingness

Some interviewers use puzzle questions as a filter to weed out candidates that flatly refuse to attempt to solve the problem. The idea is that if someone refuses to even *try* to solve a simple puzzle, how do I know if the candidate will refuse to perform tasks on the job?

This seems foolish from both sides of the interview table.

If you're sitting on the candidate's side, it would be silly to refuse to even try to solve the puzzle and to storm out in a huff. Saying something like, "I would never want to work at a company that puts job candidates through this sort of thing," won't help your cause.

Unless you're interviewing to replace Will Shortz as Puzzle Master of the New York Times, the puzzle probably has nothing to do with your job anyway. You won't be forced to solve puzzles on a daily basis, so don't think one puzzle sets the tone for your future at the company. Writing off the whole job because of one interview question is almost as silly as walking out because the interviewer is wearing the wrong colored tie. Try not to become discouraged and just do your best.

Now suppose you're an interviewer sitting on the other side of the interview table. Do you really think that someone who refuses to solve a puzzle would later refuse to perform normal job duties? Can you seriously imagine one of your team saying, "Sorry, boss. I just don't feel like documenting this procedure today?" It seems pretty unlikely. You can always look for a replacement when that unlikely event happens.

Handling Failure

I've seen several stories about interviews where candidates were given impossible problems just to see how they would handle failure. The unfortunate candidate was asked to perform some impossible task, such as solving the world's hardest Sudoku problem or predicting the next five moves in some historic chess game. The interviewer then draws some sort of conclusion about how the candidate would behave during normal work tasks such as debugging a tricky program or making a management presentation.

> This is a sort of programming version of the Kobayashi Maru training exercise given to Starfleet cadets in Star Trek. The captain–in–training must decide whether to leave the distressed ship Kobayashi Maru to face certain destruction by Klingon phasers, or to help and lose his own ship and crew in the process. The idea is to see how the cadet handles a no–win scenario.
>
> See `en.wikipedia.org/wiki/Kobayashi_Maru` for more information.

Unfortunately few jobs actually call for employees to solve impossible Sudoku puzzles, so it's unclear exactly how the candidate's performance would apply to the job. Besides, it would be much easier to just ask, "What would you do if you tried to debug a program but couldn't?"

> I'm not sure what you can learn from the Kobayashi Maru exercise either. It might make the cadet do some thinking after the fact, but this seems like one of those situations where you can't really be sure of what you'll do until you're actually stuck in the Neutral Zone surrounded by Birds–of–Prey.

That doesn't mean you can't role–play difficult situations with the candidate. However, if the situation isn't realistically related to the job, you probably won't learn much.

Note that many puzzles deal with impossible situations, but there's no reason why you can't think of things to try. For example, consider the question, "How would you empty the Pacific Ocean?" Obviously this is impossible, but that doesn't mean you can't come up with some interesting ideas.

PUZZLE–GIVING TIPS

First and foremost, use puzzles only as a small part of the interview process. Puzzles may tell you something about the candidate, but you'll learn a lot more by using normal interview techniques. For example, ask the normal interview questions, look at the candidate's degrees and previous work experience, check the candidate's references, and ask some relevant job–related questions.

Don't make decisions based solely on a puzzle question. A lack of interest and ability in card tricks doesn't make someone a bad programmer or project manager. It would be silly to disqualify a perfectly good candidate because of a glorified trivia question.

Make a written plan before you use any puzzle question. Decide what you hope to learn from the question. Don't be vague and say things such as, "I want to learn how the candidate thinks." Instead say something concrete such as, "See if the candidate asks for clarification," or "see if the candidate thinks to use linked lists." It's much easier to notice those kinds of facts if you know what you're looking for.

Be prepared to give hints if the candidate becomes hopelessly stuck. Or better still, start with an easy puzzle and then, after the candidate solves it, make the problem harder. Ask about some variations and enhancements. Discuss the problem and brainstorm about how it applies to the job or the industry.

A particularly useful technique for programmers is to ask the candidate how you could write a program to solve the problem. Some problems, such as the "Egg Drop" problem, are difficult to solve without using programming techniques. Others, such as bridge–crossing problems, also allow good programming solutions.

Be upfront with the candidate about the importance of the puzzle question. Explain that the question is only a small part of the interview. In fact, you might try to stage the question as "just for fun" to further relieve any tension. These questions are designed to be tricky. If you apply extra pressure by saying, "Unless you solve this puzzle, you won't be asked back for a follow–up interview," many perfectly good candidates will fall to pieces. It's amazing how many interviewers do just that.

Finally, don't be a jerk. Some interviewers use puzzles just to prove how clever they are. Really all those kinds of tests prove is that the interviewer is insecure. If your written plan doesn't include anything meaningful, just skip the puzzle.

PUZZLE–SOLVING TIPS

The previous sections imply that puzzle questions have a fairly limited use. That may be, but they are also a fact of life at some companies. Whether you're good or bad at solving these sorts of puzzles, or even if you absolutely hate puzzles, there's no reason why you can't attempt them calmly and with a good chance of success.

The following list describes some general problem–solving tips that can be very useful while you're working on puzzle questions.

- Stay calm. Chances are it's not the end of the world even if you can't solve the problem. A lot of these problems are easier than they seem at first, so you should at least try kicking around a few ideas and see if the interviewer gives you any hints.

- Bring pencil and paper with you to the interview. (In addition to extra copies of your resume.) Use them on the puzzles. (And to write down names, phone numbers, important dates, or anything else that comes up.)
- Know what you want to get out of the problem. Be sure you understand what the question is asking. If you're at all uncertain, ask for clarification.
- Restate the problem. This lets the interviewer verify that you understand the problem correctly.
- Consider smart aleck answers. The answers to some interview puzzles are quick one–liners. In other cases you can give a glib off–the–cuff answer before you start working on the more detailed solution. For example, if you need to find the best way around a troll blocking a bridge, you might start by saying, "I think I'd probably find another way bridge. But if I have to cross *this* bridge, ..."
- Verbalize. Let the interviewer know what you're thinking as you work through the problem. That can help the interviewer learn about the way you think. The interviewer may also give you hints to keep you on track.
- Check your work. If the interviewer says, "Yup, you've got it," then you're done. Otherwise check your work. Also verify that it makes intuitive sense. (At least to the extent that any of these puzzles makes intuitive sense.)
- Consider the big picture and the small details. In some puzzles the solution has little to do with the details. In others you need the details to grind through the math. If you verbalize about what you're doing, the interviewer may help steer you in the right direction.
- Learn techniques such as induction (described in Chapter 6) and know basic formulas for speed, distance, and so forth.

Even if you get an annoying interviewer whose hidden goal is to make himself seem smart, roll with it. Admire the puzzle's clever solution, make an insightful comment if you can, and then move along with the rest of the interview.

Summary

If you are an interviewer, puzzle questions may give you some insight into a candidate's thought process, but only under certain circumstances. You need to be there watching. You can't just give the candidate the puzzle and then leave for half an hour. It helps if the candidate vocalizes while working, but be aware that some people don't vocalize well.

You can probably learn even more about the candidate by working on a puzzle together or by having the candidate work with one of your current employees. The candidate will probably be more comfortable and that approach may create a less adversarial atmosphere.

Don't use puzzles as a test of commitment to see if the candidate is willing to do anything to get a job. If I went to an interview and you asked, "What's the first step in performing an appendectomy?" I would say, "Oops. This isn't the job I thought I was applying for," and I would leave. If a candidate doesn't know anything about puzzles, why would you expect him to flail away at some hopeless task? Using puzzles to eliminate unwilling candidates will only get you a concentrated group of sycophants.

Also don't use puzzles to test reactions to no–win scenarios. At best, if the puzzle isn't directly related to the job, you won't learn anything. At worst you'll frustrate and alienate the candidate.

If you're a job candidate, remember that the interviewer isn't an enemy. The interviewer's goal is to find a qualified candidate that can do a good job and work well with the rest of the team. Try to remain calm and focused. Your goal is to show the interviewer what you can do and how you will be a useful member of the team.

Now whether you're an interviewer or a job candidate, move on to Chapter 2 and learn a bit about the kinds of basic probabilities that you may need to calculate to solve some interview puzzles.

2

Probability Primer

Many interview puzzles deal with probability. In a real world full of relentless change and uncertainty, calculating the probabilities of events can be extremely difficult. I'm not even certain about what I'm going to have for dinner tonight. (I estimate 70% chance of sausage and steamed vegetables, 20% chance of some variation on zuppa toscana, 10% chance of something else.)

Fortunately interview puzzle scenarios occur in a fantasy world where cards are perfectly shuffled, dice never come to a stop leaning against each other, and you never drop a coin toss. (Thus starting a half hour argument about whether you can accept the result on the floor or whether you need to flip again.)

Interview puzzles also have more limited scope than most real–world scenarios. You only have two kinds of socks, ants never get confused and turn around halfway to their destinations, and sadistic guards don't lie when they tell you that someone is wearing a blue hat.

All of that means that you can solve most of these kinds of puzzles by using a few relatively simple rules for calculating probabilities. This chapter provides a brief tutorial for the techniques that you need the most while working on probabilistic interview puzzles.

> **Note:** If you already have mad probability skillz, you can just skim this chapter.

FAIR AND UNFAIR

Some puzzles mention *fair* and *unfair* objects such as coins or dice. In this context those terms have nothing to do with fairness to the interviewer, the interviewee, or the people described in the puzzle. (At some level, there's nothing fair about these kinds of interview puzzles, anyway.)

Here *fair* means that outcomes occur with equal probability. For example, if you flip a fair coin, you have a 50% chance of getting heads and a 50% chance of getting tails.

In contrast, *unfair* means the probabilities of the outcomes is not the same. If you flip an unfair coin, the chances of getting heads or tails are different. For example, the coin might come up heads up 75% of the time and tails the other 25% of the time. Or the coin might come up heads 10% of the time and tails 90% of the time. Or it might come up heads 50.001% of the time and tails 49.999% of the time. A long as the probabilities are different, it's an unfair coin.

I've seen many discussions where people incorrectly think that "unfair" means you always get the *same* outcome. In other words, they assume that an unfair coin either always comes up heads or always comes up tails.

A coin that always comes up heads is certainly unfair because the probabilities of 100% heads and 0% tails are not the same. In general, however, the probabilities need not be 100% and 0% as long as they're different.

For another example, suppose you roll a fair six–sided die. Then the chances of rolling a 1, 2, 3, 4, 5, or 6 are all 1 in 6 or 16 2/3%.

When you roll an unfair six–sided die, the chances are not equal. For example, you might have a 10% chance of rolling each of 1, 2, 3, 4, or 5, and a 50% chance of rolling a 6.

In general interview puzzles don't tell you the probabilities for unfair objects; they just tell you that they are unfair. For example, a puzzle might say that you're flipping an unfair coin, but it won't tell you the probabilities of heads or tails. You won't know those probabilities. You'll only know that they're not the same.

> **Tip:** Often you can solve these kinds of puzzles by using variables such as h and t for the probabilities of heads and tails. In the end the variables usually cancel out because it doesn't matter what the probabilities are.

Unless a puzzle states that an object is unfair, you should assume that it's fair. If you have any doubt, ask the interviewer.

ENUMERATE OUTCOMES

The following shows the mathematical definition of probability.

> **Definition:** The *probability* of an event is the ratio of the number of desired outcomes to the total number of possible outcomes.

You can solve many probability puzzles by enumerating all of the possible outcomes and then counting the desired ones. For example, suppose you want to know the probability of flipping heads three times in a row. Figure 2–1 lists of all of the possible outcomes when you flip a coin three times.

H H H

H H T

H T H

H T T

T H H

T H T

T T H

T T T

Figure 2–1: All of the possible results from flipping a coin three times.

There are eight possible outcomes and only the one shown in bold gives you the desired result of three heads. Using the definition above, that means there's a 1/8 or 0.125 probability of flipping three heads in a row.

The following list gives three ways you can report this result.

- There is a 1 in 8 chance of flipping three heads in a row.
- There is a 1/8 (or 0.125) probability of flipping three heads in a row.
- The probability of flipping three heads in a row is 12.5%.

As an exercise, you might use Figure 2–1 to calculate the probability of flipping two heads and one tail, not necessarily in that order.

PROBABILITY VERSUS ODDS

Occasionally a puzzle asks you to calculate odds instead of probabilities. Probability is given by the following.

$$Probability = \frac{\#\ Desired\ Outcomes}{\#\ Total\ outcomes}$$

For example, as Figure 2–1 shows there are 3 ways to flip two heads and one tail out of 8 possible outcomes, so the probability of that outcome is 3/8.

In contrast, odds are given by the following.

$$Odds = \#\ Desired\ Outcomes : \#\ Undesired\ Outcomes$$

For example, there are 3 ways to flip two heads and one tail, and there are 5 ways to flip something else, so the odds of flipping two heads and one tail are written 3:5 and pronounced "three to five."

Often the odds are written in the reverse order as in 5:3.

In a sense the odds tell you how much a casino would need to pay you when you win if you're going to break even over time. In this example, the odds of winning are 3:5 so, if you win, the casino should pay you $5 for a $3 bet. If you win they also let you keep the $3 that you risked.

To see why these are the break–even odds, suppose you play the game 8 times, each of the eight outcomes occurs once, and you bet $3 each time. Then you pay a total of $3×8 = $24 to play. The casino pays you $5 plus your wager of $3 each time you win. There are 3 outcomes where you win, so the casino pays you a total of 3×($5+$3) = $24 and you break even. (A real casino would shave a bit off of the odds so it can make a profit. For example, it might pay you only $4 when you win.)

Sometimes people confused probability and odds. For example, they may say that the odds of rolling a 6 on a six–sided die are 6 to 1. They really should say the probability is 1 in 6 and the odds are 5 to 1.

If there's any doubt in an interview question, ask for clarification. Then when you phrase your answer, be sure you use the correct terms.

EXPECTED VALUE

Intuitively an expected result is the average result you would expect if you were to perform the same probabilistic task many times. Normally you can't discover the value by repeating a task a huge number of times. Fortunately you can calculate the expected value by taking the average of the outcomes weighted by their probabilities.

For example, suppose a casino has a game that costs $16 to play. You roll a six–sided die and the house pays you the square of the number you roll in dollars. In other words $1 for a 1, $4 for a 2, $9 for a 3, and so forth. The questions is, "Should you play the game?"

It may be a tempting game. In half of the rolls, you lose some money, but you don't even lose all of it. In the other half of the rolls, you make money. You can make as much as $36, which includes $11 of profit.

To decide whether it's worth playing, you can calculate the expected value of a round of play. The probability of rolling any of the numbers is 1/6, so the expected value of playing once is the following.

$$\$1 \times 1/6 + \$4 \times 1/6 + \$9 \times 1/6 + \$16 \times 1/6 + \$25 \times 1/6 + \$36 \times 1/6 =$$

$$\$91 \times 1/6 \approx \$15.17$$

This is less than the $16 cost to play, so in the long run you will lose and therefore you shouldn't play. (Of course that's true of all casino games. If you didn't lose in the long run, the casino wouldn't make any profit so it would go out of business.)

ROLLING DICE

When you're flipping coins, it's easy enough to list every possible outcome. (As long as you're not flipping thousands of times.) It's sometimes a bit harder to visualize all of the possible rolls of dice.

Figure 2–2 shows the possible totals when you roll two six–sided dice.

The numbers across the top of Figure 2–2 show the result of the first die, the numbers on the left show the result of the second die, and the numbers in the middle of the table give the totals of the two dice.

For example, suppose the dice roll 3 and 4 respectively. Look down the column with 3 at the top until you reach the row with 4 on the left. The value for that row and column is 7, the sum of the two dice rolls.

	First Die					
	1	2	3	4	5	6
1	2	3	4	5	6	7
2	3	4	5	6	7	8
3	4	5	6	7	8	9
4	5	6	7	8	9	10
5	6	7	8	9	10	11
6	7	8	9	10	11	12

(The left-hand axis is labeled **Second Die**, with rows numbered 1 through 6.)

Figure 2–2: Possible totals when rolling two dice.

Now you can use the table to calculate simple probabilities. For example, there are 6 entries holding the value 7, and there are 36 possible outcomes, so the probability of rolling a 7 with two dice is 1/6.

INDEPENDENT EVENTS

Two events are independent if the outcome of one doesn't affect the outcome of the other. For example, if you roll two dice, the result of the first die doesn't affect the roll of the second die. Similarly if you flip a coin twice, the first flip doesn't affect the second.

Probability puzzles usually deal with independent events.

Coin flips and dice rolls are independent events, but card selections often are not. For example, suppose you're going to randomly draw a card from a normal 52–card deck and you want to know the probability of drawing the ace of spades. There are 52 cards and only 1 desired outcome so the probability is 1/52.

Now suppose you didn't get the ace of spades the first time around and you're going to try again. You already removed one card so now the deck only holds 51 cards. There's still 1 desired outcome so the probability of getting the ace of spades is now 1/51.

The key here is that the two events are not independent. Removing a card from the deck during your first draw changed the deck, so the probability is different the second time around.

PROBABILITY ARITHMETIC

The following sections explain a few simple rules that you should know for calculating probabilities.

Multiplying Probabilities

Let P(A) and P(B) represent the probability of the independent outcomes A and B occurring, respectively. Then you can use the following rule to calculate the probability of A and B *both* occurring.

> **Multiplication Rule:** If A and B are independent outcomes, then:
>
> P(A and B)=P(A)×P(B)

For example, you should be able to guess that the probability of flipping heads with a coin is 1/2. (If you don't see why, build a table of outcomes similar to the one shown in Figure 2–1.)

The probability of flipping a second time and getting heads is also 1/2, so the probability of flipping two coins and getting heads both times is 1/2×1/2=1/4.

If you flip the coin a third time, the probability of getting heads again is also 1/2, so the probability of getting two heads followed by a third head is 1/4×1/2=1/8. This is the same as the probability we found in the earlier section "Enumerate Outcomes."

Adding Probabilities

The Multiplication Rule described in the previous section lets you calculate the probability of two outcomes *both* occurring. There are two addition rules that let you calculate the probability of *either* of two outcomes occurring.

Which of the rules you can use depends on whether the outcomes are mutually exclusive. Two outcomes are *mutually exclusive* if they cannot both occur. For example, when you roll a six–sided die, you can't get both a 2 and a 4 at the same time.

The first addition rule is:

> **Addition Rule 1:** If A and B are mutually exclusive outcomes, then:
>
> P(A or B)=P(A)+P(B)

For example, suppose you draw a card from a normal deck of cards. There is a 1/4 chance of drawing a heart and a 1/4 chance of drawing a diamond, so there is a 1/4+1/4=2/4= 1/2 chance of drawing a red card (either a heart or a diamond).

You can verify that directly by noting that there are 26 red cards in the deck so the probability of drawing a red card is 26/52=1/2.

The second addition rule is:

> **Addition Rule 2:** If A and B are *not* mutually exclusive outcomes, then:
>
> P(A or B)=P(A)+P(B)–P(A and B)

For example, suppose you draw a card from a deck of 52 cards and you want to know the probability of getting either a heart or a face card (jack, queen, king, or ace).

There are 13 hearts in the deck, so the probability of drawing one of them is 13/52.

There are 16 face cards in the deck, so the probability of drawing one of them is 16/52.

There are 4 face cards in the deck that are also hearts, so the probability of drawing a card that is both a heart and a face card is 4/52.

That means the total probability of drawing either a heart or a face card is 13/52+16/52– 4/52=(13+16–4)/52=25/52.

> **Note:** Addition Rule 1 is really just a special case of Addition Rule 2 because, if outcomes A and B are mutually exclusive, then P(A and B) is 0.

You can verify that directly by counting the cards that are either hearts or face cards. First there are 13 hearts. There are also 4 face cards for each of the other three suits for a total of 12 non–heart face cards. That means the total number of cards that are hearts or face cards is 13 + 12 = 25, so the probability of drawing one of those cards is 25/52.

Subtracting Probabilities

The probability of an outcome *not* occurring is 1 minus the probability of the outcome occurring. If P(–A) means the probability of A *not* occurring, then you have the following subtraction rule:

Subtraction Rule: P(–A)=1–P(A)

For example, the probability of rolling a 4 on a six–sided die is 1/6, so the probability of rolling anything other than a 4 is 1–1/6=5/6.

You can verify that directly because there are 5 numbers you could roll other than 4. There are a total of 6 possible rolls, so the probability of rolling one of those other numbers is 5/6.

This rule is often useful for calculating the probability of a sequence of non–mutually exclusive outcomes occurring.

For example, suppose you roll six different six–sided dice. What is the probability that you roll a 1?

There are six possible rolls and you're rolling six times, so you might *expect* to roll a 1, but that doesn't mean you will. You could be unlucky and never roll a 1. Or you could get very lucky and roll six 1s.

The chance of rolling a 1 on any given die is 1/6. The rolls are independent, so you might think that you can simply add up the probabilities to get:

$$1/6 + 1/6 + 1/6 + 1/6 + 1/6 + 1/6 = 6/6 = 1.0$$

But that doesn't make sense. The fact that this probability is 1.0 means you would *definitely* roll a 1, but intuitively you know that there's a slim chance that you won't get any 1s. That's a clue that there's something wrong with the calculation.

The problem is that, while the outcomes are independent, they are not mutually exclusive. For example, the first and third dice could both produce 1s. Because the outcomes aren't mutually exclusive, you can't use Addition Rule 1.

This is a very common mistake and many probability puzzles are rigged to make you think you can use Addition Rule 1 when you can't. In fact, this is such a common mistake that it deserves a box.

Warning: A very common mistake is applying Addition Rule 1 with events that are not mutually exclusive. Don't make that mistake!

There's an easy strategy and a hard strategy for solving this problem correctly. Let's look at both so we can verify that they produce the same result.

The Hard Strategy

First let's use the hard strategy to calculate the probability. The hard calculation is pretty long for six dice, so we'll just look at the probability of rolling a 1 with three dice.

Suppose you're rolling only one die. The probability of getting a 1 is simply 1/6. That's easy.

Now suppose you roll a second die. It also has a 1/6 chance of rolling a 1. The Multiplication Rule says the probability of *both* dice rolling a 1 is 1/6×1/6=1/36. Then Addition Rule 2 says the probability that either die rolls a 1 is 1/6+1/6–1/36=11/36.

Next let's add a third die. Like the others, it has a 1/6 chance of rolling a 1. Before we can use Addition Rule 2, we need to know the probability of both the first two dice rolling a 1, and the third die also rolling a 1.

Figure 2–3 shows all of the possible rolls where the first two dice contain a 1 and the third die also contains a 1.

$$1,1,1$$

1,2,1	1,3,1	1,4,1	1,5,1	1,6,1
2,1,1	3,1,1	4,1,1	5,1,1	6,1,1

Figure 2–3: All of the rolls where one of the first two dice contains a 1 and the third die also contains a 1.

There are 11 such combinations and a total of 6×6×6=216 possible combinations of three dice, so the probability of getting one of these 11 combinations is 11/216.

Earlier we calculated that the probability of the first two dice rolling a 1 is 11/36, and we know the probability of the third die rolling a 1 is 1/6, so Addition Rule 2 says the probability of any one of the three dice rolling a 1 is 11/36+1/6–11/216=91/216≈42%.

Note that this is less than the 1/2 = 50% probability that you would get if you incorrectly apply Addition Rule 1 and just added up the probabilities 1/6+1/6+1/6.

The Easy Strategy

Now let's use the easy strategy to calculate the probability of rolling a 1 with three dice.

Instead of calculating the probability of at least one die rolling a 1, let's calculate the probability of all three of the dice *not* rolling a 1. Those are independent outcomes and we want them *all* to be true, so we can use the Multiplication Rule.

The probability of any single die *not* rolling a 1 is 5/6, so the Multiplication Rule says the probability of three dice not rolling 1s is 5/6×5/6×5/6=125/216.

Now the Subtraction Rule says the probability of that *not* happening is 1–125/216= 91/216. In other words, the probability of rolling at least one 1 is 91/216.

That agrees with the probability we got doing it the hard way. I think you'll agree that the easy way was a lot simpler.

You could also enumerate all of the 216 possible rolls of three dice and just count those that contain a 1. That would be straightforward, but it would also be tedious and would give you lots of chances to make mistakes.

Six Dice

Now let's go back to the original problem using six dice. The probability of *not* rolling any 1s is $(5/6)^6$=15,625/46,656. Then the Subtraction Rule says the probability of rolling at least one 1 is 1–15,625/46,656=31,031/46,656≈67%.

In other words, roughly 2/3 of the time you'll roll a one.

SUMMARY

Although the scenarios used in interview puzzles are often bizarre, they are generally simpler than real life situations. Probabilities in general can be complicated and confusing, but in interview puzzles they are usually relatively simple. Unless you're applying for a job as head statistician for Lloyd's of London, you really only need to remember a few rules to solve most of these kinds of puzzles.

The following list summarizes the probability facts that that are most useful for solving interview puzzles.

- Probability: (# Desired Outcomes)/(# Total Outcomes)
- Odds: (# Desired Outcomes) : (# Undesired Outcomes)
- Multiplication Rule[1]:   P(A and B) = P(A)×P(B)
- Addition Rule 1[2]:   P(A or B)=P(A)+P(B)
- Addition Rule 2:   P(A or B)=P(A)+P(B)–P(A and B)
- Subtraction Rule: P(–A)=1–P(A)
- If you can easily enumerate all possible outcomes, do so. That will usually be easier and less confusing than performing calculations.

[1] Outcomes must be independent.
[2] Outcomes must be mutually exclusive.

You probably can't print out the list and bring it to your interviews, but you should study it until you can remember the basic rules.

Programming Exercises

1. Write a program that displays combinations of coin flips similar to those shown in Figure 2–1. Let the user enter the number of times the coin should be flipped.
2. Write a program that lets the user enter a number of coin flips. It should then enumerate all of the possible results, count the number of heads and tails in each result, and display the counts and probabilities. For example, if the user indicates three flips, the program should display the number of results that include 0, 1, 2, or 3 heads. It should also display the probability of each result.
3. Modify the program you wrote for Exercise 2 so it displays the result counts graphically in a bar chart.
4. Write a program that simulates coin flips. Let the user enter a number of trials and a number of flips. For each trial, perform the desired number of flips and keep track of the number of heads and tails in the result. When it's done, the program should display the probability of getting each result. (The results should more or less agree with the probabilities calculated by the program that you wrote for Exercise 2.)
5. Repeat Exercise 2 for an unfair coin. Let the user enter the probability that the coin produces heads during each flip.
6. Convert the program you wrote for Exercise 5 so it displays the result counts graphically in a bar chart.
7. Write a program that converts probabilities into odds and vice versa.
8. Write a program similar to the one you wrote for Exercise 2 but for dice rolls. For example, with two dice the program should indicate that there are four ways to roll a total of eight and that the probability of rolling an eight is $4/36 \approx 0.11$.
9. Convert the program you wrote for Exercise 8 so it displays the result counts graphically in a bar chart.
10. Write a program that calculates the probability of rolling at least one 1 for various numbers of die rolls. How many rolls does it take before the probability of rolling a 1 is at least 50%? 99%?
11. If you draw five cards from a normal 52–card deck, how many ways can you get a three–of–a–kind? What is the probability of drawing a three–of–a–kind?

3

Russian Roulette

Russian roulette is a simple, albeit not very safe, game, and that makes it relatively easy to analyze probabilistically. It also provides an excellent example of the idea behind this book: that you can use variations of a puzzle to watch how a job candidate thinks. A candidate may have seen one or two of these variations, but is unlikely to have thought deeply about all of them.

In normal Russian roulette, you have a revolver that can hold up to six bullets. You place one bullet in a chamber, spin the cylinder, and pull the trigger. If the bullet is in front of the hammer, the bullet fires. If an empty cylinder is in front of the hammer, nothing happens.

When you pull the trigger, the cylinder rotates so a different chamber will be in front of the hammer the next time you pull the trigger.

In true Russian roulette, two or more players take turns pointing the revolver at their heads and pulling the trigger. In interview puzzles there is often only one player: you.

NOTE: Obviously do not try real Russian roulette or any of its variations with a real gun. These are amusing puzzles and make interesting software simulations, but they wouldn't be much fun in real life.

Then again, being chased by zombies in the real world wouldn't be much fun either. Let's just keep the puzzles imaginary, shall we?

Interview puzzles ignore several real–world issues that might interfere with a smoothly running puzzle. For example, gravity doesn't encourage the bullet to end up in the lowest position and the player can't peek at the chambers to see where the bullet lies. Spins are fair (in the probabilistic sense) and no one knows what will happen until someone pulls the trigger.

ONE BULLET, ONE PERSON

Puzzle: If you're the only player and you spin the cylinder before each round, what is the probability that you'll survive N rounds of Russian roulette?

Variation: What if you use more than one bullet?

If you use one bullet, then there's a 5/6 probability of surviving in any given round. If you spin the cylinder before each round, then the rounds are independent of each other. In that case there's a $(5/6)^N$ probability of surviving N rounds.

More generally if you use B bullets, then you have a (6–B)/6 probability of surviving in any given round and therefore a $[(6–B)/6]^N$ probability of surviving N rounds.

Figure 3–1 shows the probabilities of surviving rounds of Russian Roulette with different numbers of bullets.

Rounds	1 Bullets	2 Bullets	3 Bullets	4 Bullets	5 Bullets
1	0.8333	0.6667	0.5000	0.3333	0.1667
2	0.6944	0.4444	0.2500	0.1111	0.2780
3	0.5787	0.2963	0.1250	0.3700	0.0460
4	0.4823	0.1975	0.6250	0.1230	0.0080
5	0.4019	0.1317	0.3130	0.0410	0.0010
6	0.3349	0.8780	0.1560	0.0140	0.0000
7	0.2791	0.5850	0.0780	0.0050	0.0000
8	0.2326	0.3900	0.0390	0.0020	0.0000
9	0.1938	0.2600	0.0200	0.0010	0.0000
10	0.1615	0.1730	0.0100	0.0000	0.0000

Figure 3–1: Probability of surviving rounds of Russian roulette.

Figure 3–1 doesn't include columns for zero bullets (because the probability of survival would always be 1) or six bullets (because the probability of survival would always be 0).

ONE BULLET, ONE PERSON, NO SPINS

Puzzle: If you're the only player and you don't spin the cylinder before each round, what is the probability that you'll survive N rounds of Russian roulette?

If you don't spin the cylinder before each round, then the rounds are not independent of each other. For example, suppose you place one bullet in a chamber, perform an initial spin, and pull the trigger. For this first round, there's a 5/6 probability of survival.

Suppose there's no bang during round one. Now what's the probability of surviving the second time you pull the trigger? If you spin the cylinder again, you would again have a 5/6 chance of survival, but you've already pulled the trigger once and you didn't spin the cylinder again. That means there are only five remaining chambers that you haven't tried yet, and one of them contains the bullet. Therefore there's a 4/5 probability of survival during round two.

In round three there are four remaining chambers, one containing the bullet, so there's a 3/4 probability of survival during that round. You can use similar reasoning to calculate the probability of surviving each of the remaining rounds. Figure 3–2 shows the results.

Round	Survival Probability During This Round
1	5/6
2	4/5
3	3/4
4	2/3
5	1/2
6	0

Figure 3–2: Probability of surviving during a particular round.

Figure 3–2 shows the probabilities of surviving a round assuming you get to that round. For example, if you survive through round four, then the probability of then surviving round five is 1/2.

So what are the probabilities that you'll survive all of the rounds up to a given point? For example, what is the probability that you'll survive all of the rounds up to and including round five?

The probability of surviving through round one is simply 5/6.

You can use the Multiplication Rule to calculate the probability of surviving through later rounds.

The probability of surviving through round two is 5/6×4/5. Notice that the 5s cancel out leaving 4/6.

The probability of surviving through round three is 4/6×3/4. The 4s cancel out leaving 3/6.

You get similar cancelations in later rounds. Figure 3–3 shows the final results.

Round	Total Survival Probability
1	5/6
2	4/6
3	3/6
4	2/6
5	1/6
6	0/6

Figure 3–3: Probability of surviving for N rounds.

As you probably expect, if you only spin the cylinder before the first round, the probability of survival decreases with each round until round 6, when you're definitely dead.

Follow–up: What are the probabilities of surviving through R rounds if the gun has C chambers?

The probability of surviving the first round is $(C-1)/C$.

The probability of surviving the second round, assuming you live to see it, is $(C-2)/(C-1)$.

More generally, the probability of surviving the round R is $(C-R)/(C-R+1)$.

When you multiply the probabilities of surviving the rounds together, the terms cancel much as they did with a normal six–shooter. That means the total probability of surviving through round R is $(C-R)/C$.

SIX PEOPLE, ONE BULLET, NO SPINS

> **Puzzle:** You and five comrades have been captured by a sadistic warlord. Your captor only has five sets of shackles, so he decides to use Russian roulette to kill one of you. He places one bullet in the gun, spins the cylinder, and makes you take turns playing until one of you dies. You're not allowed to spin the cylinder between turns.
>
> Which position should you take to maximize your chance of survival?

The easiest way to solve this puzzle is to realize that the cylinder is spun only once and after that initial spin the outcome is already determined. There are six prisoners so there's an equal chance that the bullet will end up assigned to any of them. That means there's a 1/6 probability that any one of the prisoners will be the unlucky one no matter how the prisoners are ordered.

In other words, it doesn't matter what position you take. There's a 1/6 probability that you'll die no matter what.

To see this mathematically, consider turn N. To be shot in turn N, two things must happen. First turn N must occur. Second the prisoner whose turn it is must then be shot.

Round one always happens with probability 1. In that round there are six chambers, one containing the bullet, so there's a 1/6 probability that the first prisoner is shot in round one. That means the total probability of being shot in round one is $1 \times 1/6 = 1/6$.

Round two happens if the first prisoner isn't shot. The first prisoner has a 1/6 chance of being shot, so there's a 5/6 chance that the prisoner isn't shot. If we get to round two, then there are five chambers remaining, one containing the bullet, so there's a 1/5 probability that the second prisoner is shot if we get to round two. That means the total probability of being shot in round two is $5/6 \times 1/5 = 1/6$.

Round three happens if the first two prisoners aren't shot. The probability of the first prisoner not being shot is 5/6. In round two there are five remaining cylinders so the chance of the second prisoner surviving is 4/5. That means the probability of both the first and second prisoners surviving is $5/6 \times 4/5 = 4/6$.

If round three happens, there are only four cylinders remaining, one containing the bullet, so there's a 1/4 probability that the third prisoner is shot. That means the total probability of being shot in round three is $4/6 \times 1/4 = 1/6$.

You can use similar calculations to find the remaining probabilities. Figure 3–4 shows the probabilities for all six rounds.

Round	Probability of Round Happening	Probability of Being Shot in this Round	Total Probability of Death
1	6/6	1/6	1/6
2	5/6	1/5	1/6
3	4/6	1/4	1/6
4	3/6	1/3	1/6
5	2/6	1/2	1/6
6	1/6	1/1	1/6

Figure 3–4: Probabilities during each round of Russian roulette.

So it doesn't matter which position you take in the order. Your chances are the same no matter what.

Since there's no probabilistic difference, your choice of position is a matter of preference. You could go first to avoid as much suspense as possible. Or you could go last to lengthen your life by a few seconds.

Or you could go last and, if you get to round 6, turn and shoot the warlord because at that point you know that the bullet is ready to fire. Then it's a question of whether you're faster than the warlord instead of a question of probability.

Follow–up: What is the probability of surviving if the gun has C chambers, there are C prisoners, and there are C–1 shackles?

Logic similar to the reasoning above shows that you have a $1/C$ probability of death no matter what position you take.

Follow–up: Suppose there are seven prisoners. The sadistic warlord decides it would be unfair to make six of you play Russian roulette and leave the seventh person out of the fun, so he decides to modify the game. Each of you will spin the cylinder and then pull the trigger. You'll keep taking turns until two of you have been shot.

Is the new game fair?

Not quite. Anyone who plays has a 1/6 probability of death, so that part is fair. However, after the second person dies, anyone who hasn't played yet in that round doesn't face the same risk as everyone else. For example, suppose the first two prisoners die on their first tries. Then the other prisoners never have to play.

To see that this is true mathematically, suppose we only need one prisoner to be shot and consider the second prisoner to play. There's a 1/6 probability that the first prisoner will die and in that case the second prisoner is safe. There's also a 5/6 probability that the first prisoner survives. In that case the second prisoner must play and faces a 5/6 probability of survival. That makes the second prisoner's total probability of survival $1/6+(5/6)\times(5/6)=31/36\approx0.86$. The first prisoner's probability of survival is only $5/6\approx0.833$ so the second prisoner has an advantage.

The game would be fairer if everyone must play out the round that is in progress when the second person dies. For example, if the first two prisoners immediately die, then everyone else still has to pull the trigger once.

If this was an "engineer, physicist, and statistician" joke, the statistician would probably tell the sadistic warlord and spoil someone's (probably his own) chance at skipping a turn.

SIDE–BY–SIDE BULLETS

> **Puzzle:** Suppose a guard places two bullets in adjacent chambers in a six–shooter and then spins the cylinder. He points the gun at you and pulls the trigger while chuckling evilly. Luckily for you, the chamber is empty.
>
> Now the guard says, "I'm going to pull this trigger again. Do you want me to spin the cylinder again first?"

If you spin the cylinder again, then the probability of surviving round two is simply $4/6=2/3$ because four of the six cylinders are empty. The question is, "What is the probability of surviving round two if you *don't* spin the cylinder?"

To calculate the probabilities, first number the chambers 1 through 6 and assume the bullets are in chambers 5 and 6. Also assume that each time you pull the trigger the cylinder rotates so the next higher numbered chamber is in front of the hammer.

For example, if the hammer starts at chamber 1 and you pull the trigger, nothing happens and then the cylinder rotates so chamber 2 is now in front of the hammer. (And yes I know that the cylinder normally rotates just before the shot not afterward, but I think it's easier to visualize this way.)

Now think about where the hammer might be. The first pull of the trigger didn't kill you, so the hammer must have started in position 1, 2, 3, or 4.

If the hammer started in position 4, then you're in trouble because the cylinder rotated so now the hammer is in position 5 and there's a bullet there.

If the hammer started in position 1, 2, or 3, then you're safe because the hammer is now in position 2, 3, or 4, none of which holds a bullet.

There are three safe positions out of four possible positions, so there's a 3/4 probability that you're safe in round two if you don't spin the cylinder.

You have a $4/6 \approx 0.67$ probability of surviving if you do spin the cylinder and a $3/4 = 0.75$ probability of surviving if you don't spin the cylinder, so you're slightly better off if you don't spin the cylinder.

LONG—TERM SURVIVAL

> **Puzzle:** Suppose a guard places two bullets in adjacent chambers in a six–shooter, spins the cylinder, and then makes you play rounds of Russian roulette. Before each round, you have the option of spinning the cylinder if you like.
>
> What's your best strategy to maximize your chance of survival?

In round one you have a $4/6 = 2/3$ probability of survival.

The solution to the preceding puzzle showed that you have a slightly better probability of survival in round two if you don't spin the cylinder. In that case you have a 3/4 probability of survival in round two.

Now consider round three. If you assume the bullets are in chambers 5 and 6, and the first two rounds didn't kill you, then the hammer must have started in position 1, 2, or 3. If it started in position 3, then in round three it is in position 5, which contains a bullet, and you're a goner. There are three possible positions for the hammer and two will let you survive, so there's a 2/3 chance of survival if you don't spin the cylinder.

That's the same probability you get if you do spin the cylinder, so it doesn't matter whether you spin or not before round three, at least as far as survival in round three is concerned. Let's look at the two cases of spinning or not spinning before round three.

Suppose you don't spin before round three and you survive to play round four. Then the hammer must have started in position 1 or 2. If it started in position 2, then round four will kill if you don't spin the cylinder. There is one position that lets you live out of two possible positions, so you have a 1/2 probability of survival if you don't spin before round four.

If you do spin in round four, then you have a 4/6=2/3 chance of survival. That's better than 1/2 so you should spin before round four.

Figure 3–5 shows the probabilities of surviving each round if you *don't* spin before round three.

Action	Probability of Survival in this Round
Spin	
Round 1	2/3
Round 2	3/4
Round 3	2/3
Spin	
Round 4	2/3

Figure 3–5: Probability of survival if you don't spin before round three.

Now suppose you *do* spin before round three and you survive to play round four. Then you're back to the situation you had when you played round two. You spun before round one (the guard spins at the start) so your best strategy is to not spin now. We already saw that this approach gives you a 3/4 probability of survival if you don't spin.

Figure 3–6 shows the probabilities of surviving each round if you *do* spin before round three.

Action	Probability of Survival in this Round
Spin	
Round 1	2/3
Round 2	3/4
Spin	
Round 3	2/3
Round 4	3/4

Figure 3–6: Probability of survival if you do spin before round three.

In round four, the 3/4 probability you get if you do spin before round three is better than the 2/3 probability you get if you don't spin, so you should spin before round three and not before round four.

The long–term pattern is: Spin, Don't Spin, repeat.

SEPARATED BULLETS

Puzzle: Suppose a guard places two bullets in non–adjacent chambers in a six–shooter and then spins the cylinder. He points the gun at you and pulls the trigger. Luckily for you, the chamber is empty.

Now the guard is going to pull the trigger again. Do you want him to spin the cylinder again first?

As in the previous puzzles, the gun contains four chambers with no bullets so the probability that you survive in round 1 is 4/6=2/3.

This time the two bullets are not adjacent to each other, so each of them has an empty cylinder in the next smaller numbered position. That means two of the four empty chambers come right before a bullet. If the hammer is initially behind one of those two positions, then round two will kill you if you don't spin the cylinder.

The hammer started behind one of four empty positions, two of which will kill you in round two, so the probability of surviving round two is 2/4=1/2 if you don't spin.

The probability of survival is 4/6=2/3 if you do spin. That's greater than 1/2 so you should always spin.

Notice that this solution doesn't depend on whether the bullets are separated by 1 or 2 empty chambers. As long as they aren't adjacent, you're always better off spinning.

THREE BULLETS

Puzzle: Suppose a guard places three bullets in adjacent chambers in a six–shooter and then spins the cylinder. He points the gun at you and pulls the trigger. As usual, the chamber is empty. (It wouldn't be much of a puzzle if you died before it started.)

Now the guard is going to pull the trigger again. Do you want him to spin the cylinder again first? What about before round three?

Number the chambers 1 through 6 as before and assume the bullets are in chambers 4, 5, and 6. Because you survived round one, the hammer must have started in position 1, 2, or 3.

If you don't spin again, then when the guard pulls the trigger in round two you'll die if the hammer started in position 3 and you're safe if the hammer started in position 1 or 2. There are three positions where the hammer might have started and two are safe, so there's a 2/3 probability of survival if you don't spin before round two.

If you do spin, there are six positions where the hammer could land and three are safe, so you have a 3/6=1/2 probability of survival if you spin before round two.

That means you should not spin before round two.

If you survive round two, then the hammer began in position 1 or 2. If you don't spin before round three, there are two possible positions where the hammer started and one of those is safe, so there's a 1/2 probability of surviving round three. That's the same as the probability if you do spin.

At this point the problem is similar to the one the "Long–term Survival" puzzle. It doesn't matter whether you spin before round three as far as round three is concerned, but if you do spin then you get a higher probability of survival in round four. Figure 3–7 shows the probabilities of surviving each round if you do spin before round three.

Action	Probability of Survival in this Round
Spin	
Round 1	1/2
Round 2	2/3
Spin	
Round 3	1/2
Round 4	2/3

Figure 3–6: Probability of survival during each round if you spin before round three.

As was the case in the "Long–term Survival" puzzle, the long–term pattern is: Spin, Don't Spin, repeat.

DOUBLE TAP

Puzzle: Suppose your sadistic jailer places one bullet in a chamber, spins the cylinder, and then makes you and two other prisoners play Russian roulette with the following rules. Each of you must pull the trigger twice, once pointing at yourself and once pointing at the ceiling. You can decide whether you point the gun at yourself first or at the ceiling first. After the bullet eventually fires, the survivors can return to their cells.

Should you point the gun at yourself first or at the ceiling first?

Some people think they should point the gun at the ceiling first. Then if the bullet is in the first chamber, you don't need to point the gun at yourself. Somehow that seems like it should give you better odds of survival.

Unfortunately that logic doesn't work. When the guard spins the cylinder, the location of the bullet is fixed. After that point there is a 1/6 probability that the bullet will fire during any one of the first six trigger pulls. That means the probability doesn't change depending on whether you point the gun at yourself or the ceiling first.

You may prefer to point the gun at the ceiling first anyway so you don't have to pull the trigger again if the gun fires, but that doesn't change the probability.

> **Follow–up:** Is it better to go first, second, or third in this game?

As in the "Six People, One Bullet, No Spins" puzzle, it doesn't matter which position you take. The probability of you being shot is 1/6 no matter what order you use. You may prefer to go first to get it over with, or you might want to go last to delay the inevitable, but the probability is the same in any case.

> **Follow–up:** What is the probability of you surviving this game?

There's a simple 1/6 probability that the bullet will fire when it's pointed at you, so there's a 5/6 probability that you will survive.

> **Follow–up:** What is the probability that all three prisoners will survive the game?

There are three bullet positions that will result in a prisoner's death and three that result on no death, so the probability that all three prisoners will survive is 3/6=1/2.

> **Follow–up:** If you play this game once per day, what is the probability that at least one prisoner will be shot within the first N days?

Each day there is a 1/2 probability that all three prisoners survive each time you play the game. After N days, there's a $(1/2)^N$ probability that all of you will be alive. That means there's a $1-(1/2)^N$ probability that at least one of you will have been shot.

> **Follow–up:** On what day does the probability of someone being shot exceed 0.9?

If you plug in the values N=1, 2, 3, and 4 in the equation $(1/2)^N$, you get 0.5, 0.75, 0.875, and 0.9375, so the probability of a fatality exceeds 0.9 during the fourth day.

SUMMARY

At its most basic, Russian roulette is a simple game, but its variations provide wonderful opportunities for probabilistic interview puzzles. You can create all sorts of interesting twists on the basic puzzle by varying the number of chambers, bullets, and people; and by changing the conditions at the start and between pulls of the trigger.

Russian roulette puzzles are also relatively easy to convert into programming challenges. They let you simulate different situations and verify the probabilities that you calculate mathematically.

PROGRAMMING EXERCISES

1. Write a program that calculates and displays probabilities similar to those shown in Figure 3–1. Let the user enter the number of chambers in the gun. (After all, not all revolvers have six chambers. Some have five, seven, eight, nine, ten, or even twelve!)

2. Write a program that simulates Russian roulette to verify the values shown in Figure 3–1. (Or for the program you wrote for Exercise 1.) Let the user enter the number of trials, cylinders, bullets, and rounds each game should last. The program should run the indicated number of trials and display the percentage of times the player survived for the given number of rounds.

3. Write a program that simulates the situation in the "Side–by–side Bullets" puzzle. Let the user enter the number of trials, chambers, and bullets. The program should run the indicated number of trials with and without spinning after round one. It should then display the percentage of times the player survived through the second round with and without spinning.

4. Write a program to simulate the seven prisoners variation of the "Six People, One Bullet, No Spins" puzzle. Let the user enter the number of trials, prisoners, and shackles. For the indicated number of trials, the program should use the "fairer" version of the game until the number of prisoners is no greater than the number of shackles. The program should display the average number of rounds it took and the average number of prisoners killed.

5. Write a program to simulate the situation in the "Side–by–side Bullets" puzzle. Let the user enter the number of trials, chambers, and bullets to be placed side–by–side. After running the trials, the program should display the percentage of times that you survived two rounds with and without spinning before round two. What results do you get when the number of chambers is large? For example, with 100 chambers and two bullets?

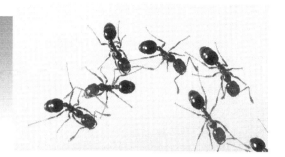

Accomplished Ants

Ant puzzles deal with ants (or your bugs of choice) crawling around in some sort of geometric environment. For example, the ants may be crawling around on the edges of a triangle or across the sides of a box.

Sometimes the paths that the ants can take form a network, although often network algorithms won't provide much help in solving the puzzle.

In many ant puzzles, you need to be aware of what many ants are doing at the same time. For example, some puzzles ask you how ants can move without bumping into each other.

You can easily generalize the basic puzzles to more complicated shapes. For example, the first puzzle described in this chapter is a classic about ants walking along the edges of a triangle. You can easily generalize that to ants walking along the edges of a square, tetrahedron, or even more complicated shapes.

Think carefully before you use more complicated shapes, however, because the puzzles become much more complicated when you do. Calculating expected numbers of moves or the probability of a lucky ant finding the shortest path to a can of soda might be possible on a dodecahedron, but calculating the probability of collisions might be very hard during an interview.

ANTS ON A TRIANGLE

Puzzle: Three ants are sitting on the corners of an equilateral triangle. Each ant flips a tiny coin and moves along a randomly chosen edge. What is the probability that the ants don't collide?

The fact that the triangle is equilateral is irrelevant. What matters is that the ants are on a triangle.

This puzzle may seem confusing because it involves a lot of ants all acting randomly at the same time. Fortunately the situation is much simpler than it seems. The ants will collide unless they either all move clockwise or they all move counterclockwise.

One way to solve the puzzle is to divide the number of successful outcomes by the total number of possible outcomes. There are only two successful outcomes: clockwise or counterclockwise.

In practice you don't actually need to list the possible outcomes; you just need to know how many there are. Each ant picks its direction independently and each has two possible choices. That means there are $2^3=8$ possible combinations of ant directions and therefore 8 possible outcomes.

Therefore the probability that the ants don't collide is $2/8=1/4$.

Another way to solve the puzzle is to let one ant pick a random direction and then ask, "What is the probability that the other ants pick the same direction?" Each of the other two ants has a $1/2$ probability of picking the first ant's direction. There are two other ants and they pick their directions independently, so the Multiplication Rule says the probability that they both pick the correct direction is $1/2 \times 1/2 = 1/4$. That agrees with the probability we calculated by counting outcomes.

ANTS ON A POLYGON

> **Puzzle:** N ants are sitting on the corners of an N–sided polygon. Each ant flips a tiny coin and moves along a randomly chosen edge. What is the probability that the ants don't collide?

This is a generalization of the "Ants on a Triangle" puzzle and the same logic works. The ants don't collide if they either all move clockwise or they all move counterclockwise.

Let one ant pick a direction and then ask, "What's the probability that the other ants all pick the same direction?" Each of the other ants has a $1/2$ probability of picking the first ant's direction. There are N–1 other ants and they pick their directions independently, so the Multiplication Rule says the probability that they all pick the correct direction is $(1/2)^{N-1}$.

If you plug in the value N=3 for a triangle, then this value is $1/2^2=1/4$, which is the answer we got for the previous puzzle.

ANTS ON A TETRAHEDRON

Puzzle: Four ants are sitting on the vertices of a tetrahedron. Each ant moves along a randomly chosen edge. What is the probability that the ants don't collide?

For this puzzle, it may help to draw a picture similar to Figure 4–1.

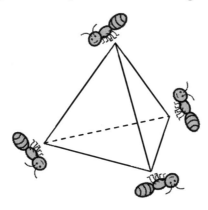

Figure 4–1: Four ants on the vertices of a tetrahedron.

First, notice that there are no notions of clockwise or counterclockwise in three dimensions. That means you can't say, "This ant starts walking clockwise and continues walking clockwise at each vertex." Each time the ant reaches a new vertex, it would have to pick a new random direction.

Because each ant picks new random directions each time it reaches a vertex, there's no way the ants can walk indefinitely without colliding. Eventually one of them will pick a random direction that will cause a collision.

That makes this puzzle slightly different from the "Ants on a Triangle" puzzle. Instead of requiring the ants to move indefinitely without collision, as we can on a triangle, we can only ask, "What is the probability that the ants move to an adjacent vertex without collision?"

Finding non–colliding moves for the ants is equivalent to finding a set of non–intersecting closed paths along the tetrahedron's edges that include all of the vertices. Ants that follow a closed path in the same direction won't collide with each other because each ant moves to a vertex that has just been vacated by another ant on the same closed path.

Figure 4–2 shows a closed path that the ants can follow without colliding.

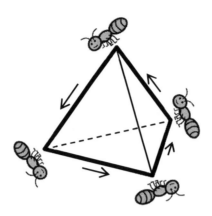

Figure 4–2: A path where the ants don't collide.

To calculate the probability of not colliding, we can count the number of successful outcomes and the number of total outcomes. A closed path similar to the one shown in Figure 4–2 is a successful outcome, so we need to count those kinds of paths.

Every such path on the tetrahedron passes through every vertex, so if we count the paths that start at a particular vertex, then that will give us all of the paths. Let's count the paths that start with the topmost vertex.

The topmost ant can start in three directions. After moving along one edge, the ant then has two choices for its second move.

Figure 4–3 shows the situation after the topmost ant has moved along one edge to vertex A. From this point the ant can move to vertex B or vertex C.

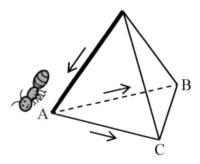

Figure 4–3: The top ant after moving along one edge.

After the ant has made its second move, it has visited three of the tetrahedron's vertices. For example, if the ant moves to vertex B in Figure 4–3, then in its next move it must move to vertex C.

After that the ant must return to its starting vertex at the top of the tetrahedron.

The total number of possible paths is:

$$[\#choice\ 1] \times [\#choice\ 2] \times [\#choic\ 3] \times [\#choice\ 4] =$$
$$3 \times 2 \times 1 \times 1 = 6$$

Next we need to count the total number of possible outcomes. Each ant has three choices and there are four ants, so the total number of possible outcomes is $3^4 = 81$.

Therefore the probability of the ants not colliding during their first move is $6/81 = 2/27$.

ANTS ON A CUBE

Puzzle: Eight ants are sitting on the vertices of a cube. Each ant moves along a randomly chosen edge. What is the probability that the ants don't collide?

This is a variation of the "Ants on a Tetrahedron" puzzle. Figure 4–4 shows the two types of closed paths that the ants can follow to avoid a collision.

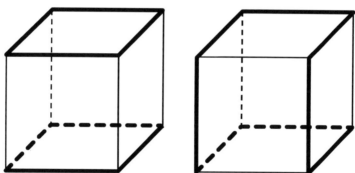

Figure 4–4: Two types of paths that the ants can follow to avoid colliding.

The left side of Figure 4–4 shows two square paths. The right side shows a single path that visits all of the cube's vertices. If the ants follow either of these kinds of paths, they won't collide.

To calculate the probability of the ants colliding, we need to count the number of successful outcomes and the number of total possible outcomes.

First, let's count the number of paths similar to the one shown on the left in Figure 4–4.

This solution uses two square paths that are each parallel to the X–Y, Y–Z, or X–Z planes. There are three possible coordinate planes to which they can be parallel, so there are three possible choices for the squares.

Now we need to consider the directions that the ants could move along any pair of squares. The ants could move clockwise or counterclockwise along any square when viewed from outside of the cube looking at the square. Each pair includes two squares, so each pair gives four possible directions for the ants: CW–CW, CW–CCW, CCW–CW, and CCW–CCW.

Multiplying the three possible pairs of squares by four possible directions gives 12 possible paths that the ants could follow.

Now let's count the number of paths similar to the one shown on the right in Figure 4–4. If you look at the cube from the top, that path makes a sort of inverted U as shown on the left in Figure 4–5. If you rotate the cube around the vertical axis, you get 3 other paths. Figure 4–5 shows the four U–shaped variations.

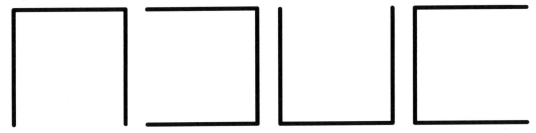

Figure 4–5: Rotations of the path on the right in Figure 4–4.

Rotating around the X, Y, and Z axes gives you four paths for each axis, for a total of 12 paths.

Unfortunately that's not quite the end of the story. Each of the paths makes the U–shape when you look at it along *two* of the coordinate axes.

Figure 4–6 shows an exploded view of one of the paths with the cube removed to reduce clutter. The gray curves show the U–shapes as seen along the vertical and left–to–right axes.

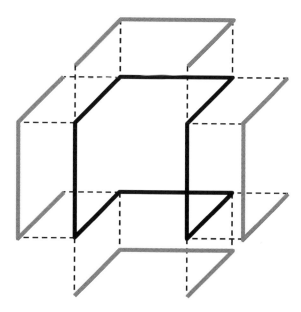

Figure 4–6: A path's U–shapes along two axes.

Each of the 12 curves we counted earlier was counted twice, once for each of two axes. That means the number of undirected curves of this kind is actually 12/2=6.

Finally, the ants can traverse each of these curves in two directions, so we need to count each of these curves twice. That means the true total number of directed curves of this kind is 6×2=12.

Adding that to the 12 curves that include two squares, we get a grand total of 24 curves that the ants could follow to avoid collisions.

We now know that there are 24 successful outcomes. We still need to count all of the possible outcomes. Fortunately that's a lot easier.

There are eight ants and each picks one of three possible directions to move, so there are 3^8=6,561 possible outcomes.

That means the final probability of the ants not colliding is 24/6,561=8/2,187≈0.0037. In other words, there's only about a 0.37% chance that the ants won't collide.

ONE ANT ON A CUBE

> **Puzzle:** An ant and a can of soda are positioned on opposite corners of a cube. For each move, the ant travels along a randomly selected

edge until it reaches the next vertex. What is the expected number of moves the ant makes before it reaches the soda?

Figure 4–7 shows the initial situation.

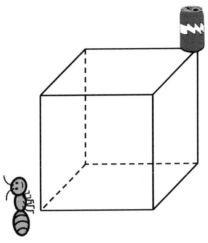

Figure 4–7: An ant and can of soda sit on opposite corners of a cube.

This is an intimidating puzzle because there are an infinite number of paths that the ant could take. A lucky ant could reach the soda in three moves. An extremely unlucky ant could move back and forth across the same edge thousands of times before it finds the soda.

Recall that the expected number is the probability–weighted average of the number of moves across all possible moves. The trick here is to not think about all of the infinitely many possible paths and to just think about the expected path lengths.

Let E_1, E_2, and E_3 be the expected number of moves the ant makes to reach the soda when it starts 1, 2, or 3 edges away from the soda respectively. Figure 4–8 shows the cube vertices labeled with their expected numbers of moves. The ant begins at the vertex labeled E_3, so our goal is to calculate E_3.

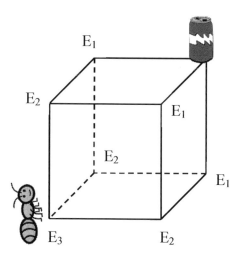

Figure 4–8: E_1, E_2, and E_3 are the expected number of moves the ant makes to reach the soda.

Now suppose the ant is at the node labeled E_3. After making one move, the ant will end up at a node labeled E_2 no matter which edge it follows. The expected distance from that vertex to the soda is E_2, so the expected distance from the E_3 vertex is 1 move to get to the E_2 vertex plus E_2.

There are 3 possible paths out of the E_3 vertex, and the ant follows them with $1/3$ probability each, so the weighted average of the three possible paths is:

$$E_3 = \frac{1}{3} \times (1 + E_2) + \frac{1}{3} \times (1 + E_2) + \frac{1}{3} \times (1 + E_2) = 1 + E_2$$

Now suppose the ant is at an E_2 vertex. Two of the paths out of that vertex lead to E_1 vertices and the third path leads back to the E_3 vertex. The weighted average of the three possible paths is:

$$E_2 = \frac{1}{3} \times (1 + E_1) + \frac{1}{3} \times (1 + E_1) + \frac{1}{3} \times (1 + E_3) = 1 + \frac{2}{3} \times E_1 + \frac{1}{3} \times E_3$$

Finally suppose the ant is at an E_1 vertex. Two of the paths out of that vertex lead back to E_2 vertices and the third path leads to the soda. The weighted average of the three possible paths is:

$$E_1 = \frac{1}{3} \times (1 + E_2) + \frac{1}{3} \times (1 + E_2) + \frac{1}{3} \times (1) = 1 + \frac{2}{3} \times E_2$$

Now we have the following three equations with three unknowns:.

$$E_3 = 1 + E_2$$

$$E_2 = 1 + \frac{2}{3} \times E_1 + \frac{1}{3} \times E_3$$

$$E_1 = 1 + \frac{2}{3} \times E_2$$

You can solve these equations to find the expected number of moves from each type of vertex.

$$E_3 = 7$$

$$E_2 = 9$$

$$E_1 = 10$$

So the expected number of moves the ant makes to reach the soda is 10.

It's interesting to note that there are no paths of exactly 10 steps that end at the soda.

THE LUCKY ANT

Puzzle: An ant and a can of soda are positioned on opposite corners of a cube. For each move the ant travels along a randomly selected edge until it reaches the next vertex. What is the probability that the ant will get lucky and reach the soda in exactly three moves?

If you want to see a picture of the initial situation, look at Figure 4–7 again.

To determine the probability of the ant finding the lucky path, we need to count the number of three–move paths that reach the soda and the total number of three–move paths.

The ant has three possible choices for the first move. No matter which choice it makes, the ant ends up at one of the vertices labeled E_2 in Figure 4–8.

From an E_2 vertex, the ant must move to an E_1 vertex in the second move if it is going to reach the soda by the third move. Each E_2 vertex has two choices for the E_1 vertex to visit next.

From the E_1 vertex, the ant has only a single choice for the third move: it must move to the soda.

The ant has three viable choices for its first move, two for its second, and one for its third, so the total number of paths that reach the soda in three moves is $3\times2\times1=6$.

The ant has three possible edges that it could follow during each move, so the total number of possible three–move paths is $3^3=27$.

Together those numbers mean that the probability of the ant finding a lucky path is $6/27=2/9\approx0.22$.

THE UNLUCKY ANT

> **Puzzle:** An ant and a can of soda are positioned on opposite corners of a cube. For each move the ant travels along a randomly selected edge until it reaches the next vertex. What is the probability that the ant will reach the soda in exactly 100 moves?

If you want to see a picture of the initial situation, look at Figure 4–7 again.

This puzzle is intimidating because there are a huge number of possible 100–move paths and surely many of those must end at the soda, right?

However, there's a trick. Before you read about it, try finding a path that reaches the soda in exactly four moves. You'll probably quickly discover the solution to the puzzle.

Suppose you orient the cube so it's centered at the origin with each of its faces parallel to the X–Y, Y–Z, and X–Z planes. If you assume the cube is 2 units wide, then the coordinates of its vertices are $(\pm1, \pm1, \pm1)$.

Also assume that the ant is initially at the vertex $(-1, -1, -1)$ and the soda is at $(+1, +1, +1)$.

Each time you follow one of the cube's edges, you change the sign of one of the coordinates of the ant's location. For example, from the initial position $(-1, -1, -1)$, if the ant moves parallel to the X axis, its new position is $(+1, -1, -1)$.

The only way the ant can get from $(-1, -1, -1)$ to $(+1, +1, +1)$ is to switch the signs of its position's coordinates an odd number of times. It could do it in three moves (as shown by "The Lucky Ant" puzzle), or it could do it in five moves, or 17 moves, or 111 moves. With a little work, you can show that the ant can reach the soda in any odd number of moves greater than one.

However, you can never switch the signs from $(-1, -1, -1)$ to $(+1, +1, +1)$ in an even number of moves. That means it's impossible for the ant to reach the soda in exactly 100 moves, and therefore the probability of that happening is 0.

Whenever a puzzle involves a large number that makes it seem impossible, look for a trick. Often there's some detail that lets you skip the daunting calculation and jump to the solution relatively easily.

> **Note:** If a puzzle involves a large number that makes it seem impossible, look for a trick. There may be an easier way to solve the puzzle than the obvious one.

Now if the puzzle had asked for the probability of the ant reaching the soda in exactly 99 moves, that would have been another matter.

ANTS ON AN OCTAHEDRON

> **Puzzle:** Six ants are sitting on the vertices of an octahedron. Each ant moves along a randomly chosen edge. What is the probability that the ants don't collide?

This is a variation of the "Ants on a Cube" puzzle. To solve the puzzle, you need to count the number of arrangements of ants that avoid collision and the total number of possible arrangements of ants.

As is the case with a cube, there are two kinds of arrangements that the ants can follow to avoid collisions on an octahedron. Figure 4–9 shows the first kind of arrangement.

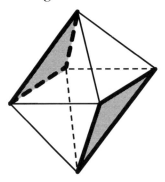

Figure 4–9: Ants following these two closed paths don't collide.

In Figure 4–9, the ants follow the edges of the two shaded triangles. To enumerate these arrangements, you can pick any of the four triangles on the top half of the octahedron and then match it with the opposite triangle on the bottom half. There are four possible orientations for each pair of triangles (CW–CW, CW–CCW, CCW–CW, and CCW–CCW), so there are a total of 4×4=16 arrangements of this kind.

Figure 4–10 shows the other kinds of arrangements that avoid collisions.

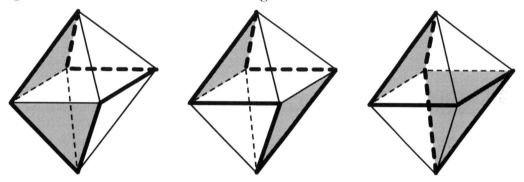

Figure 4–10: Ants following these paths don't collide.

To build these arrangements, start by choosing one of the four triangles on the top half of the octahedron. Add to the path the triangle's edges that are not on the octahedron's equator.

Next add one of the three triangles on the bottom half of the octahedron that doesn't share a common edge with the top triangle. In Figure 4–10 the pairs of triangles are shaded to make them easier to see.

You can't pair a top triangle with a bottom triangle that shares an edge with it because the path including those two triangles would be closed, so you couldn't reach the other two vertices that aren't part of those triangles.

Figure 4–11 shows another kind of path that lets the ants avoid collisions.

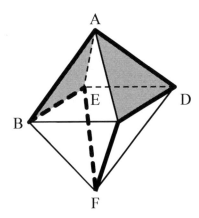

Figure 4–11: This path is the same as another path that has been rotated.

The paths shown in Figure 4–10 each have 2 shaded triangles where the edge that isn't part of the path lies on the octahedron's equator. The path shown in Figure 4–11 has no such triangles, so this path is different from the others.

For example, consider the shaded triangle ΔABE in Figure 4–11. Its edge BE lies on the octahedron's equator and that edge is part of the closed path drawn in bold.

You could try to enumerate all of the paths of this type directly, but the symmetry of the octahedron gives you an easier way to count them.

It's fairly obvious that you can rotate a *cube* around the X, Y, and Z axes to get another cube with a different orientation. That allows you to create paths on the cube that have different orientations.

It's less obvious that you can do the same thing with an octahedron. If you place the octahedron's vertices along the axes, then you can rotate to move any of the vertices to the top.

If you rotate the octahedron appropriately, then paths of the type shown in Figure 4–11 become paths similar to those shown in Figure 4–10. In this example, if you rotate the octahedron so vertex B is on top, then the square □ACFE becomes the octahedron's equator. Then triangle ΔABE becomes a top triangle and triangle ΔACD becomes a bottom triangle similar to those shown on the right in Figure 4–10.

To enumerate all of the paths similar to those shown in Figure 4–10, you can rotate the octahedron so each of the vertices A, B, and C are on top and then generate the paths shown in Figure 4–10.

You don't need to move vertices D, E, and F to the top because then you would duplicate the paths generated with vertices A, B, and C on top.

Taking all of this into account, the number of paths similar to those shown in Figure 4–10 is:

$$[\text{\# top triangles}] \times [\text{\# allowed bottom triangles}] \times [\text{\# orientations}]$$

$$= 4 \times 3 \times 3 = 36$$

Each path can also be oriented clockwise or counterclockwise, so the total number of paths of this type is $2 \times 36 = 72$.

Then the total number of paths that avoid collisions is:

$$[\text{\# paths similar to Figure 4-9}] \times [\text{\# paths simil   to Figure 4-10}]$$

$$= 16 + 72 = 88$$

There are six ants and each has four choices for the direction it moves, so there are $4^6 = 4{,}096$ possible outcomes.

Therefore the probability that the ants don't collide is $88/4{,}096 = 11/512 \approx 0.02$.

Remember when I said at the beginning of the chapter that the puzzles get more complicated when you use more complicated shapes? I wasn't kidding!

ONE ANT ON AN OCTAHEDRON

Puzzle: An ant and a can of soda are positioned on opposite corners of an octahedron. For each move the ant travels along a randomly selected edge until it reaches the next vertex. What is the expected number of moves the ant makes before it reaches the soda?

This is a variation of the "One Ant on a Cube" puzzle.

Let E_1 and E_2 be the expected number of moves that the ant makes to reach the soda when it starts 1 or 2 edges away from the soda respectively. Figure 4–12 shows the octahedron with its vertices labeled with their expected numbers of moves. The ant begins at the vertex labeled E_2, so our goal is to calculate E_2.

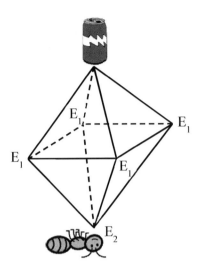

Figure 4–12: An ant and can of soda sit on opposite corners of an octahedron.

If the ant is at the E_2 node, then it has a 1/4 probability of moving to any one of the E_1 nodes during its next move. The expected number of moves it makes from the E_2 node is:

$$E_2 = \frac{1}{4} \times (1 + E_1) + \frac{1}{4} \times (1 + E_1) + \frac{1}{4} \times (1 + E_1) + \frac{1}{4} \times (1 + E_1) = 1 + E_1$$

If the ant is at an E_1 node, then it has a 1/4 probability of moving back to the E_2 node, a 2/4 probability of moving to another E_1 node, and a 1/4 probability of moving to the soda. That means the expected number of moves it makes from the E_1 node is:

$$E_1 = \frac{1}{4} \times (1 + E_2) + \frac{2}{4} \times (1 + E_1) + \frac{1}{4} \times (1) = 1 + \frac{1}{4} \times E_2 + \frac{1}{2} \times E_1$$

That gives you the following two equations and two unknowns.

$$E_2 = 1 + E_1$$

$$E_1 = 1 + \frac{1}{4} \times E_2 + \frac{1}{2} \times E_1$$

You can solve those equations to find the following values for E_2 and E_2.

$$E_1 = 5$$

$$E_2 = 6$$

Therefore the expected number of moves the ant makes to reach the soda is 6.

Two Move Soda

> **Puzzle:** An ant and a can of soda are positioned on opposite corners of an octahedron. For each move the ant travels along a randomly selected edge until it reaches the next vertex. What is the probability that the ant will get lucky and reach the soda in exactly two moves?

In its first move, all of the ant's choices lead to a vertex that is one move away from the soda. In other words, all of the ant's choices for its first move are correct. That means the probability of the ant making a correct choice for its first move is 1.

In its second move, the ant has a 1/4 probability of picking the correct edge to follow to get to the soda.

The ant's choices for its two moves are independent, so the Multiplication Rule lets us multiply their probabilities and the total probability of the ant achieving the lucky two–move path is 1×1/4=1/4.

Three Move Soda

> **Puzzle:** An ant and a can of soda are positioned on opposite corners of an octahedron. For each move the ant travels along a randomly selected edge until it reaches the next vertex. What is the probability that the ant will reach the soda in exactly three moves?

All of the ant's possible first moves lead to a three–move path, so the ant will pick a valid start with probability 1.

In its second move, the ant cannot move back to its starting vertex or else it won't be able to reach the soda in its third move. The ant also cannot move to the soda in its second move or it won't arrive at the soda in its third move. That gives the ant a probability of 2/4=1/2 that it will move to one of the other adjacent vertices that is neither the starting vertex nor the soda's vertex.

In its third move, there is a 1/4 probability that the ant will move to the soda.

The ant's choices in its three moves are independent, so the Multiplication Rule lets us multiply their probabilities and the total probability of the ant achieving the three–move path is 1×1/2×1/4=1/8.

TWO OR THREE MOVE SODA

> **Puzzle:** An ant and a can of soda are positioned on opposite corners of an octahedron. For each move the ant travels along a randomly selected edge until it reaches the next vertex. What is the probability that the ant will reach the soda in at most three moves?

The ant cannot reach the soda in one move, so to reach the soda in at most three moves, it must do so in either two or three moves. The preceding two puzzles give the probabilities of the ant stumbling across paths with lengths of two or three.

Those outcomes are exclusive (the ant can't reach the soda in exactly two moves *and* in exactly three moves), so Addition Rule 1 lets us add the probabilities and the total probability of reaching the soda in at most three moves is 1/4+1/8=3/8.

ANTS ON A STAR

> **Puzzle:** Suppose five ants are sitting on the corners of a star as shown in Figure 4–13. Each ant flips a tiny coin and moves at the same speed along a randomly chosen edge. What is the probability that the ants don't collide?

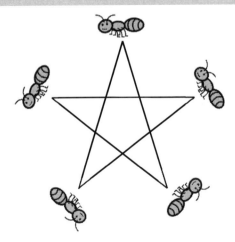

Figure 4–13: Five ants on the corners of a star.

There are a couple of issues that you should consider here. First, all of the ants need to move in the same direction, either clockwise or counterclockwise. There are five ants so the probability of them all moving clockwise is $(1/2)^5$. Similarly there is a $(1/2)^5$ probability of them all picking counterclockwise. Those events are mutually exclusive, so there's a $(1/2)^5+(1/2)^5=1/16$ probability that the ants all move in the same direction.

Next, even if the ants all move in the same direction, you should consider whether they collide when their paths cross at the star's interior corners. If the ants move at the same speed, then they each reach the closer of the two points of intersection along their paths at the same time. At that point the ants are each sitting on a different interior corner so they don't collide.

A short while later each ant reaches the second point of intersection along its path. Again they are each sitting at a different interior corner so they still don't collide.

The ants basically move past each other in a well–coordinates maneuver something like a synchronized swimming routine.

SUMMARY

Ant puzzles usually ask you to perform one of three tasks: calculating the probability of a particular situation, such as the ants moving without colliding; finding the probability of a certain event occurring, such as an ant finding a lucky path; or calculating the expected distance an ant travels to reach a goal.

The examples shown in this chapter demonstrate methods that you can use to solve all three of those kinds of puzzles.

You can easily make variations on these puzzles by changing the location of the goal, the number of moves the ant is allowed to make to reach the goal, of the object on which the ant is walking. Be careful, however, if you change the object. As you can see from the solutions shown here, working with a polygon or tetrahedron isn't too hard, but using a cube or an octahedron makes things much more difficult. Calculating the expected number of moves needed to go from one side of an icosahedron to another would be extremely difficult. And I don't even want to think about how many ways ants could move on an icosahedron without colliding with each other.

PROGRAMMING EXERCISES

1. Write a program that simulates ants on a triangle. Let the user enter a number of trials. For each trial, move each ant randomly and see whether any collide. Keep in mind that ants collide if they move across the same edge even if they end up at

different vertices. (In other words, if they swap positions.) After finishing the trials, the program should display the percentage of times that there were no collisions.

2. Repeat Exercise 1 for general polygons. Let the user enter the number of the polygon's sides.

3. Repeat Exercise 1 for a cube. It may be helpful to build a table of allowed moves so you can tell which vertices are accessible from which others.

4. Write a program that simulates a single ant on a cube. Let the user enter a number of trials and a number of moves. For each trial, move the ant randomly through the indicated number of moves and then see if the ant arrived at the soda on the cube's opposite vertex. Calculate the percentage of times the ant arrives at the soda. Does the probability tend toward a limit as the number of moves grows large?

5. Repeat Exercise 4 but counting the number of times the ant returns to its starting position instead of the number of times it reaches the soda.

6. Write a program that simulates a single ant on a cube. Let the user enter a number of trials. For each trial, move the ant randomly until it reaches the soda on the cube's opposite vertex. After the trials are finished, calculate the average number of steps the ant needed. How does the result relate to the expected number of steps calculated for the "One Ant on a Cube" puzzle?

7. Repeat Exercise 6 but counting the number of times the ant returns to its starting position instead of the number of times it reaches the soda. Calculate the expected distance the ant must travel to return to its starting point and compare that value to the result found by the program.

For Exercises 8 through 12, repeat Exercises 3 through 7 for an octahedron.

5

Subtle Selections

For these puzzles you need to make some sort of selection. For example, you might need to pick random socks from a drawer, or you might need to arrange marbles to maximize the probability of your later picking certain colors. These puzzles typically ask you to calculate probabilities or to make selections that guarantee a certain result, such as knowing that you have two matching socks.

Often you can change these puzzles by renaming the objects that you're selecting. For example, instead of marbles you could use crystals or donuts. You won't baffle someone who truly understands the puzzle, but you might make things harder for someone who only knows the puzzle by name and doesn't understand the underlying principles.

RED AND BLUE MARBLES

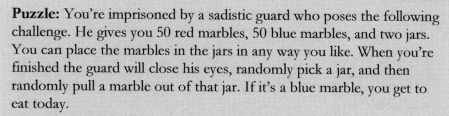

Puzzle: You're imprisoned by a sadistic guard who poses the following challenge. He gives you 50 red marbles, 50 blue marbles, and two jars. You can place the marbles in the jars in any way you like. When you're finished the guard will close his eyes, randomly pick a jar, and then randomly pull a marble out of that jar. If it's a blue marble, you get to eat today.

How can you arrange the marbles to maximize your chances of eating today? How many arrangements can give you the maximum probability?

There are many possible arrangements of marbles that give various probabilities of getting a blue marble. To see which arrangement will work the best, let's consider a few sample strategies.

Blue in One Jar, Red in the Other

Suppose you put all of the blue marbles in the first jar and all of the red marbles in the second.

The guard has a 1/2 probability of picking the first jar, and in that case he gets a blue marble because that jar only contains blue marbles.

There's also a 1/2 probability that the guard picks the second jar, in which case he gets a red marble because that jar only contains red marbles.

This strategy gives you a 1/2 probability of getting a blue marble (when the guard picks the first jar) and being allowed to eat.

All Marbles in One Jar

Another strategy would be to place all of the marbles in the first jar.

Now the guard has a 1/2 probability of picking the first jar. If that happens, he has a 50/100=1/2 probability of getting a blue marble. Those picks are independent so the Multiplication Rule says that the total probability of getting a blue marble in this way is 1/2×1/2=1/4.

The guard also has a 1/2 probability of initially picking the second jar. That jar doesn't hold any marbles so he can't pull a blue marble out of it and therefore you go hungry.

That makes the final probability of picking a blue marble 1/4, which is worse than the first strategy.

Most Blue Marbles in One Jar

Suppose you modify the first strategy by moving some of the blue marbles into the second jar. For example, suppose the first jar contains 40 blue marbles and the second jar contains all of the other marbles.

There's a 1/2 probability that the guard picks the first jar and then gets a blue marble because that jar only contains blue marbles.

There's also a 1/2 probability that the guard picks the second jar. In that case, there's a 10/60=1/6 probability that the guard pulls a blue marble from the second jar.

The two successful outcomes are mutually exclusive (the guard can't pick from both jars) so Addition Rule 1 says that the total probability of picking a blue marble is 1/2+1/6=4/6=2/3. That's bigger than the 1/2 probability given by the first strategy so it's an improvement.

The Best Strategy

Now let's take the "Most Blue Marbles in One Jar" strategy to the extreme. Let's place one blue marble in the first jar and put all of the other marbles in the second jar.

First, there's a 1/2 probability that the guard picks the first jar. That jar contains only a single blue marble, so there's probability 1 that the guard then picks that marble. The total probability of picking that marble from the first jar is $1/2 \times 1 = 1/2$.

There's also a 1/2 probability that the guard picks the second jar. That jar contains 49 blue marbles and 50 red marbles, so the probability of the guard then picking a blue marble is 49/99. The total probability of picking a blue marble from the second jar is $1/2 \times 49/99 = 49/198$.

The two successful outcomes are mutually exclusive, so Addition Rule 1 says the total probability of picking a blue marble $1/2 + 49/198 = 148/198 \approx 0.75$.

This is a greater probability than the other strategies.

Other Strategies

Proving that this is the best possible strategy is fairly complicated.

Intuitively suppose you move blue marbles from the second jar into the first. That doesn't change the probability of the first jar yielding a blue marble (it's still 1), but it lowers the probability of the second jar giving you a blue marble.

Suppose instead you move red marbles from the second jar into the first. That slightly increases the probability of the second jar giving you a blue marble, but it greatly reduces the probability of the first jar giving you a blue marble.

The best strategy is to place 1 blue marble in the first jar and all of the other marbles in the second.

The only other strategy that gives the same roughly 0.75 probability of success is if you switch the roles of the two jars. Place a single blue marble in the second jar and place all of the remaining marbles in the first.

RED, GREEN, AND BLUE MARBLES

Puzzle: Suppose you're imprisoned by the same sadistic guard from the "Red and Blue Marbles" puzzle, but this time he has two jars and

50 marbles of each of three colors: red, green, and blue. As before, you only get to eat if he picks a blue marble.

How can you arrange the marbles to maximize your chance of eating today?

The solution to this puzzle is actually quite simple. Just treat the red and green marbles as if they are the same. Place a single blue marble in the first jar and place all of the remaining marbles in the second jar. Then the odds of picking a blue marble are:

$$1/2 \times 1 + 1/2 \times 49/149 = 99/149 \approx 0.66$$

This is less than the 0.75 probability that you can get with just two colors, but it's a lot better than the roughly 0.33 probability you would get if you just mixed the marbles together.

MATCHING SOCKS

Puzzle: You wake up early and want to leave for work. You need to find a pair of matching socks, but you don't want to turn on the lights and wake your roommate. If your sock drawer contains 20 red socks and 17 blue socks all jumbled together, how many socks do you need to take into the hallway to be sure that you have a matching pair?

The number of socks of each color is irrelevant. You only need to know the number of colors. This example uses two colors, red and blue, so you need to pick three socks. If the first two socks don't match, then the third must match one of the first two.

Note: This is an example of the pigeonhole principle.

The pigeonhole principle says, if you have N items and you divide them into M groups, and N > M, then at least one group must contain more than one item. For example, if you have a group of 10 mail slots (sometimes called pigeonholes) and you need to place 11 letters in them, then at least one mailbox must contain more than one letter.

In the sock example, you have two colors so if you pick three socks then at least one color must "contain" two socks.

This puzzle is easy to generalize. For example, suppose the drawer contains red, blue, green, and orange socks. In that case there are four colors so you could pick up to four socks without getting a match. In that case, sock number five must match one of the others, so you need to pick at least five socks. You can also make variations of the puzzle by using other objects that come in matching sets such as gloves, shoes, or chopsticks.

Of course you can avoid the whole problem if you only buy one kind of sock.

FOUR OF A KIND

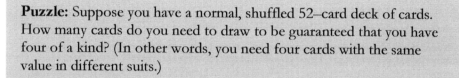

> **Puzzle:** Suppose you have a normal, shuffled 52–card deck of cards. How many cards do you need to draw to be guaranteed that you have four of a kind? (In other words, you need four cards with the same value in different suits.)

This is similar to the "Matching Socks" puzzle. The differences are that you have 13 different values analogous to sock colors, and you need to find four matching values instead of a pair.

One way to solve these kinds of puzzle in general is to think about the worst possible case. For this puzzle, how long can you pick cards before you get four of a kind?

You could start with three aces. That's as many aces as you can have without getting four of a kind, so you need to add another type of card.

To be methodical, you can add cards in order so add a 2. As long as you have a single 2, you may as well have three of them, so add two more. That's as many 2s as you can have without getting four of a kind, so move on to the next value: 3.

If you continue that way, you can draw three aces, three 2s, three 3s, and so on up to three kings. That's $3 \times 13 = 39$ cards.

At this point no matter what card you add next, you'll have a four of a kind.

That gives you the solution to the puzzle. You need to draw 39 cards plus 1 more for a total of 40 cards to guarantee that you have four of a kind.

FOUR OF A KIND, PART 2

> **Puzzle:** Suppose you have six normal 52–card decks shuffled together. How many cards do you need to draw to be guaranteed that you have four of a kind?

The logic is the same as it is for the original "Four of a Kind" puzzle. The number of decks doesn't matter. All that matters is the number of values the cards can have: ace, 2, 3, ..., queen, king.

The worst case is three aces, three 2s, three 3s, ..., three queens, and three kings. That gives you three of 13 different values for a total of $3 \times 13 = 39$ cards.

Adding one more card to ensure a four of a kind gives you 40 cards. The number of decks of cards that you use doesn't matter.

FOUR OF A KIND, PART 3

> **Puzzle:** Suppose you have six normal 52–card decks shuffled together. How many cards do you need to draw to be guaranteed that you have an exact four of a kind? For example, four aces of spades or four queens of hearts.

Again the number of decks doesn't matter. All that matters is the number of values that the cards can have. This time, however, we're considering cards with different suits to be different. For example, the ace of diamonds is different from the ace of clubs.

The worst case is three aces of spades, three 2s of spades, three 3s of spades, ..., three kings of spades. It would also include three aces of hearts, three 2s of hearts, and so forth.

In the end it would include three of each of the 52 distinct cards for a total of $3 \times 52 = 156$ cards.

Adding one more to ensure a four of a kind gives you a total of 157 cards.

MATCHING CHECKERS

> **Puzzle:** Suppose you have a bag containing 50 red checkers and 50 black checkers. The bag is deep and its neck is small so you can't see what color checker you've grabbed until it's completely out of the bag.
>
> In the worst case, how many checkers might you need to pull from the bag before you have at least 12 red and 12 black checkers?

This puzzle is a bit different from the previous ones for two reasons. First, instead of matching two objects to make a pair, you essentially need to make "pairs" of 12 checkers. Second, you need to make "pairs" of both red and black checkers.

In the worst case, you could pick all 50 checkers of one color before you pick any of the other color. For example, you might be unlucky and pull out all of the 50 red checkers first. In that case you would need to pick 12 more to be sure you have enough black checkers. That means you need to pull 50+12=62 checkers out of the bag to be sure you have 12 of each color.

Variation: Suppose the bag contains 60 red checkers and 40 black checkers. Now how many checkers do you need to pull from the bag to be sure you have at least 12 red and 12 black?

In the worst case, you pick all 60 red checkers before you pick any black checkers. In that case you need to pick another 12 checkers before you're sure you have enough of both colors making the total 60+12=72 checkers.

Variation: Suppose the bag contains 100 checkers but you don't know how many are red and how many are black. Now how many checkers do you need to pull from the bag to be sure you have at least 12 red and 12 black?

In this case you can't really tell how many checkers you might need to pull from the bag. For example, if there are no black checkers, then you won't have enough of each color even if you pull them all out.

Assuming there are enough checkers of each color in the bag, then the worst case is if there are only 12 of one of the colors. In that case you would need to take every checker from the bag before you were sure you had 12 of each color.

Of course in real life you would stop picking checkers when you had 12 of each color. Or you could just dump the whole bag on the floor and pick out the colors you need. Then you can make whoever loses the game clean up the mess.

Variation: Suppose you're not going to play a game of checkers, but you only want 10 matching checkers to use as tokens for some other game. (Perhaps Munchkin. See www.worldofmunchkin.com/game.) How many checkers do you need to pick to guarantee that you have 10 matching checkers?

You essentially need to make a 10–checker "pair." In the worst case, you could initially pick nine red checkers and nine black checkers. The next checker would make a 10–checker match, so you need to pick a total of 9+9+1=19 checkers.

CAR OR GOAT

Puzzle: Suppose you're on a game show. You can win one of three prizes: a fabulous car, a goat, or a different goat. Obviously you want the car. The prizes are randomly hidden behind three doors.

Initially you're allowed to pick a door. Without showing you what's behind the door you picked, the host then opens one of the other two doors and reveals a goat.

While the crowd loudly shouts useless advice, you're given a chance to switch doors if you like. Should you switch doors or should you stick with your original choice?

You initially had a 1/3 probability of picking the door with the car. Showing you the goat behind one of the other doors didn't change what was behind your door, so intuition says it shouldn't have changed the probability that you picked the car.

In this case intuition is wrong and you should switch doors. The following sections use two different methods to explain why. Hopefully one of them will make enough sense to overrule your intuition.

Solution 1

Suppose you initially pick door 1. There's a 1/3 probability that the car is behind door 1 and a 2/3 probability that the car is somewhere else.

Now the host shows you a goat behind one of the other doors. Suppose it's door 2.

After the host shows you one of the goats, there's still a 1/3 probability that the car is behind door 1 and a 2/3 probability that car is somewhere else. But you now know that the car isn't behind door 2, so if it is somewhere else it must be behind door 3. That means there's a 2/3 probability that the car is behind door 3, so you should switch.

Solution 2

When in doubt, it's often useful to enumerate every possible outcome in a probability puzzle. Figure 5–1 shows all of the possible arrangements of the car and two goats.

Door 1	Door 2	Door 3
Car	Goat 1	Goat 2
Car	Goat 2	Goat 1
Goat 1	Car	Goat 2
Goat 2	Car	Goat 1
Goat 1	Goat 2	Car
Goat 2	Goat 1	Car

Figure 5–1: All of the possible arrangements of a car and two goats.

Now suppose you pick door 1. The analysis for the other doors would be similar.

First suppose the car and goats are placed in one of the first two arrangements with the car behind door 1. In that case if you switch doors, you lose the car and win a goat.

Next suppose the car and goats are placed in the third or fourth arrangement with the car behind door 2. In that case the host will show you the goat behind door 3. If you switch you'll end up with door 2 and you'll win the car.

Finally suppose the car and goats are placed in the fifth or sixth arrangement with the car behind door 3. In that case the host will show you the goat behind door 2. If you switch you'll end up with door 3 and you'll also win the car.

So if you switch doors, you lose for two of the arrangements and you win for the other four. That means the probability of winning with this strategy is 4/6=2/3.

MULTIPLE GUESS

Puzzle: What is the probability of randomly picking the correct answer to this question from the following list?

A. 1/4

B. 1/2

C. 1

D. 1/4

Understanding this puzzle is a bit of a puzzle in itself.

The easiest way to solve this puzzle is to look at each of the listed solutions. They are 1/4, 1/2, and 1.

First, suppose the correct answer is 1/4. Then you must have probability 1/4 of randomly picking that solution from the list of answers. But the answer 1/4 appears in two of the four choices, so the probability of actually picking that solution randomly is 1/2. That means this cannot be the correct solution.

Next, suppose the correct answer is 1/2. Then you must have probability 1/2 of randomly picking that solution from the list of answers. But the answer 1/2 appears in only one of the four choices, so the probability of actually picking that solution randomly is 1/4. That means this cannot be the correct solution.

Finally, suppose the correct answer is 1. Then you must have probability 1 of randomly picking that solution from the list of answers. But the answer 1 appears in only one of the four choices, so the probability of actually picking that solution randomly is 1/4. That means this cannot be the correct solution.

At this point, you've eliminated all of the listed solutions so you might think you're in trouble. Fortunately the puzzle doesn't actually ask you to pick an answer from the list. Instead it asks you to determine the *probability* of picking the correct answer from the list. Because none of the answers in the list is correct, the probability of picking the correct answer from the list is 0.

MULTIPLE GUESS FIGHTS BACK

> **Puzzle:** How could you change the answers in the "Multiple Guess" puzzle to make one of them correct?

This question has a bit of a trick to it. If you read carefully, you'll see that it asks you to make *one* of the answers correct. If only one answer is correct, then there is a 1/4 probability that you will pick that answer randomly. That means the correct answer must be 1/4.

You can fix the puzzle by making exactly one of the answers be 1/4, but there's a little bit more to it. When you make one of the answers 1/4, you cannot also make one of the other answers correct at the same time. For example, you can't change answer A or D to 1/2 because then there would be a 1/2 probability of picking one of those answers so they would also be correct.

The following answers work.

A. 1/4

B. 1/2

C. 1

D. 1

Now there's a 1/4 probability of picking 1/4 (the right answer), a 1/4 probability of picking 1/2 (a wrong answer), and a 1/2 probability of picking 1 (another wrong answer).

There are other possible solutions to this version of the problem.

THE RETURN OF MULTIPLE GUESS

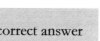

Puzzle: What is the probability of randomly picking the correct answer to this question from the following list?

A. 1/4

B. 1/2

C. 1/2

D. 1

The solution to this puzzle is practically philosophical because you can make good arguments in favor of each of these answers. The answer 1/4 appears in 1/4 of the answers. Your probability of picking it is clearly 1/4, so it's reasonable to consider it an answer.

Similarly the answer 1/2 appears in 1/2 of the answers, so the probability of picking it is 1/2 and it also makes sense as an answer.

Can you consider both 1/4 and 1/2 to be answers? After all, if I asked, "Which of the numbers 1, 2, 3, and 4 is even?" you would confidently answer 2 and 4.

If you consider both 1/4 and 1/2 to be answers, then if you also assume that 1 is an answer, the probability of randomly picking an answer is 1, thus confirming your designation of 1 as an answer.

This is all pretty confusing, so let's go back to the beginning. You're trying to find the probability of an event occurring. That event is you randomly picking the correct answer. Normally a single event can have only a single probability, so it may not make sense to allow all three solutions.

If you can't allow multiple solutions, then 1 is definitely off the table, but 1/4 and 1/2 still seem promising.

You could just declare, "The solution is 1/4," and then you have a consistent answer. Unfortunately the logic that proves that 1/4 is correct also proves that 1/2 is correct, so you could say, "The solution is 1/2," with equal confidence.

There's only one probability that is an unambiguous candidate for a solution: 0. If you assume the answer is 0, then all of the listed answers are wrong and you have 0 probability of randomly picking 0.

Note that if I were an interviewer, I would much rather hear the candidate working through all of this rather than simply stating an answer.

MULTIPLE GUESS, THE SEQUEL

Puzzle: How could you change the answers in the "Multiple Guess" puzzle to make all of them correct?

This is actually quite easy. Just use the following answers.

A. 1
B. 1
C. 1
D. 1

MISLABELED JARS

Puzzle: Suppose you have three jars, one containing red marbles, one containing blue marbles, and one containing a mix of red and blue marbles. Unfortunately all of the jars are mislabeled.

What is the minimum number of marbles that you can pick from the jars to figure out where the labels should be?

We can fix the labels by selecting a single marble from the jar labeled "Mix." Suppose we get a red marble. Then we know that this jar doesn't contain only the blue marbles. The jar was labeled "Mix" and we know that every jar was incorrectly labeled, so this jar also cannot contain the mix. If it doesn't contain the blue marbles or the mix, then it must contain the red marbles.

Next, because every jar is mislabeled, the jar labeled "Blue" must contain either the red marbles or the mix. But we just showed that the jar labeled "Mix" contains the red marbles, so the jar labeled "Blue" must contain the mix.

By process of elimination the jar labeled "Red" must contain the blue marbles. Figure 5–2 shows the correct contents for each off the incorrect labels.

Label	Contents
Mix	Red
Red	Blue
Blue	Mix

Figure 5–2: The contents of the mislabeled jars if you pick a red marble from the jar labeled "Mix."

If you pick a blue marble from the jar labeled "Mix," then Figure 5–3 shows the jars' contents.

Label	Contents
Mix	Blue
Red	Mix
Blue	Red

Figure 5–3: The contents of the mislabeled jars if you pick a blue marble from the jar labeled "Mix."

Instead of marbles, the jars can contain two kinds of fruits, two flavors of jelly beans, or two types of just about any other kind of object.

The puzzle probably wouldn't work well with two liquids such as water and milk. It would be hard to remove one water from a jar.

MAXIMAL SUBARRAYS

Puzzle: Suppose you have an array that contains positive and negative integers in any order. How can you find the subarray (contiguous entries) that holds the largest total of values?

This is really a programming puzzle so it would probably be too confusing for a candidate who's applying for a non–programing position.

For an example, suppose the array contains the values {2, –5, 7}. Figure 5–4 shows all of the possible subarrays and their total values.

Subarray	Total
{2, –5, 7}	4
{2, –5}	–3
{–5, 7}	2
{2}	2
{–5}	–5
{7}	7
{ }	0

Figure 5–4: All of the subarrays of the array containing the values {2, –5, 7}.

It's easy to see in Figure 5–4 that the maximal subarray contains the single item with value 7. For longer arrays, such as {–5, 5, 2, 6, –4, 9, –4, 8, 1, 2}, it's not as easy to find the maximal subarray.

Kadane's algorithm is one of the easier ways to find a maximal subarray. In this algorithm you scan through the array from start to finish. For each position P, you calculate the best subtotal that you can make by using subarrays that end at position P.

Suppose you're moving through the array and you're at position P. You've already passed position P–1, so you already know the largest possible subtotal for any subarray that ends at position P–1. Call that largest subtotal S_{P-1}.

Now consider subarrays that end at position P.

If S_{P-1} is positive, then the best subtotal you can make ending at position P is the previous subtotal S_{P-1} plus the array's value at P. You simply use the largest subarray ending at position P–1 and extend it by one position to include the value at position P.

If S_{P-1} is negative, then the best subtotal you can make ending at position P includes the single entry at position P. Adding S_{P-1} to it would only make the total at position P smaller.

The following text shows the algorithm in pseudocode.

```
best_ending_here = -infinity
best_overall = -infinity
For Each Value X In array:
    best_ending_here = Max(X, best_ending_here + X)
    best_overall = Max(best_ending_here, best_overall)
```

When this code finishes, the value `best_overall` holds the total of the maximal subarray.

If you implement this in code, you can also keep track of the start and end of the maximal subarray as you go along.

MIXED BAG

> **Puzzle:** Suppose you have a bag containing 15 red marbles and 15 blue marbles, and now you're going to play a little game. You reach into the bag and pull two out marbles. If the two marbles are the same color, you place a blue marble in the bag and discard the two you pulled out. If the two are of different colors, you put the red marble back in the bag and discard the blue marble.
>
> Each time you repeat this process, you replace two marbles with one, so the number of marbles decreases until you're eventually left with a single marble. What color is that marble?

Because this puzzle involves a known mix of marbles, you might be tempted to calculate some probabilities. After you start making replacements, however, the number of red and blue marbles changes and the calculations quickly become extremely complicated.

A better approach is to look for some condition on the marbles that remains unchanged by the replacements. In this puzzle, the key fact is that the number of red marbles is always odd. There are two cases depending on which type of replacement you make.

If you pull out two matching marbles, then you remove them and replace them with a blue one. In that case you either removed zero or two red marbles, so if the number of red marbles was odd before the replacement, then it is still odd after the replacement.

If you pull out two different colored marbles, then you put the red one back in the bag and you remove the blue one, so the number of red marbles is unchanged.

Because the number of red marbles is always odd, when you have only one left it must be red.

Follow–up: When only two marbles are left, what colors are they?

You can't have two red or two blue marbles because then the number of red marbles would be even. That means you must have one red marble and one blue marble.

SUMMARY

Some selection puzzles ask you to arrange objects to make a particular selection more likely, as in the case of the jars of red and blue marbles. You can often solve those puzzles by calculating the probabilities for a few possible arrangements and then deciding in which direction the best solution lies.

Other selection puzzles ask you to determine how many objects you need to guarantee a result, such as finding matching socks or four of a kind. Often you can solve those puzzles by thinking about the worst case.

PROGRAMMING EXERCISES

1. Write a program to study the "Red and Blue Marbles" puzzle. It should try putting between 0 and 50 blue marbles in the first jar, calculate the probability of randomly selecting a blue marble for each arrangement, and then display the results so you can see which strategy is best.
2. Consider a puzzle similar to the "Red and Blue Marbles" puzzle but with three jars. What strategy do you think would give the guard the best chance of randomly picking a blue marble? After you make your guess, repeat Exercise 1 with three jars and find out. The program should place N blue marbles in the first jar, where N is between 0 and 50. Then it should put M marbles in the second jar, where M is between 0 and 50–N.
3. Write a program to study the "Car or Goat" puzzle. Let the user enter a number of trials. Then for each trial, the program should simulate one instance of the game with and without switching doors. When it's done, it should display the probability of winning for the two strategies.
4. Write a program to implement Kadane's algorithm for finding maximal subarrays. The program should let the user enter the values in the array separated by spaces. It should then find the items in the maximal subarray and its total value.
5. Write a program that simulates picking checkers from a bag. Let the user enter the number of trials, and the numbers of red and black checkers. For each trial the program should randomly pick checkers until it has 12 of each color. When it is finished, it should display the average number of checkers it needed to pick.

6

Pure Probability

The puzzles in this chapter generally require you to make probability calculations. Many of the actual calculations are relatively straightforward, but often it's hard to figure out what calculations to perform because your intuition leads you in the wrong direction. Other puzzles use wording to imply the wrong approach.

Good techniques for solving these kinds of puzzles include figuring out what is actually important, working on the problem incrementally or in steps, and enumerating all of the possible outcomes to see what's actually happening.

GENDER MINDBENDER

Puzzle: Suppose you live in a country where every couple wants to have a girl. Each couple has children until they get a girl and then the couple stops having children.

Assuming the probability of having a girl or boy is the same for every birth, what is the country's ratio of girls to boys in the long term?

This puzzle is tricky because the result defies intuition. No couple will ever have three girls but they could have three boys, so obviously there should be more girls than boys, right?

Unfortunately in this case your intuition is completely wrong. The following sections describe three strategies for understanding that the country ends up with the same number of girls as boys. (Barring accidents.)

Quick but Unsatisfying Strategy

First, here's a quick but mostly unsatisfying explanation. If the probability of each baby being a girl or boy is 1/2, then the ratio of girls to boys in a large population will be 1:1. If there are N babies, then there will be roughly N/2 girls and N/2 boys.

This is correct but somehow seems unconvincing. After all, this scheme allows a family to have 10 boys a row but it doesn't allow a family to have even two girls in a row. Somehow that intuitively seems like it would skew the population.

More Satisfying Strategy

Here's a more satisfying explanation.

For simplicity, suppose the couples have babies in synchronized rounds. In round one, half of the couples have girls and half have boys. At this point, half of the babies are girls and half are boys.

The couples that had girls in round one stop and the other couples try again in round two. Of those couples, half have girls and half have boys. Again the country has the same number of girls and boys.

At this point you can probably see where we're heading. At any round R, half of the couples have girls and stop, while the other half have boys and try again in round R+1. In round R (and all of the previous rounds), half of the new babies are girls and half are boys.

That means in the long term, the country will have roughly the same number of boys as girls.

Mathematical Strategy

This solution is basically the same as the preceding one except it includes numbers.

Suppose the country has N couples. In round one, those couples have N/2 girls and N/2 boys.

In round two, the N/2 couples who had boys in round one try again. They produce (N/2)/2=N/4 girls and (N/2)/2=N/4 boys. That makes the total number of girls N/2+N/4. The total number of boys is the same.

In round three, the N/4 couples who had boys in round two try again. They produce (N/4)/2=N/8 girls and the same number of boys. That makes the total number of girls N/2+N/4+N/8. Again the total number of boys is the same.

In round four, the N/8 couples who had boys in round three try again. They produce (N/8)/2=N/16 girls and the same number of boys. That makes the total number of girls N/2+N/4+N/8+N/16. And, as you can probably guess, the total number of boys is the same.

In the long term, the total number of girls is:

$$\sum_{R=1}^{\infty} \frac{N}{2^R} = N \sum_{R=1}^{\infty} \frac{1}{2^R}$$

As the number of rounds R tends towards infinity, the summation on the right tends towards 1, so the total expected number of girls is simply N. Similarly the total expected number of boys is N.

This shows not only that the ratio of girls to boys is 1:1, but also that the couples have just enough children to replace themselves.

Note that this only works for relatively large populations. For small populations, the actual numbers of girls and boys may not match the expected numbers very closely. For example, if the country consists of a single couple, then there's a 1/2 probability that their first child is a girl, making the ratio of girls to boys undefined.

GENDER MINDBENDER, REDUX

> **Puzzle:** Suppose you live in the country described in the "Gender Mindbender" puzzle, but now any couple who has five boys in a row gives up and stops having children. Now what is the country's ratio of girls to boys in the long term?

As strange as it may seem, the result is the same as in the previous version of the puzzle. The expected ratio of girls to boys is 1:1.

Like the original "Gender Mindbender" puzzle, this one defies intuition. You might think that the numbers of girls and boys would only match if you allow fewer and fewer couples to have more and more children. You might assume that if you stop the process early, there would be unmatched boys to skew the population.

In fact, the same logic used to solve the original puzzle still applies. The only difference is that you don't need to use an infinite number of steps.

The first, somewhat unsatisfying explanation still holds. If there are N babies, then there will be roughly N/2 girls and N/2 boys. In the new version of the puzzle, N will just be smaller than it is in the previous version.

The second, more satisfying explanation, which uses rounds of births still holds. The only difference is that, in the new version of the puzzle, couples stop after at most five rounds. The number of girls and boys is the same after each round. If you're worried about the couples that stop after having five boys, note that for each of those couples there's another couple who stopped after five rounds because they had a girl in round five.

The third solution, which calculates the number of girls and boys, can still use a summation, but now the variable R only goes up to 5. The total number of girls (and boys) is now:

$$N \sum_{R=1}^{5} \frac{1}{2^R} = N \times \left(\frac{1}{2} + \frac{1}{4} + \frac{1}{8} + \frac{1}{16} + \frac{1}{32} \right) = N \times \frac{31}{32} = N \times 0.96875$$

This is not quite as many children as in the previous version, but it's pretty close.

PROBABILISTIC CARS

Puzzle: If the probability of a car passing a certain intersection in a 20–minute window is 0.9, what is the probability of a car passing the intersection in a five–minute window? (Assuming the probability is uniform throughout the puzzle.)

The tricky part of this puzzle is figuring out what equation to use. Unless you've seen this sort of problem before, you may not know where to start.

Often when you need to calculate one probability in terms of another, you need to find a way to recast one of the events in terms of the other. In this puzzle, a 20–minute window consists of four five–minute windows.

Exactly how you compose one event from four other events depends on the relationships among the events. In this case, the probability of a car passing within a 20–minute window is the same as the probability of one or more cars passing in any of the four five–minute sub–windows.

Let P be the probability of at least one car passing inside a given five–minute window.

Intuitively you might like to add the probabilities, but adding probabilities isn't that simple because the five–minute sub–windows aren't mutually exclusive. For example, cars could pass in both the first and third five–minute windows. In order to add the probabilities, we would need to subtract out the probabilities of all of the combinations of multiple cars passing during any of the sub–windows, and that sounds like a lot of work.

A better approach is to examine the probabilities of cars *not* passing during the sub–windows. No cars passing during 20 minutes is the same as no cars passing during *any* of the five–minute sub–windows. Those events are independent, so we can multiply their probabilities.

We let P be the probability of a car passing during a five–minute sub–window, so the probability of no car passing is 1–P.

In that case the probability of no car passing during all four of the five–minute sub–windows is $(1–P)^4$.

This is the same as the probability of *no* cars passing during the larger 20–minute window, so the probability of at least one car passing during that window is 1 minus this probability or

$1–(1–P)^4$.

The problem statement says that this probability is 0.9, so we get the following equation.

$$0.9 = 1–(1–P)^4$$

Solving this for P gives:

$$P = 1 - \sqrt[4]{0.1} \approx 0.4377$$

In other words, there's almost a 44% chance that a car will pass in any given five–minute window.

PROBABILISTIC BYTE

Puzzle: Suppose you're watching a stream of an unknown number of bytes flowing past you on a network. When the stream finishes, how can you pick one of the bytes randomly and with equal probability?

If you could store the entire stream, then you could wait until it was finished and then pick one of the bytes randomly. Easy peasy, high fives all around, and we can all go home early.

Unfortunately you don't know how long the stream will be. It might be long enough to fill all of the memory and disk space at your disposal, and in that case you can't store the whole stream anyway.

If you knew how long the stream was going to be ahead of time, then you could just pick a random byte number, wait for that byte to float past, and grab it. But again, you don't know how long the stream will be ahead of time.

The solution is to always keep track of a byte chosen from those you've seen so far. Then when you see the next byte, switch to the new one with a probability that makes it equally likely that you'll pick any given byte from the stream.

To make this work, if you're looking at the Nth byte, switch to it with probability 1/N.

To see why this works, consider the first byte in the stream. At this point you've only seen one byte, so you pick it with probability 1/1=1. There's only one byte, so you don't have much choice anyway.

Now the second byte floats by, and you switch to it with probability 1/2. At this point there's probability 1/2 that you keep the first byte and probability 1/2 that you switch to the second byte, so the probability of picking either byte is the same, which is what we want.

You've still only seen two bytes, however, so this isn't terribly impressive.

Now the third byte comes along, and you switch to it with probability 1/3. At this point there's a 1/3 probability that you switched to the new byte and a 2/3 probability that you kept the old byte.

But which one was the old byte? There was a 1/2 probability that it was the first byte and a 1/2 probability that it was the second byte. That means the probability that you keep the first byte is 1/2×2/3=1/3. The probability that you keep the second byte is the same: 1/3. That means the probability that you kept any of the first three bytes is identical: 1/3.

Now you can probably see where this is heading. If so, you might want to stop reading and try to figure out the general case on your own before you read further.

> **Claim:** After you see N bytes, this scheme guarantees that you have picked any one of those bytes with probability 1/N.

We can prove this claim by induction.

> **Note:** *Induction* is a mathematical technique for proving statements that involve an integer N. In an inductive proof, you must do two things.
>
> First, you must prove a *base case* that ensures that the claim is true for some value N=B. Often B is 0 or 1.
>
> Second, you must show that, if the claim is true for any value k where k>B, then it must also be true for the value k+1.
>
> If you do those two things, then induction proves that the claim is true for all values N≥B.

Now back to the "Probability Byte" puzzle. First the base case. We saw earlier that the scheme worked for N = 1, 2, and 3. To make the claim cover as many values as possible, we can use B=1 as the base case.

Next we need to perform the inductive step. Suppose the claim holds true for the value N=k, and suppose you're now looking at byte number k+1. We need to show that the probability of picking any one of the first k+1 bytes is $1/(k+1)$.

When we see byte number k+1, the scheme tells us to switch to the new byte with probability $1/(k+1)$. That's what we need to show for the new byte, so we're done proving the claim for the most recent byte. What about the earlier bytes?

When we see byte number k+1, the scheme tells us to keep the previously selected byte with probability $[(k+1)-1]/(k+1)=k/(k+1)$.

Because we know the property holds for value k, we know that the probability of picking any one of the earlier k bytes was $1/k$.

Combining those two probabilities, we can calculate the probability of picking any one of the earlier bytes *and then keeping it* when we see byte k+1. That probability is:

$$k/(k+1)\times 1/k=1/(k+1)$$

That's what we were trying to prove, so the claim is true by induction.

Induction is a powerful theorem–proving technique, so you should add it to your interview puzzle toolkit. Search the internet for "induction proof examples" to see other examples of inductive proofs.

AIRPLANE SEATING

Puzzle: Suppose you're about to business take a trip to Wichita Kansas on a completely booked 100–seat airplane. You're last in line and your manager Arthur is first. Unfortunately Arthur is rather clueless (he is a manager, after all) and he succeeds in loosing his boarding pass between check–in and the plane. Rather than asking for help, he picks a random seat, sits down, and glares belligerently at anyone who later tries to claim that seat.

The other passengers don't want to cause trouble so, as they board, each passenger takes his or her assigned seat if it's available. If that seat is already taken, the passenger picks an empty seat at random.

> What is the probability that you end up in your assigned seat? (In real life you can predict which seat you'll end up in because it's next to the screaming baby.)

This problem is tricky because your intuition steers you in the wrong direction. There are 100 passengers and it seems like a lot of random selections must be happening, so it seems unlikely that you'll land in your assigned seat.

Actually there's a 1/2 probability that you'll end up in your assigned seat.

Part of the reason that your intuition is wrong is that there aren't as many random seat assignments happening as you might imagine. For example, suppose Arthur sits in a random seat and then consider the next passenger. There's only a 1/100 probability that Arthur is in that passenger's seat, so that passenger probably sits in his assigned seat. In general, lots of passengers probably end up in their assigned seats before someone is blocked by Arthur.

The following sections describe three strategies for understanding the puzzle's solution. The first uses a quick explanation, the second uses a more detailed description of what happens, and the third may seem more intuitive to you.

Quick Strategy

The quick explanation is to note that when you eventually board the plane, there is only one seat available, because you're the last in line. At that point the empty seat is either yours or Arthur's because every other seat has either been taken by its rightful occupant or by Arthur.

Because there is no reason for anyone to prefer one of those seats over the other, there must be an equal probability that it's either one. That means there is a 1/2 probability that the available seat is your assigned seat.

If you think this is a sort of "hand–waving" style of explanation that doesn't seem very rigorous, perhaps the next explanation will be more satisfying.

Detailed Strategy

The quick explanation is correct, but it glosses over the fact that the last available seat is either yours or Arthur's. Here's why that's true.

The key is to note that, at any given moment, there is at most one passenger who still hasn't boarded the plane whose seat is blocked by someone else.

Suppose some passenger, call her Betty, is waiting to board and is blocked by someone who's already sitting in her seat. The other passengers board the plane and sit in their assigned seats until it's Betty's turn. Because her seat is blocked, she picks another seat at random. Say it's Christopher's seat.

Now Betty is no longer waiting to board and Christopher is blocked, so there is still only one person waiting to board who is blocked. Every time a blocked person (such as Betty) boards, he or she picks a random empty seat and blocks someone new (such as Christopher). That shows that there is always at most one person blocked.

So how does this fact help solve the puzzle?

Eventually someone (call her Debbie) randomly picks either your seat or Arthur's. It might happen early on, or at the latest it will happen when those are the only two empty seats remaining.

Suppose Debbie picks your seat. In that case, you're blocked. Because only one person at a time can be blocked, all of the other passengers in line can sit in their assigned seats. They do so and the only empty seat remaining at the end is Arthur's. (We know that no one has taken Arthur's seat because Debbie was the passenger who first took either your seat or his.)

Now suppose Debbie picks Arthur's seat. In that case, Debbie is no longer blocked (because she's not waiting any more) but she didn't block anyone new because Arthur is already sitting smugly in someone else's seat. Because no one is blocked, all of the remaining passengers including you can sit in their assigned seats.

All of this proves that you will either sit in your seat or in Arthur's seat.

Now let's go back to when Debbie picked either your seat or Arthur's. Suppose there were N empty seats remaining at that point. Then there's a $1/N$ probability that she picks your seat and a $1/N$ probability that she picks Arthur's seat. The probabilities are the same, so the chances are equal that she picks your seat or Arthur's and you end up in the other one.

All of this logic also applies if Arthur randomly picks either your seat or his own seat at the very beginning.

Intuitive Strategy

Here's another way to think about the puzzle that may be more intuitive. In this version, when a passenger boards the plane and finds Arthur in his seat, the blocked passenger politely asks Arthur to move to a new random seat.

Eventually Arthur randomly picks either your seat or his. After that point the previous logic shows that you will end up in either his seat or yours (the one that Arthur didn't take) with equal probability.

This situation is the equivalent to the previous one except in this version anyone who is blocked is blocked by Arthur instead of by different passengers.

No matter how the seating arrangements turn out, the flight crew thanks you all for handling all of this civilly without a lot of shouting and complaining.

THREE HATS FOR THREE PRISONERS

Puzzle: The traditional sadistic jailer is at it again. In a few minutes you and two other prisoners will be taken into a room. As each of you enters, the jailer will flip a coin to decide whether you will be given a red hat or a blue hat.

Once you're all in the room, you can see the other prisoners' hats but you can't see your own. Each of you must then write down a guess about your own hat color. You can write "red," "blue," or "pass."

If all of you pass or if one of you guesses the wrong color, then you all go hungry today.

You have two minutes to discuss the problem with the other prisoners before the game begins and you're taken to the room. What strategy should you use to maximize your chance of eating?

For example, one strategy would be for you to guess red and for the other prisoners to pass. You would have a 1/2 chance of guessing correctly and eating.

Here's a better strategy. If you see two hats of the same color, guess that your hat is the other color. If you see one hat of each color, pass.

Because each hat can be one of two colors, there are 8 possible color combinations. (You can enumerate them if you like.) In two of those combinations (red–red–red and blue–blue–blue), all three hats have the same color. That means there's a 2/8=1/4 probability that the hats have the same color and a 3/4 probability that the hats include both red and blue.

If the hats are all the same color, then all three of you guess the other color, you lose, and you go hungry.

If the hats are not all the same color, then one of you sees two hats of the same color. That person correctly guesses that he's wearing the other color. The other prisoners see one of each color and pass. Because the only prisoner who picked a color was correct, you get to eat.

The probability of the hats including both colors is 3/4 so this strategy gives you a 3/4 probability of eating.

> **Follow–up:** What happens if there are four prisoners and a prisoner guesses the opposite of the majority of the colors he sees? For example, if you see two or three red hats, you guess that your hat is blue.

With this strategy, the prisoners guess correctly only if there are two red hats and two blue hats. That happens in eight of the 16 possible hat assignments, so there's a 1/2 probability of eating.

You may as well just have everyone pass except one prisoner who guesses "red."

> **Follow–up:** What happens if there are four prisoners and if a prisoner sees three hats of the same color he guesses the oppositecolor? For example, if you see three blue hats, you guess that your hat is red.

With this strategy, the prisoners guess correctly only if there are three red hats or three blue hats. That happens in eight of the 16 possible hat assignments, so there's a 1/2 probability of eating.

This is the same probability given by the previous strategy and again is no better than a random guess.

TWO HEADS ARE BETTER THAN ONE

> **Puzzle:** Suppose you have two coins, one normal and one with heads on both sides. You close your eyes, shake up the coins, and put them on the table.
>
> If the first coin shows heads, what is the probability that the other coin also shows heads?

You can solve this puzzle by enumerating all of the possible arrangements of coins. Let H and T represent heads and tails for the normal coin, and let H1 and H2 represent the two different sides of the two–headed coin. Then the possible arrangements where the first coin shows heads are:

H	H1
H	H2
H1	H
H1	T
H2	H
H2	T

There are six possible arrangements and four of them have the second coin showing heads, so the probability of the second coin showing heads is 4/6=2/3.

BEWILDERING BIRTHDAYS

Puzzle: Suppose you're a professor at the Nostradamus School of Prognostication and you're teaching Underwater Divination. You roll your eyes and moan theatrically, and then in a mysterious voice announce that at least two of the 40 students in the class have the same birthday.

What is the probability that you are correct?

As is the case with many complicated probability puzzles, the trick is to look at the probability of the event *not* happening and subtract that value from 1.

In this case, you should first look at the probability of N people not having the same birthday. To calculate the probability that N people have different birthdays, you can use the following definition of probability.

$$Probability \quad \frac{\# \, Desired \; Outcomes}{\# \, Total \; outcomes}$$

Start by considering two people. There are 365 ways you can pick the first person's birthday (assuming it's not a leap year). After you make that choice, there are 364 ways you can pick a second birthday that is different from the first. That means there are 365×364 ways you can pick two different birthdays.

There are a total of 365×365 ways you can pick two arbitrary birthdays, so the probability that two birthdays will be different is $\frac{365\times364}{365\times365} = \frac{364}{365} \approx 0.9973$.

In that case the probability that two birthdays will *not* be different is 1 minus that value or roughly 1–0.9973=0.0027.

Now consider three birthdays. There are 365×364×363 ways you can pick three distinct birthdays and there are a total of 365^3 ways you can pick three arbitrary birthdays, so the probability that the three birthdays are all different is:

$$\frac{365 \times 364 \times 363}{365^3} \approx 0.9918$$

Then the probability of three birthdays *not* all being different is 1 minus that value or roughly 1–0.9918=0.0082.

The probabilities look pretty small (less than 1%), so you might think that you made a mistake in predicting that at least two students share the same birthday. Or if your powers of premonition are genuine, you may have a feeling that you won't be issuing an apology and you can continue the calculation.

The following equation shows the general equation for the probability of N birthdays all being different.

$$\frac{365 \times 364 \times ... \times (365 - N + 1)}{365^N}$$

Subtracting that from 1 gives the following formula for the probability that at least two out of N students share the same birthday.

$$1 - \frac{365 \times 364 \times ... \times (365 - N + 1)}{365^N}$$

You can calculate some values by hand, but it's a pretty complicated computation. Besides, this is an ideal task for a computer. The following pseudocode shows how a program could list the probabilities for different values of N.

```
For i = 1 To 366
    prob_no_match = 1.0
    For j = 1 To i
        prob_no_match = prob_no_match * (365 - j + 1) / 365

    prob_match = 1.0 - prob_no_match
    Write i + ": " prob_match
```

Figure 6–1 shows the calculated probability of two or more students sharing a birthday in classes with 1 through 40 students.

# Students	Probability of Match	# Students	Probability of Match
1	0.00	21	0.44
2	0.00	22	0.48
3	0.01	23	0.51
4	0.02	24	0.54
5	0.03	25	0.57
6	0.04	26	0.60
7	0.06	27	0.63
8	0.07	28	0.65
9	0.09	29	0.68
10	0.12	30	0.71
11	0.14	31	0.73
12	0.17	32	0.75
13	0.19	33	0.77
14	0.22	34	0.80
15	0.25	35	0.81
16	0.28	36	0.83
17	0.32	37	0.85
18	0.35	38	0.86
19	0.38	39	0.88
20	0.41	40	0.89

Figure 6–1: Probabilities that at least two students share the same birthday for different class sizes.

From Figure 6–1 you can see that the probability of some students sharing a birthday in your class of 40 students is roughly 0.89, so your prediction is probably safe.

Variation: How many students must a class contain before the probability of at least two students sharing a birthday is at least 50%?

You can see from Figure 6–1 that the probability of matching birthdays first exceeds 50% when the class has 23 students.

If you continue the calculation, the probability exceeds 0.99 when there are 57 students, 0.999 when there are 70 students, and 0.9999 when there are 80 students. A 64–bit floating–point number cannot tell the difference between the probability and 1 for 149 students, although the probability doesn't truly reach 1 until you have 366 students.

Follow–up: The previous pseudocode is the most obvious way to calculate the probabilities. Can you think of a method that is more efficient?

Hint: Write the probability of no match for N students in terms of the probability of no match with N–1 students.

The following pseudocode produces the same results as the previous version.

```
prob_no_match = 1.0
For i = 1 To 366
    prob_no_match = prob_no_match * (365 - i + 1) / 365
    prob_match = 1 - prob_no_match
    Write i + ": " prob_match
```

This pseudocode produces the same output as the first version but doesn't require the inner For loop.

PROBABILISTIC SOCKS

Puzzle: If you have 10 blue socks and 10 white socks in a drawer and you pull out two at random, what is the probability that they match?

One approach for solving this puzzle is to calculate the number of ways you can pick two socks, the number of ways you can pick two blue socks, and the number of ways you can pick two white socks. That works but there's an easier way to solve the puzzle.

After you pull out one sock, the drawer contains 19 socks, 9 of which match the one that you pulled out. That means the probability of the second sock matching is 9/19.

SUMMARY

When you see a probability problem, check your intuition at the door. These problems are often designed to work against your instincts or to suggest the wrong approach. If a puzzle seems obvious, then you're probably looking at it incorrectly. Do the calculations and trust the mathematics and not your feelings.

When in doubt, see if you can calculate probabilities by enumerating the possible outcomes and counting those that are desired and undesired. If you can't actually enumerate the outcomes, you may be able to calculate their numbers.

PROGRAMMING EXERCISES

1. Write a program that simulates births in the "Gender Mindbender" puzzle. Let the user enter the number of couples and then make the program run until every couple has a girl. The program should display the percentage of girls in the population for each round of births and at the end of the simulation.

2. Write a program that demonstrates the algorithm in the "Probabilistic Byte" puzzle. Let the user enter a string of characters and a number of trials. For each trial the program should consider each of the characters in the string and use the algorithm to pick a character randomly. After it finishes the trials, the program should display the number of times each character was selected.

3. Modify the program you wrote for Exercise 2 so it displays the character counts in a bar graph.

4. Write a program that simulates the "Airplane Seating" puzzle. After performing the number of trials entered by the user, the program should display the number of times you ended up in your seat, Arthur's seat, or someone else's seat.

5. Write a program that simulates the "Three Hats for Three Prisoners" puzzle. After performing the number of trials entered by the user, the program should display the percentage of times that the strategy allowed the prisoners to eat.

6. Write a program that calculates probabilities similar to those shown in Figure 6–1 for classes with up to 366 students. Use both pseudocode implementations and verify that they give the same results.

7. Write a program that simulates classes for the "Bewildering Birthdays" puzzle. Let the user enter a number of trials. Then for each number of students between 1 and 366, it should perform the indicated number of trials. For each trial the program should randomly pick birthdays for the students (you can just pick a number between 1 and 365) and see if any are shared. When it finishes, the program should show the fraction of times each class size had a match, and it should compare its results to those calculated by the program you wrote for exercise 6.

8. Modify the program you wrote for Exercise 8 so it lets the user enter a number of birthdays and then looks for classes with the indicated number of shared birthdays. For example, what is the probability that three of 40 students share a birthday?

7

Clever Crossings

The puzzles in this chapter deal with crossings. Sometimes you're crossing a bridge over a raging river or a ravine. Sometimes you're using a boat to cross a river full of crocodiles. Sometimes you're being chased, have a leaky boat, or have a torch that's burning low.

The puzzles' restrictions make things interesting. For example, some puzzles require you to carry animals that can't be left alone in certain combinations.

The most useful trick for these puzzles is to realize that you can cross back over the bridge or take the boat back across the river.

WOLF, GOAT, AND CABBAGE

Puzzle: Suppose you are taking a wolf, a goat, and a cabbage to market and you come to a river. There's a boat, but it's only big enough for you to take one item across at a time.

If you leave the wolf and goat alone together, the wolf eats the goat. If you leave the goat and cabbage alone together, the goat eats the cabbage.

How can you get all three safely across the river?

This is a very old puzzle. The first known occurrence is in the medieval manuscript *Propositiones ad Acuendos Juvenes*, which translates as *Problems to Sharpen the Young* and which has been around since at least the late 9th century. (See en.wikipedia.org/wiki/Propositiones_ad_Acuendos_Juvenes for more information.)

Variations of the puzzle involve a fox, goose, and bag of beans; a fox, chicken, and grain; a fox, goose, and corn; and the alliterative panther, pig, and porridge. Basically any three objects A, B, and C where you can't leave the pairs A–B or B–C unguarded.

This problem actually includes so many restrictions that it practically solves itself. All you need to do is ask yourself, "What is possible at this step?" You really only have one choice that makes progress and that is safe.

At the start, you can't leave the wolf and goat alone together or the goat and cabbage alone together. The only item that you can take across the river without disaster is the goat. You take the goat across the river, leave it on the other side, and return.

You can take either the wolf or the cabbage next. Let's assume that you take the cabbage. The logic is the same but reversed if you take the wolf.

When you take the cabbage across, you now have the goat and the cabbage on the far side of the river. You can't leave them both there or the goat will eat the cabbage, so you have to take one of them back. Taking the cabbage back would be silly because you just bright it across. That only leaves the goat, so you take the goat back.

When you bring the goat back, you now have the wolf and goat on the original side of the river. You can't leave them both there or the wolf will eat the goat, so you need to take one of them to the other side of the river. Taking the goat across would be a waste of time because you just bright it back. That only leaves the wolf, so you must take the wolf across.

Now you have the wolf and the cabbage on the far side of the river. The wolf won't eat the cabbage (and the cabbage won't eat the wolf, unless this is a really low–budget horror film), so you can leave them alone together. You go back across the river alone.

Finally you take the goat across and you're done. (Hopefully the boat's owner won't mind when you leave it on the other side of the river.)

Notice that the goat is the item that can't be left with either of the other two, so it is the one that needs to make three trips across the river. If you're working with some other kinds of objects, such as a panther, pig, and porridge, then the item that can't be left with the other two needs to cross the river three times.

Figure 7–1 shows the crossings that you need to make to bring the wolf, goat, and cabbage safely cross the river. The left and right columns represent the near and far banks of the river. The middle column represents you and the boat, usually carrying the wolf, goat, or cabbage.

For example, in the second row in the table, the wolf and cabbage are on the river's near bank as you and the goat row across to the far bank.

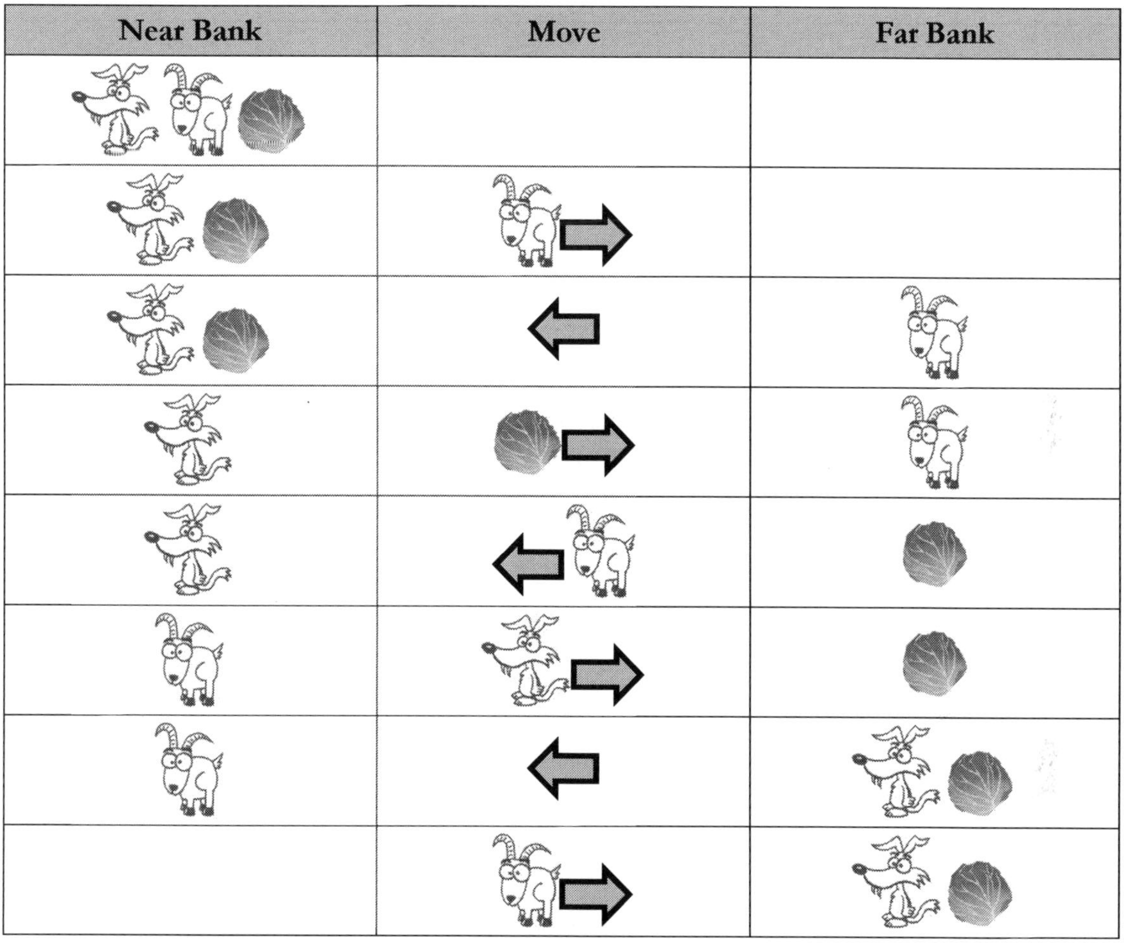

Near Bank	Move	Far Bank
wolf, goat, cabbage		
wolf, cabbage	goat →	
wolf, cabbage	←	goat
wolf	cabbage →	goat
wolf	← goat	cabbage
goat	wolf →	cabbage
goat	←	wolf, cabbage
	goat →	wolf, cabbage

Figure 7–1: Moving a wolf, goat, and cabbage across a river.

You can verify that all of the boat uses are valid by checking that the boat in the middle column in Figure 7–1 always contains zero or one items, and that the left and right columns never contain the wolf–goat or goat–cabbage pairs.

I can imagine rowing a boat across a river carrying a cabbage and perhaps a goat, but I'm not sure how I would keep a wolf under control.

FAMILY OUTING

> **Puzzle:** A family consisting of a father, mother, son, and daughter come to a river. There's a boat, but it can only hold 180 pounds, enough for one adult or two children. How can the family cross the river safely?

The key to this puzzle is to realize that, if two children cross together, then one can bring the boat back. Like the "Wolf, Goat, and Cabbage" puzzle, this puzzle has so many constraints that it practically solves itself.

Having an adult cross first won't help because then that adult would need to immediately come back. You could have one child cross, but again that child would need to immediately return so you wouldn't gain anything. The only alternative is to have both of the children cross. Then one child returns.

Next it would be silly for the child cross again, so an adult crosses.

Now it would be a waste of time for the adult to cross back. Your only alternative is for the other child to return to the original side of the river.

Now you can repeat those steps. Both children cross and one returns. The second adult crosses and the other child returns.

At this point both of the children are on the starting side of the river. They cross together and the whole family is on the far side of the river.

Figure 7–2 shows crossings that let the family cross the river.

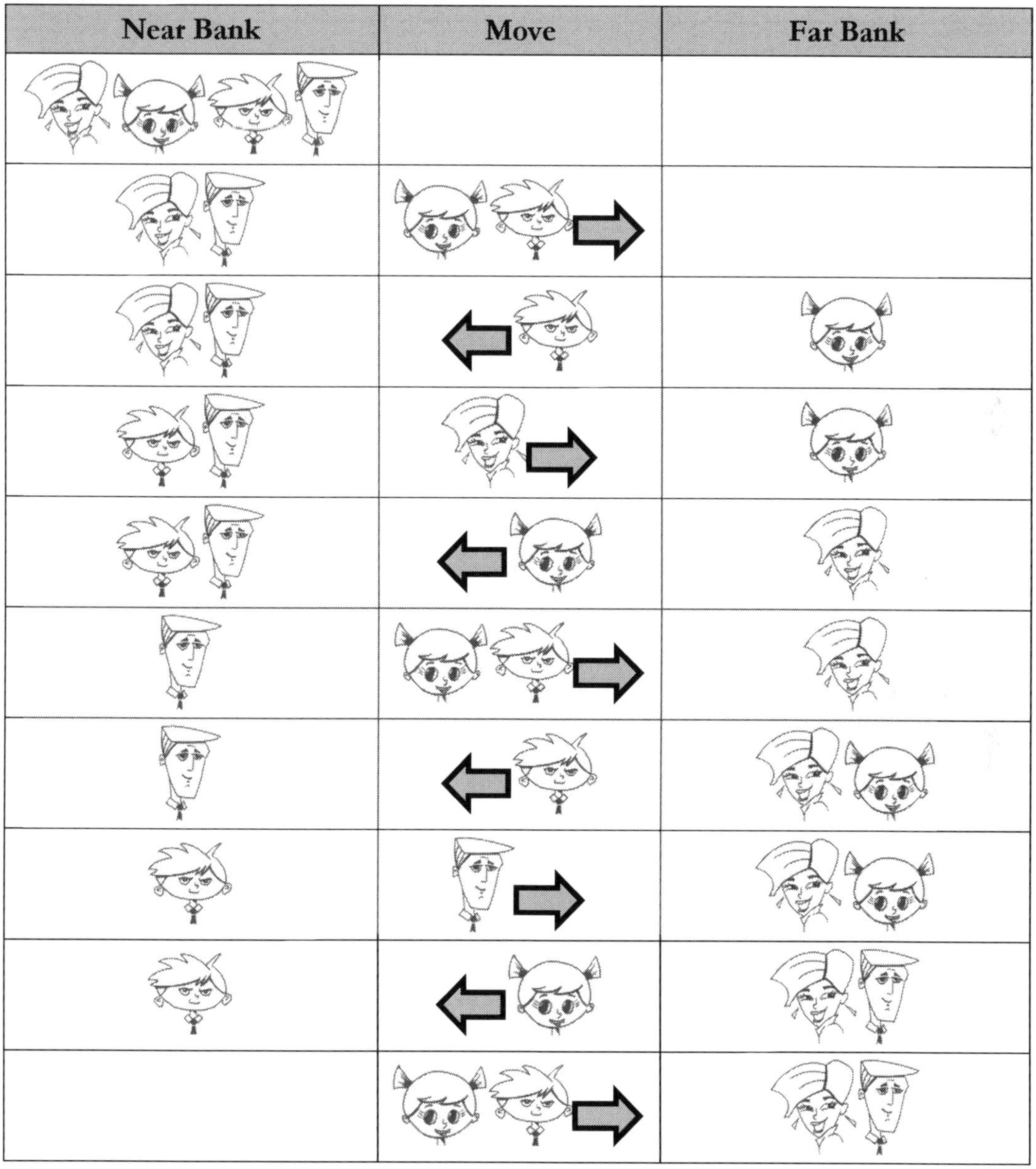

Figure 7–2: Moving a family across a river.

You can verify that all of the boat uses are valid by checking that every cell in the middle column in Figure 7–2 either contains one adult, or one or two children.

As in the "Wolf, Goat, and Cabbage" puzzle, we have to hope that the owner of the boat doesn't mind it being left on the far side of the river. Perhaps there's some sort of shuttle service that tows boats back to their owners.

CANNIBAL CROSSING

> **Puzzle:** Three anthropologists and three cannibals need to cross a river. There's a boat but, as so often seems to be the case, it's only big enough to hold two people.
>
> The cannibals will do as they are instructed, but if the cannibals ever outnumber the anthropologists on either side of the river or in the boat for even an instant, the cannibals eat the anthropologists!
>
> How can the party cross the river?

First, two cannibals cross the river and then one returns. Next two more cannibals cross the river so all three cannibals are on the far side.

One of the cannibals returns. Now there are two cannibals on the far side, so if a single anthropologist crosses he will be eaten. That means the only choice is for two anthropologists to cross.

At this point the near bank holds one cannibal and one anthropologist, and the far back holds two of each. If one anthropologist returns to the near bank, the remaining anthropologist on the far bank will be eaten. Making two anthropologists return to the near bank would be a waste of time because they just left there. Finally if one or two cannibals return to the near bank, then the anthropologist on the near bank will be eaten.

The only other option is to make one anthropologist and one cannibal return to the near bank. After that crossing, the near bank holds two anthropologists and two cannibals, and the far side holds one of each.

Now the two anthropologists cross to the far bank. When they arrive, the near bank holds two cannibals and the far bank holds one cannibal and all three anthropologists.

At this point the cannibal returns to the near bank. Now all of the anthropologists are on the far bank and all of the cannibals are on the near bank.

The rest is fairly obvious. Two cannibals cross and one returns to the near bank. Finally the last two cannibals cross and the party can go on its way.

Figure 7–3 shows the crossings used to move the party across the river.

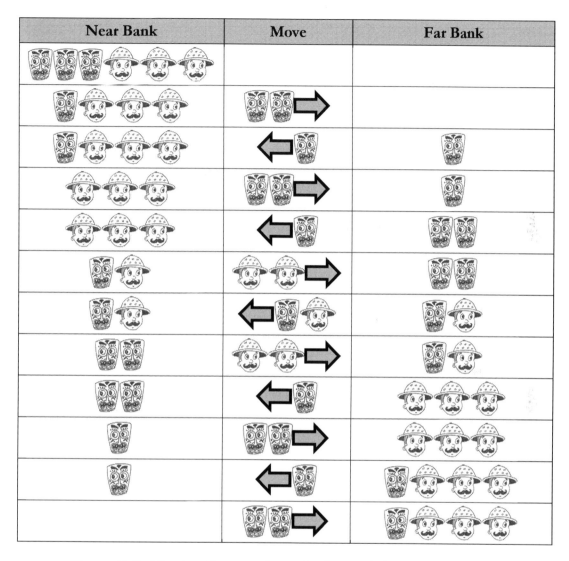

Figure 7–3: Moving three anthropologists and three cannibals safely across a river.

To check that all of the crossings are valid, you should verify that none of the cells in Figure 7–3 contain more cannibals than anthropologists.

CANNIBAL CROSSING, PART 2

Puzzle: The solution to the "Cannibal Crossing" puzzle shown in the preceding section doesn't work if there are more than three pairs of cannibals and anthropologists. Why?

In the beginning of that solution, one of the cannibals ferries the other cannibals to the river's far bank. If you try that approach with four or more cannibals, then at some point there are three cannibals and no anthropologists on the far bank.

At that point there is no way to move the anthropologists across. Even if two of them cross together, they will be outnumbered on the far bank and served up with a roll and salad.

That's not a proof that there is *no* way for the group to cross; it only shows that the previous approach won't work. One way to prove that there is no possible solution would be to try all of the possible sequences of allowed moves and verify that none leads to a solution.

CANNIBAL CROSSING, PART 3

Puzzle: You can solve the "Cannibal Crossing" puzzle with any number of pairs of cannibals and anthropologists if there is an island in the middle of the river. How?

In the first part of the original solution to the "Cannibal Crossing" puzzle, one cannibal acts as a ferry pilot and ferries the cannibals to the river's far bank. Basically two cross and then one returns until all of the cannibals are on the far bank.

In the new puzzle you can use a similar technique to move all of the cannibals except the ferry pilot onto the island. Next the ferry pilot takes the anthropologists to the far bank. Finally the pilot fetches the other cannibals and brings them to the far bank.

CANNIBAL CROSSING, PART 4

Puzzle: Suppose four pairs of cannibals and anthropologists need to cross a river with an island as in the "Cannibal Crossing, Part 3." This time, however, the boat isn't allowed to cross directly from one bank to the other; it must stop on the island along the way. In that case, how can the party cross?

Figure 7–4 shows the beginning of one possible solution. To save space, the Figure represents cannibals and anthropologists with the letters C and A respectively. The people who are about to move at each step are underlined.

CCC<u>CA</u>AAA		
CCCAAA	C<u>A</u>	
C<u>CC</u>AAAA	C	
CAAAA	<u>CC</u>C	
CCAA<u>AA</u>	CC	
CCAA	CC<u>AA</u>	
CCAA	CA	C<u>A</u>
CCAA	C<u>AA</u>	C
CC<u>A</u>AA	CA	C
CAA	CC<u>AA</u>	C
CAA	CC	<u>C</u>AA
CAA	<u>C</u>CC	AA
CC<u>AA</u>	CC	AA
CC	<u>CC</u>AA	AA
CC	AA	<u>CC</u>AA
CC	C<u>AA</u>	CAA
CC	C	<u>C</u>AAAA
CC	<u>C</u>C	AAAA
C<u>CC</u>	C	AAAA
C	<u>CC</u>C	AAAA
<u>CC</u>	CC	AAAA

Figure 7–4: Moving four anthropologists and four cannibals safely across a river with an island.

After this point the cannibals on the island spend six more moves ferrying themselves across to the far bank for a total of 26 crossings.

JEALOUS HUSBANDS

Puzzle: Three couples are on a hike at a marriage retreat and the come to a river. They need to cross the river by using the classic undersized boat that can hold up to two people at a time. The catch is that the husbands are extremely jealous so no wife can ever be left with a man unless her husband is also present.

How can the couples cross the river?

This seems like a new and extra–complicated puzzle, but it's actually a disguised version of the "Cannibal Crossing" puzzle. The jealously condition basically means that husbands cannot outnumber wives on either side of the river or in the boat. If they did, then one of the wives present would be without her husband. There are no bushes on the river, so her husband would see and throw a temper tantrum, undoing days of productive counseling.

To solve this puzzle, use the solution from the "Cannibal Crossing" puzzle treating the husbands like cannibals and the wives like anthropologists. The only remaining detail is that you need to be sure to match up the right husbands and wives during the crossings, but that isn't hard.

IN A HURRY

Puzzle: You and three others are running from a hoard of zombies at night when you come to a rickety bridge across a deep chasm. The bridge is only strong enough to hold two of you at a time. To make matters worse, you only have a single flashlight and it's far too dark to cross the bridge safely without a light. (Zombies or no zombies, safety comes first!)

The final twist is that the four of you run at different speeds. You and Alice are the fastest and will need 1 and 2 minutes to cross the bridge, respectively. Bob and Cindy are loaded down with loot they picked up on the way, so they'll need 7 and 10 minutes to cross, respectively.

How can all four of you cross the bridge and keep the biggest possible lead over the zombies?

There are two key observations that make this puzzle solvable.

First, someone will need to cross the bridge and then return to bring the flashlight back to the others. To save time, anyone who crosses the bridge multiple times should be as fast as possible. For example, you don't want Cindy to do it.

Second, if two people cross at the same time, then the faster of the two essentially gets a free crossing and you're only charged for the time required by the slower person.

Those two observations give you the following solution.

First you and Alice cross. You need 1 minute and Alice needs 2 minutes, so this takes 2 minutes.

Next you spend 1 minute returning to the original side with the flashlight.

Bob and Cindy then cross. Bob needs 7 minutes and Cindy needs 10 minutes, so this takes 10 minutes. Here's where Bob essentially gets a free trip.

Now Alice returns to your side of the chasm, taking 2 minutes, and you both run across to the far side, taking another 2 minutes.

The total time is 2 + 1 + 10 + 2 + 2 = 17 minutes.

IN A BIG HURRY

> **Puzzle:** Suppose you and three others are fleeing from zombies as described in the puzzle "In a Hurry." You and Alice are faster than the zombies, but Bob and Cindy are not. Furthermore, the zombies are closing in fast. They'll reach the near end of the bridge in 15 minutes.
>
> What strategy lets as many of you as possible escape?

If it comes to a prolonged chase, the zombies will catch Bob and Cindy because they're faster. If there is going to be a long chase, you and Alice may as well run across the bridge and abandon the others to their fate. Sorry Bob and Cindy. That's what you get for looting.

Fortunately, there may be a better solution. If you follow the same strategy used in the previous puzzle, then the zombies reach the near end of the bridge in 15 minutes, just as you and Alice begin your final trip across the bridge. You sprint out of their clutches at the last possible second and, because you're both faster than the zombies, you reach the far side of the bridge first.

Then you destroy the bridge. The bridge is rickety, so hopefully you can destroy it before the zombies reach the far side and catch you.

ROOM FOR ONE MORE

Puzzle: Suppose you're fleeing from zombies as in the puzzle "In a Hurry," but this time you have five people. You can cross the bridge in 1 minute; Alice can cross in 3 minutes; Bob, who keeps dropping his machete, can cross in 6 minutes; Cindy, who's carrying loot, can cross in 8 minutes; and Dan, who for some reason is dragging a sofa along with him, can cross in 12 minutes.

How quickly can the group cross the bridge?

The same ideas that let you solve the "In a Hurry" puzzle also work here. Some people will need to cross the bridge twice so you want those people to be the fastest people possible. The slower people should cross together to save time.

First the two fastest people, you and Alice cross. You need 1 minute and Alice needs 3 minutes, so this takes 3 minutes.

Next you spend 1 minute returning to the original side with the flashlight.

Now Cindy and Dan cross together. Cindy needs 8 minutes and Dan needs 12 minutes, so this takes 12 minutes.

Next Alice spends 3 minutes returning to the original side with the flashlight.

Now you, Alice, and Bob are all on the original side. Whoever crosses with Bob will need to come back to get the last person, so you want this person to be as fast as possible. That's you. You and Bob cross. You need 1 minute and Bob needs 6 minutes, so this takes minutes.

You return to the original side, taking 1 minute.

Finally you and Alice cross together. You need 1 minute and Alice needs 3 minutes, so this takes 3 minutes.

The total time to cross is $3+1+12+3+6+1+3=29$ minutes. You'd better hope the zombies are slower than the ones in the "In a Big Hurry" puzzle.

WORLD'S LONGEST ROPE BRIDGE

> **Puzzle:** Suppose you're driving a truck carrying a precious cargo of curling stones through the Amazonian jungle when you come to the world's longest rope bridge, which is 20 miles long. The sign says, "Load Limit 10 Tons."
>
> The bridge attendant tells you that the bridge can hold exactly 10 tons and not a milligram more. To make sure that everything is completely safe, the attendant weighs your truck. He finds that the truck (including you, the cargo, the bugs on the radiator, the dirt on the windows— everything) weighs exactly 10 tons, so he waves you forward.
>
> Being a rational person, you're more than a bit concerned, but you're in a hurry so you drive on.
>
> Halfway across the bridge, a swallow (without a coconut) sees you and comes down for a closer look. You frantically shout and wave at the bird to try to scare it off, but that only seems to encourage it and it's about to land on the truck's hood ornament!
>
> You're not allowed to dump any cargo (you'd be fired) and no, there are no loose items in the cab such as a map, thermos, or Batman lunchbox that you can discard. What can you do to save yourself?

A quick calculation reveals that the swallow won't be a problem.

Swallows weigh between around 1/3 of an ounce and 2 ounces. Let's assume this swallow has just finished lunch and weighs 2 ounces.

Gasoline and diesel weigh a bit more than 6 pounds per gallon. There are 16 ounces per pound, so that's about 8 swallows per pound. That means the truck's fuel weighs around 8×6=48 swallows per gallon.

Even if the truck gets 100 miles per gallon, after 10 miles it will have used up 1/10 of a gallon of fuel, which weighs about as much as 4.8 swallows. Therefore you should be safe with a single swallow as a passenger.

Unfortunately a Harpy Eagle sees the swallow and decides it might make a nice snack. Harpy Eagles can weigh more than 20 pounds, so you better step on the gas.

SUMMARY

Many river crossings are so tightly constrained that the solution is practically forced on you. At each step, think about which moves are allowed and which moves take you closer to a solution.

PROGRAMMING EXERCISES

These puzzles make interesting programming challenges, but they're quite difficult. Even the easiest may take a candidate a few hours to implement. You may be better off asking the candidate to design the program but not implement it. Or you could have the candidate work with you (after you've written the program yourself so you know exactly what you need to do) as an exercise in pair programming.

1. Write a program that searches for solutions to the "Wolf, Goat and Cabbage" puzzle.
2. Write a program that searches for solutions to the "Family Outing" puzzle.
3. Write a program that searches for solutions to the "Cannibal Crossing" puzzle.
4. Modify the program you wrote for Exercise 3 so the user can enter the number of cannibals and anthropologists that need to cross the river. Test the program with four pairs (it should find no solutions), and with four cannibals and five anthropologists.
5. Write a program that searches for solutions to the "In a Hurry" puzzle.
6. Modify the program you wrote for Exercise 5 so the user can enter any number of crossing times and the program then finds an optimal crossing strategy.
7. Write a program that calculates mileage in swallow–weights of fuel per mile. The user should input a number of gallons used and miles driven. Use constants in the code to store the density of the fuel (6.073 lbs/gal for gasoline, 6.943 lbs/gal for diesel) and the weight of a swallow (0.63 oz).
8. Modify the program you wrote for Exercise 7 so the user can enter values in gallons, liters, miles, or kilometers. The user should be able to select output in miles or kilometers per gallon, liter, or swallow-weight.

Mystifying Measurements

These puzzles deal with measuring things. Generally you need to use known measurements of distance or volume to make unknown measurements.

To solve these puzzles, first determine how you can use the known measurements in unobvious ways. In water–measuring puzzles, for example, you can subtract values by pouring one container's contents into another. In rope–burning puzzles, you can cut a rope's burn time in half by lighting it at both ends.

Once you've discovered your non–obvious options, look at combinations of the values that you can create. By adding, subtracting, and halving, you should be able to come up with the result you need.

Note that ropes are generally assumed to have varying thicknesses so different parts of a rope burn at different rates. That means, for example, that you can't cut a rope in half and expect the halves to burn in half of the time that the whole would take. You only know the rope's total burn time. (How you predict the total time for a rope that burns non–uniformly is a mystery to me.)

Normally in water–measuring puzzles you must assume that the containers have arbitrary shapes. For example, you can't assume a container is a perfect cylinder.

FORTY–FIVE MINUTE ROPES

Puzzle: Suppose you're on a secret mission and your team is infiltrating enemy headquarters. Your mission is to disable the alarm system exactly 45 minutes from now.

Unfortunately you remembered to bring your night vision goggles, shoe phone, exploding chewing gum, laser cutter, and other specialized spy gadgetry, but you forgot your watch. All you have to help you measure time are two ropes that you know take 60 minutes each to burn from end to end.

How can you use the ropes to measure exactly 45 minutes?

Start by lighting the first rope at both ends and the second rope at one end. After the first rope finishes burning, 30 minutes have passed so the second rope is half burned and has 30 minutes left. At that point, light the second rope's second end so it takes 15 more minutes to finish burning.

When the second rope has finished burning, the 45 minutes are up and you can disable the alarm system. Now you only have to hope that the rest of your team neutralized the gate guards, tower snipers, and free–ranging Dobermans.

FIFTEEN MINUTE COOKIES

Puzzle: Suppose you're making pecan sandies (cookies) and they need to bake for exactly 15 minutes. You have the mixer, bowls, ingredients, cookie sheets, oven, and everything else you need to make the cookies except a timer.

Fortunately your roommate has two ropes that take exactly 60 minutes to burn. They're not your ropes, so why not use them?

How can you use the ropes to time exactly 15 minutes?

Start by lighting the first rope at both ends and the second rope at one end. While the ropes are burning, preheat the oven, mix the ingredients, and drop the dough in one–inch balls onto your cookie sheets.

After the first rope finishes burning, 30 minutes have passed so the second rope is half burned so it has 15 minutes left. At that point, place the cookies in the oven and light the second rope's second end so it takes 15 more minutes to finish burning.

When the second rope is done burning, remove the cookies from the oven and transfer them to a wire rack to cool. When cool, roll in powdered sugar and store in an airtight container.

(I actually have a good recipe for pecan sandies. Email me at RodStephens@CSharpHelper.com if you want a copy.)

CATCHING THE TRAIN

> **Puzzle:** Suppose you need to leave to catch a train to work in 15 minutes, but you're not finished reading the comics yet. Your clock is broken and you've lost your cellphone, but you have two hourglass–style egg timers that run for 11 minutes and 13 minutes, respectively.
>
> How can you use the two egg timers to measure exactly 15 minutes?

Although this puzzle measures time, it's more similar to a water–measuring puzzle than it is to a rope–burning puzzle because you can't make the egg timers measure from both ends. You can, however, run both timers and then turn one over to essentially "subtract" time from the sand that it has remaining.

To measure 15 minutes, start both timers. When the 11–minute timer finishes, the 13–minute timer has 2 minutes remaining. At that point, flip the 11–minute timer over so it starts again.

When the 13–minute timer runs out, the 11–minute timer has been flipped for 2 minutes. Flip it again so it runs for 2 more minutes.

When the 11–minute timer finishes again, the total elapsed time is 13+2=15 minutes. Put down the comics and go catch your train.

Alternatively just leave right away and take the comics with you to read while you wait for the train at the station.

SHEPHERD'S PIE

> **Puzzle:** Suppose you're making shepherd's pie from a recipe translated from an ancient Celtic runestone. After substituting lamb for wild beaver and making a few minor adjustments to the spices (you just can't get good sliphium any more), you need to bake it for 15 minutes.
>
> The bad news is that the clock on your traditional clay oven is broken. The good news is that you have three ropes that take exactly 40 minutes each to burn. How can you use the ropes to time 15 minutes?

First light rope 1 from both ends and light ropes 2 and 3 from one end each.

After 20 minutes, rope 1 will finish burning. Ropes 2 and 3 will be half burned, so they will each have 20 minutes left. At that time, put the pie in the oven and light the second end of rope 2.

After 10 more minutes, rope 2 will finish burning and rope 3 will have 10 minutes left. Now light the second end of rope 3.

After an additional 5 minutes, both rope 3 and the shepherd's pie will be finished.

FOUR–QUART MELTDOWN

Puzzle: Suppose you're a nuclear technician and your reactor is about to go full Chernobyl. To stop it, you need to pour *exactly* four quarts of water into the cooling system. While you have a faucet that gives you as much water as you need, you unfortunately only have a five–quart bucket and a three–quart bucket with which to measure. (You would think that nuclear power plants would keep a bucket of the correct size handy.)

How can you use the buckets to measure exactly four quarts of water?

First fill the three–quart bucket and pour its water into the five–quart bucket.

Next fill the three–quart bucket again and pour its water into the five–quart bucket until that bucket is full. The five–quart bucket previously held three quarts, so it can hold two more. After this step, the five–quart bucket is full and the three–quart bucket holds one quart.

Dump the five–quart bucket down the drain. Then pour the one quart of water that's in the three–quart bucket into the five–quart bucket.

Finally fill the three–quart bucket again and add its water into the five–quart bucket. At this point the five–quart bucket contains four quarts. Pour it into the cooling system and take a well–deserved coffee break.

Figure 8–1 shows a summary of the moves that let you measure exactly four quarts.

Move	5–Quart Bucket	3–Quart Bucket
Fill 3–quart bucket		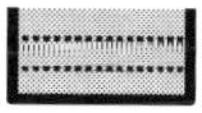
Pour 3 → 5	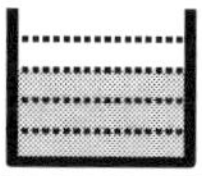	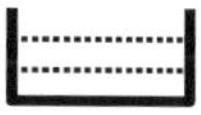
Fill 3–quart bucket	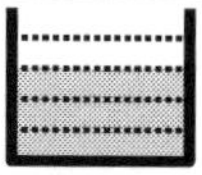	
Pour 3 → 5	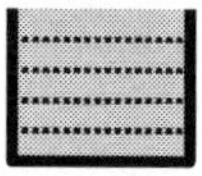	
Empty 5–quart bucket		
Pour 3 → 5		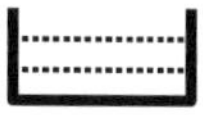
Fill 3–quart bucket		
Pour 3 → 5	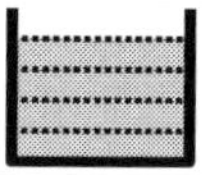	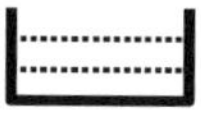

Figure 8–1: Measuring four quarts of water.

This method uses one simple operation: fill the three–quart bucket and pour its water into the five–quart bucket. When the five–quart bucket is full, empty it. After any given move, the five–quart bucket holds some multiple of three quarts modulo five. The following equation shows the values the five-quart bucket can hold for any non–negative integer N.

$$Q \equiv 3 \times N \bmod 5$$

To measure a particular number of quarts, you can set this equation equal to that number. For example, to measure four quarts, you need to find a value for N that makes the following equation true.

$$4 \equiv 3 \times N \bmod 5$$

This equation is true if N=3, so you can measure four quarts by repeating the operation three times.

If you look at Figure 8–1, you'll see that the steps actually pour water from the three–quart bucket into the five–quart bucket four times. The difference is that two of those pours are part of a single operation. The second and third pours move the water from the three–quart bucket into the five–quart bucket with a pause in the middle to empty the five–quart bucket.

Now that we have a formula for modeling the buckets, what amounts of water can we measure? If you set N = 0, 1, 2, 3, and 4, you can make Q equal 0, 3, 1, 4, and 2.

You can also measure five quarts by simply filling the five–quart bucket. The equation doesn't generate the value 5 because $5 \equiv 0$ mod 5.

The numbers of quarts you can measure this way are simply the multiples of 3 mod 5. Those multiples generate all possible values below 5 because 3 and 5 are relatively prime. (In other words, they have no common factors other than 1.)

The equation won't generate all possible values if the generator and the modulus are not relatively prime. For example, suppose you have a six–quart bucket and a four–quart bucket. Because you only have the values 4 and 6 to work with, it's fairly obvious that you can never measure an odd amount of water.

The equation for those buckets is:

$$Q \equiv 4 \times N \bmod 6$$

If you list the multiples of 4 mod 6, you get 0, 4, 2, and then the numbers repeat. That means you can't use those buckets to measure 1, 3, or 5 quarts of water.

SIX–LITER SPAGHETTI

Puzzle: Suppose you've volunteered to cook spaghetti for your annual beekeeping school banquet. You need 6 liters of water but the school's only bowls hold 7 liters and 11 liters, respectively. How can you use the bowls to measure 6 liters of water?

This is easy if you use the equation from the "Four–Quart Meltdown" puzzle. For this problem, the equation is:

$$Q \equiv 7 \times N \bmod 11$$

If you enumerate the multiples of 7 mod 11, you get 0, 7, 3, 10, 6, 2, 9, 5, 1, 8, 4, and then the numbers repeat. The number 6 appears fifth in this list, so to measure 6 liters you fill the seven–liter bowl and empty it into the 11–liter bowl four times, stopping to empty the 11–liter bowl whenever it's full.

EIGHT–LITER SPAGHETTI

Puzzle: Suppose your previous dinner was such a hit that your beekeeping school asks you to make spaghetti again for the summer festival. This time they want you to make more spaghetti so you need 8 liters of water. Unfortunately they still only have the 7 and 11 liter bowls.

How can you use the 7 and 11 liter bowls to measure 8 liters of water with the fewest measurements?

As in the "Six–Liter Spaghetti" puzzle, the appropriate equation is:

$$Q \equiv 7 \times N \bmod 11$$

If you enumerate the multiples of 7 mod 11, you get 0, 7, 3, 10, 6, 2, 9, 5, 1, 8, 4, and then the numbers repeat. The number 8 appears tenth in this list, so one solution would be to fill the seven–liter bowl and empty it into the 11–liter bowl nine times, stopping to empty the 11–liter bowl whenever it's full.

Because you fill the 7–liter bowl nine times, you use 7×9=63 liters of water. You keep the last 8 liters, so you discard 63–8=55 liters of water. You also need to pour water into the 7–liter bowl nine times and you need to empty the 11–liter bowl 5 times. That's a lot of work and a lot of wasted water.

Instead of moving forward through the list of values, you can move backward through the list by pouring water the other way: from the 11–liter bowl into the 7–liter bowl.

Fill the 11–liter bowl, pour 7 liters into the 7–liter bowl, and then empty the 7–liter bowl.

That leaves 4 liters in the 11–liter bowl. Pour that into the 7–liter bowl.

Next fill the 11–liter bowl again and use it to fill the 7–liter bowl. That requires 3 liters, so the 11–liter bowl now contains 8 liters as desired.

With this solution you fill the 11–liter bowl twice with a total of 22 liters of water. You keep 8 liters so you discard 22–8=14 liters. The 7–liter is even left containing 7 liters of water, which you can save if you have a use for it. This solution is much faster and wastes a lot less water than the original one does.

SEVEN DRAMS

> **Puzzle:** Suppose you're an alchemist's apprentice. Your master gives you two cruets that hold 6 drams and 15 drams, respectively, and then asks you to measure exactly 7 drams of aqua vitae. You can't discard any of the precious liquid, but you can pour it back into the decanter that originally holds it.
>
> Why does the alchemist want the aqua vitae?

Some interview questions use this format. They begin with a problem statement that sounds reasonable, but then they end with what seems to be a non–sequitur. Instead of asking you to measure the aqua vitae, the puzzle asks you why your master wants it.

Sometimes the initial problem statement is intended to make you focus on its details and distract you from the rest of the story. Initially try to ignore those details and think about the problem as a whole to see if there's some obvious conclusion you can make.

For example, one famous riddle asks you to pretend that you're a bus driver. It then gives you details about the numbers of passengers getting on and off at several stops. Most people spend a lot of time concentrating on the number of people currently on the bus and the total number of those who have gotten off over time. The puzzle then finishes by asking you how old the bus driver is. If you were distracted by the passenger details, you may have forgotten that the riddle initially asked you to pretend that *you* are a bus driver. In that case the bus driver's age is your age. The details about the passengers are just noise designed to make you forget the original assumption.

If you can't solve the puzzle by ignoring the details and looking at the big picture, examine the details to see if you can solve the puzzle or at least understand it. In this example, you would try to measure 7 drams with the 6–dram and 15–dram cruets.

For this puzzle you can use the equation from the "Four–Quart Meltdown" puzzle. When you apply it to this puzzle, the equation becomes:

$$Q \equiv 6 \times N \bmod 15$$

If you enumerate the multiples of 6 mod 15, you get 0, 6, 12, 3, 9, and then the numbers repeat. The value 7 doesn't appear in the list, so you *can't* measure 7 drams with the 6–dram and 15–dram cruets.

To answer the puzzle's question, you need to figure out why the alchemist asked you to make an impossible measurement. The following statements are reasonable possibilities.

1. The alchemist wants to test your intelligence to see if you start pouring aqua vitae back and forth without making a plan.
2. The alchemist wants to get you out of the way for a bit while you try and fail to measure the aqua vitae.
3. The alchemist is in a bad mood and wants to annoy you by assigning an impossible task.
4. The alchemist has already drunk too much aqua vitae and didn't think the problem through. (Aqua vitae is any strong alcoholic solution such as brandy.)

Almost any vaguely plausible answer should satisfy the interviewer as long as you explain your reasoning. The real point here is that you figured out that the measurement is impossible.

EIGHT OUNCES OF GOLD

Puzzle: Suppose you're a prospector and you and your partner want to evenly divide eight ounces of gold dust. In addition to the eight–ounce bowl that is initially holding the dust, you have a five–ounce bowl and a three–ounce bowl.

How can you use the bowls to evenly divide the gold?

This problem is different from previous liquid measuring puzzles for several reasons. Obviously you're not measuring a liquid, but you can measure dust much as you do a liquid so that's not a big difference. Far more importantly, you have three bowls, you don't have an unlimited supply of gold dust (wouldn't that be nice?), and you don't want to discard any of the dust.

However, you can still use the equation used in earlier puzzles if you only work with the smaller bowls. For this puzzle, the equation is:

$$Q \equiv 3 \times N \bmod 5$$

If you enumerate the multiples of 3 mod 5, you get 0, 3, 1, 4, 2, and then the numbers repeat. Now you can solve the puzzle as before, pouring gold from the 3–ounce bowl into the 5–ounce bowl. Whenever the 5–ounce bowl becomes full, pour its contents back into the 8–ounce bowl.

To finish measuring more quickly, work backwards as in the solution to the "Eight–liter Spaghetti" puzzle.

Figure 8–2 shows one possible solution.

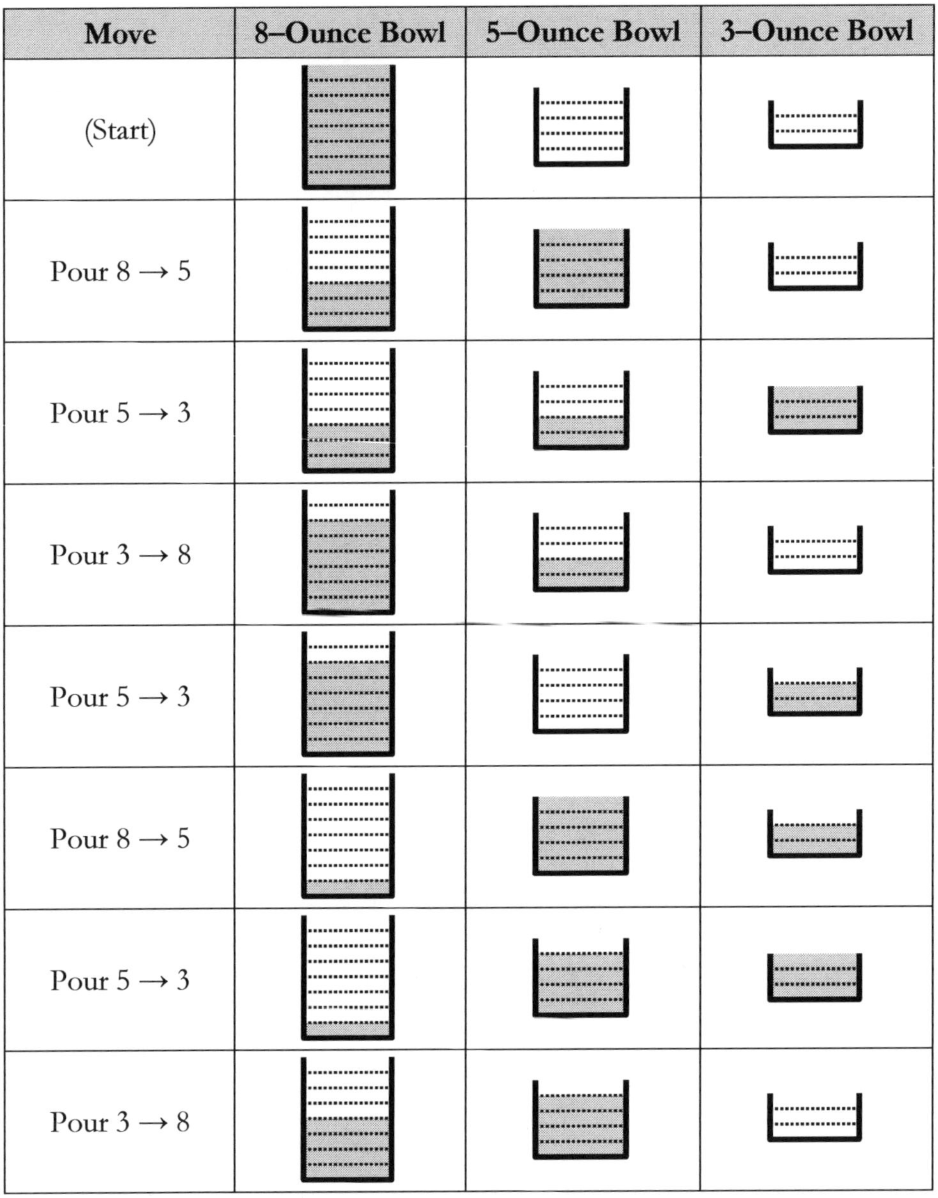

Move	8–Ounce Bowl	5–Ounce Bowl	3–Ounce Bowl
(Start)			
Pour 8 → 5			
Pour 5 → 3			
Pour 3 → 8			
Pour 5 → 3			
Pour 8 → 5			
Pour 5 → 3			
Pour 3 → 8			

Figure 8–2: Dividing eight ounces of gold dust without spilling.

To verify that no gold is gained or lost, you can check that each row of the table holds eight ounces of gold. (Then you should probably check your partner's pockets.)

SEVEN GILLS

Puzzle: Suppose you're an herbalist and you need to measure exactly seven gills of deer antler velvet extract. Unfortunately you only have 6–gill, 10–gill, and 15–gill measuring bowls. How can you measure exactly seven gills?

Figure 8–3 shows one solution. The numbers inside the pictures of the bowls indicate how many gills of extract each is holding.

Move	6–Gill Bowl	10–Gill Bowl	15–Gill Bowl
(Start)	0	0	0
Fill 10–gill bowl	0		0
Pour 10 → 15	0	0	
Fill 6–gill bowl		0	
Pour 6 → 15	1	0	15
Pour 6 → 10	0	1	15
Fill 6–gill bowl		1	10
Pour 6 → 10	0	7	15

Figure 8–3: Measuring seven gills of extract.

Follow–up: Can you measure seven gills of extract without using all three bowls?

It turns out that you can't measure seven gills by using only two of the bowls. None of the pairs of numbers (6, 10), (6, 15), or (10, 15) is relatively prime, so there are some measurements that the pairs of bowls cannot measure.

Figure 8–4 shows the values that you can generate by using pairs of bowls. The left column shows the bowls used. The middle column holds the equations that tell which values you can measure. The right column shows the values generated by the equations. The values repeat after 0 appears for the second time.

Bowls	Equation	Values Generated
6–Gill, 10–Gill	$Q \equiv 6 \times N \bmod 10$	0, 6, 2, 8, 4, 0, ...
6–Gill, 15–Gill	$Q \equiv 6 \times N \bmod 15$	0, 6, 12, 3, 9, 0, ...
10–Gill, 15–Gill	$Q \equiv 10 \times N \bmod 15$	0, 10, 5, 0, ...

Figure 8–4: Values you can measure by using only two bowls.

The values 1, 7, 11, 13, and 14 don't appear in any of the values in the right hand column, so you cannot measure those numbers by using only pairs of measuring bowls.

FOURTEEN GILLS

Puzzle: The follow–up to the "Seven Gills" puzzle says you cannot measure 14 gills by using any two of the 6–, 10–, and 15–gill measuring bowls. You actually can measure 14 gills using two of the bowls if you have a third output bowl. How can you do that?

If you look at the values in the right column of Figure 8–4, you won't see the value 14, but you will find values that add up to 14. For example, in the first row you can see the values 6+6+2=14.

Figure 8–5 shows one way you can use the 6– and 10–gill bowls to measure 14 gills.

Move	6–Gill Bowl	10–Gill Bowl	Output Bowl
(Start)	0	0	0
Fill 6–gill bowl		0	0
Pour 6 → Output	0	0	6
Fill 6–gill bowl		0	
Pour 6 → Output	0	0	12
Fill 6–gill bowl	6	0	12
Pour 6 → 10	0	6	12
Fill 6–gill bowl	6	6	12
Pour 6 → 10	2	10	12
Pour 6 → Output	0	10	14

Figure 8–5: Measuring 14 gills with an output bowl.

You could also measure 14 gills by adding 6 gills and 8 gills. Move 6 gills into the output bowl as before. Then if you fill the 6–gill bowl and pour its contents into the 10–gill bowl three times, emptying the 10–gill bowl when it fills, you'll be left with 8 gills in the 10–gill bowl. Add that to the output bowl and you have the required 14 gills.

SUMMARY

In measurement puzzles, you have some measuring devices such as buckets, bowls, or inflammable ropes. You know the amounts that those objects can measure.

If you're working with rope–burning puzzles, you can light a rope at both ends to decrease the time it measures. You can measure other durations by burning multiple ropes at the same time.

If you're measuring volumes, you can repeatedly pour water (or whatever you're measuring) from one bowl into another, emptying the second bowl when it becomes full. If the bowls hold A and B volumes, use the following equation to calculate values that you can measure.

$$Q \equiv 6 \times N \bmod 10$$

PROGRAMMING EXERCISES

Like the crossing puzzles described in Chapter 7, these puzzles make interesting programming challenges, but they can be quite difficult. Using modular arithmetic lets you measure quantities relatively easily, but that doesn't guarantee the quickest solution.

For example, suppose you have 6–liter and 10–liter flasks. By filling the 6–liter flask and pouring it into the 10–liter flask four times, emptying the 10–liter flask when it becomes full, you can measure 4 liters. However, a faster solution would be to fill the 10–liter flask and then pour its contents into the 6–liter flask, leaving 4 liters in the 10–liter flask.

Using a more general dynamic programming approach to search for the shortest possible solution, or to search for rope–burning solutions, could be quite difficult. For those types of challenges you may want to have the candidate outline a program instead of writing one.

1. Write a program that lets the user enter multiple rope burn times and a goal duration. The program should find a way to use the ropes to measure the goal duration if it is possible.
2. Write a program that lets the user enter two bucket sizes and a goal amount. The program should show a way to use the buckets to measure the goal amount if it is possible. (The program need not find the *shortest* method for measuring the goal.)
3. Repeat Exercise 1 but find the shortest way to achieve the goal.
4. Repeat Exercise 2 but allow the user to enter more than two bucket sizes.
5. Write a program to solve the "Eight Ounces of Gold" problem. It should let the user enter multiple bowl sizes and the amount of available gold. It should find a way to divide the gold evenly if possible without spilling any of the gold. For simplicity each share of gold should each end up in a single bowl.
6. Repeat Exercise 5 but allow each share to be contained in multiple bowls if necessary. For example, four ounces might be contained in a one–ounce bowl and a three–ounce bowl.

Worrisome Weights

These puzzles deal with weighing things. They include puzzles that use pan balances and spring scales. Some ask you to compare objects to each other, for example to find the one that has a different weight. Others ask you to pick standard weights to counterbalance other objects that you need to weigh.

In double pan balance puzzles, it's important to remember that objects can be in three places: in the left pan, in the right pan, and in neither pan. That also applies to known weights. For example, if you're using known weights to try to balance objects with unknown weights, you can place the known weights in the left pan, the right pan, or neither pan.

COUNTERFEIT COIN

> **Puzzle:** Suppose you have eight gold coins that look identical. Of the coins, seven are solid gold and one is a counterfeit made of gold–plated silver. How many weighings with a double pan balance do you need to find the counterfeit coin?

Because a double pan balance has two pans, people often think they should divide the objects into two piles of equal size and then use some sort of binary search to find the solution. The fact that this puzzle involves eight coins, and eight is a power of two, is another false hint that you should divide the coins into two piles and use a binary search.

In double pan balance puzzles, it's important to remember that objects can be in three places: in the left pan, in the right pan, and in neither pan. Often that means you should divide the objects into three groups and use a trinary search.

For this puzzle, place three coins in the left pan, three in the right pan, and leave two on the table. There are two cases: the pans balance or they don't.

If the pans balance, you know that the counterfeit coin is one of the two on the table, so you compare them. Silver is lighter than gold (10.5 gm/cm^3 versus 19.3 gm/cm^3) so the lighter coin is the counterfeit.

If the pans don't balance in your first weighing, then the lighter pan holds the counterfeit coin. Weigh two of those coins against each other. If they balance, then the third coin from that pan is the counterfeit. If the coins don't balance, then the lighter one is the counterfeit coin.

Whether the pans balance or not in the initial weighing, you only need two weighings to find the counterfeit.

They key to this puzzle is using a single weighing to find the lighter coin among three groups. In the first weighing, you use that technique to figure out which of three groups of coins contains the counterfeit. In the second weighing, you figure out which coin in the group is the counterfeit.

In the first weighing, one of the groups only contains two coins. Because the second group can find the counterfeit with up to three coins, that group *could have* contained three coins and the solution would still work. That means the same weighings would work with up to nine coins instead of just eight.

To see how many coins you can check with a given number of weighings, you can consider the weighings in reverse order. The last weighing can pick out the counterfeit from among three coins.

The second–to–last weighing can examine three groups of three coins to find the lighter group for use in the last weighing. That means you can find the counterfeit in up to $3 \times 3 = 9$ coins with two weighings.

Extending that technique, the third–to–last weighing could examine three groups of nine coins each to find the lighter one for use in the second–to–last weighing. That lets you test up to 27 coins with three weighings.

To check 27 coins, you would weigh nine coins against nine other coins with nine coins left over sitting on the table. You would then take the lighter group of nine coins and weigh three against three with three left over. Finally you would take the lighter three and weigh one against one with one left over to find the counterfeit coin.

More generally if you use N weighings, then you can find the counterfeit coin in a group of up to 3^N coins.

Conversely if you have C coins, then you need $\lceil Log_3(C) \rceil$ weighings to find the counterfeit coin. Here [x] is the ceiling function that returns the smallest integer that is at least as large as x. In other words, calculate $Log_3(C)$ and then round up to the next higher integer.

COUNTERFEIT EGG

> **Puzzle:** Suppose you have 12 gold eggs that look identical, but you know that one of them is either lighter or heavier than the others. How can you use a double pan balance to find the odd egg and learn whether it is lighter or heavier than the others?

This puzzle is different from the preceding one because we don't know whether the odd egg is heavier or lighter than the others.

Because we're using a double pan balance, we should divide the eggs into three groups of four eggs each. For weighing 1, weigh eggs {1, 2, 3, 4} against {5, 6, 7, 8}, leaving {9, 10, 11, 12} on the table. Now consider the following three cases.

1. Suppose {1, 2, 3, 4} balances with {5, 6, 7, 8}. Then {9, 10, 11, 12} contains the odd egg, but we don't know whether it's light or heavy. To find out, weigh {6, 7, 8} against {9, 10, 11}, leave {12} on the table, and consider the following cases.

    a. If {6, 7, 8} balances with {9, 10, 11}, then we know that egg 12 is the odd one, but we still don't know if it's heavy or light. Weigh it against any other egg (which we know has the normal weight) to find out.

    b. If {6, 7, 8} is lighter than {9, 10, 11}, then we know that {9, 10, 11} contains the odd egg and it's heavier than normal (because 6, 7, and 8 have normal weights). Weigh {9} against {10}. If they balance, then 11 is the heavy egg. If {9} and {10} don't balance, then the heavier one is the odd egg.

    c. If {6, 7, 8} is heavier than {9, 10, 11}, then reverse the logic used in part 1b. We know that {9, 10, 11} contains the odd egg and it's lighter than normal (because 6, 7, and 8 have normal weights). Weigh {9} against {10}. If they balance, then 11 is the light egg. If {9} and {10} don't balance, then the lighter one is the odd egg.

2. Suppose {1, 2, 3, 4} is lighter than {5, 6, 7, 8}. In this case we know that either {1, 2, 3, 4} is light or {5, 6, 7, 8} is heavy. For the second weighing, weigh {1, 2, 5} against {3, 6, 12}, leaving {4, 7, 8} on the table, and consider the following outcomes.

a. If {1, 2, 5} balances with {3, 6, 12}, then we know that {4, 7, 8} contains the odd egg. Weigh {7} against {8}. If they balance, then we know that 4 is the odd egg and it's light (because we know that {1, 2, 3, 4} is light). If {7} and {8} don't balance, then the heavier one is the odd egg (because we know that {5, 6, 7, 8} is heavy).

b. If {1, 2, 5} is lighter than {3, 6, 12}, then we know that this is either because 1 or 2 is lighter, or because 6 is heavier (because we know that either {1, 2, 3, 4} is light or {5, 6, 7, 8} is heavy). Weigh {1} against {2}. If one of them is lighter, that's the odd egg. If they balance, then egg 6 is the heavy one.

c. If {1, 2, 5} is heavier than {3, 6, 12}, then we know that either 5 is heavy or 3 is light (because we know that either {1, 2, 3, 4} is light or {5, 6, 7, 8} is heavy). Weigh {5} against {1}. If egg 5 is heavier, then it is the odd egg. If they balance, then egg 3 is the light one.

3. Suppose {1, 2, 3, 4} is heavier than {5, 6, 7, 8}. In that case, reverse the logic used for case 2. Or if you prefer, swap the labels on eggs 1, 2, 3, 4 with those on eggs 5, 6, 7, 8 and use the steps for case 2.

There are two tricks in this solution. First, it sometimes compares eggs that are known to have the normal weight to eggs with unknown weights. Second, it sometimes puts suspected light eggs and suspected heavy eggs in the same pan.

POISONED PILLS

Puzzle: Suppose you're an apothecary and you have 10 bottles of pills, nine containing vitamins and one containing poison. Unfortunately your assistant made up the bottles and forgot to label them. You consider making him taste them one at a time until you find the poison, but then you would have to hire a new assistant.

A vitamin weighs 1 gram and a poisoned pill weights 1.1 grams. Using a spring scale, how many weighings do you need to identify the poisoned bottle?

This puzzle is different from the previous ones because it uses a spring scale instead of a pan balance. In a spring scale, you place an object on the scale and it tells you the object's weight.

One approach would be to use 10 weighings to weigh one pill from each of the bottles until you find a pill that weighs 1.1 grams.

If you're really lucky, you'll find the poisoned pill in the first weighing. If you're unlucky, you might need to perform nine weighings. If none of the first nine pills is poisoned, then you know that the tenth jar contains the poisoned pills so you don't need to weigh one of its pills. On average you would expect to perform around four or five weighings before you find the poisoned bottle.

A quicker approach would be to weigh one pill from bottle 1, two pills from bottle 2, three pills from bottle 3, and so on up to ten pills from bottle 10.

If all of the pills were vitamins, then the total weight would be 1+2+3+...+9+10=55 grams, but the weight will be bigger by 0.1 grams for each poisoned pill present. Just subtract 55 grams from the measured weight and divide the result by 0.1 to find the number of the poisoned bottle.

For example, if the measured weight is 55.4 grams, then the pile contains (55.4–55)/0.1=4, so the balance is holding four poisoned pills and bottle 4 is the poisoned bottle.

Variation: What if the pills look identical and you can't keep the pills separated on the balance? In other words, after you dump the pills on the balance, you can no longer tell which pills came from which bottles.

You can still perform the measurement to identify the poisoned bottle, but you can't tell which of the pills you weighed is safe so you have to discard all of the pills that you weighed. To avoid discarding more pills than necessary, don't place any pills from bottle 10 on the scale. Then if the total weight is exactly 1+2+...+9=45 grams, you know that the tenth bottle contains the poison. Then you discard 45 pills instead of 55.

Variation: What if you don't know how much the pills weigh? You know that the vitamins all have the same weight and that the poisoned pills have a different weight, but you don't know what the weights are.

In this case the previous technique won't tell you much because you don't know how much the total should weigh and you don't know how different the poisoned pills are from the vitamins. You need to learn the weights.

One way to do that is to weigh a pill from bottle 1, then weigh a pill from bottle 2, and so on until you find 2 bottles containing pills of the same weight and another bottle with pills of a different weight. The pills of the different weight are poisoned. In the worst case, you might need to perform nine weighings. (If the first nine bottles' pills all have the same weight, then bottle 10 contains the poison.)

A better approach is to treat this as a sort of awkward double pan balance problem. First weigh a pill from bottle 1. Second weigh a pill from bottle 2.

If the weights are different, use a third weighing learn the weight of a pill from bottle 3. The pill with the odd weight is poisoned. In this case you use 3 weighings.

If the pills from bottles 1 and 2 have the same weight, then they are vitamins and you know the weight of a vitamin. Call that weight V. Now you can perform a binary search of the remaining eight bottles to find the poison.

For the third weighing, place one pill from each of bottles 3, 4, 5, and 6 on the scale. If their combined weight is 4×V, then they contain vitamins so one of bottles 7, 8, 9, and 10 contains the poison. If the sum of the weights of the pills from bottles 3, 4, 5, and 6 is not 4×V, then one of those bottles contains poison. In either case you've narrowed the search down to four candidate bottles that may contain the poison. Suppose the candidates are bottles 3, 4, 5, and 6.

For the fourth weighing, place one pill from each of bottles 3 and 4 on the scale. If their total weight is 2×V, then you know that either bottle 5 or bottle 6 contains the poison. If the total weight isn't 2×V, then you know that either bottle 3 or 4 contains the poison.

For the fifth weighing, simply weigh a pill from one of the remaining two candidate bottles and its weight will tell you whether it or the other candidate contains the poison.

This method uses at most five weighings.

> **Follow–up:** In the worst case, how many pills do you need to discard if you can't tell the pills apart in the previous method?

If the first two pills have different weights, then you only weigh three pills and you weigh them individually so you don't need to discard any of them.

If the first two pills have the same weight, then you perform a binary search. If the group of four pills contains poison, you need to discard them. Then if the next group of two candidate pills contains poison, you also need to discard them. The final weighing includes a single pill, so you don't need to discard it.

In the worst case you discard 4+2=6 pills.

> **Variation:** What if the non–poisoned pills contain life–saving medicine and you can't afford to discard even one?

If each bottle is identical and contains the same number of pills, you can still use the previous binary search if you weigh entire bottles instead of pills. If the bottles are different (some bottles are heavier than others), you'll need to weigh pills one at a time.

If the bottles are identical but contain different numbers of pills, then you can still use the binary search with some modification. First remove all of the pills except one from bottle 1 and set them aside. Weigh bottle 1 and restore its pills.

Next repeat those steps with bottle 2.

If bottle 1 with one pill and bottle 2 with one pill have different weights, then weigh bottle 3 with one pill. The bottle with the different weight contains the poison and you're done with only three weighings.

If bottle 1 with one pill and bottle 2 with one pill have the same weight, then they contain medicine. Use a third weighing to weigh a single pill from bottle 1. That gives you the weight of a pill and from that you can calculate the weight of a bottle. Now perform the binary search with closed bottles, doing a little math to figure out how much each bottle should weigh for the number of pills it contains.

The binary search takes three weighings, so you use a total of six weighings. That's one more than before, but you don't need to discard any pills.

Alternatively, if you can take pills out of the bottles and place them on a table without mixing them up, then you can leave one pill in each bottle and then use the normal binary search method on them.

In any case you should give your assistant a sound reprimand and possibly dock his wages for the hour and a half that you spent trying to figure out how to use the fewest possible weighings.

TRIPLE PAN BALANCE, PART 1

> **Puzzle:** Suppose you have a triple pan balance with three pans connected to the corners of a triangle. If one of the three pans is light, it rises. If one is heavy, it sinks.

Now suppose you have 15 eggs, one of which is either heavier or lighted than the others. How many weighings do you need to find the odd egg and to determine whether it's heavy or light?

Place four eggs in each of the three pans, leave three eggs on the table, and consider the following cases.

1. If all of the pans balance, then the three eggs on the table contain the odd egg. In that case weigh those three eggs against each other. If one egg is higher than the others, then it is light. If one is lower than the others, then it is heavy.
2. If one of the pans is higher than the others in the initial weighing, then it contains the odd egg and that egg is light. Weigh three of those four eggs. If they balance, then the fourth egg is the light one. If they don't balance, then the egg in the higher pan is the light one.
3. If one of the pans is lower than the others in the initial weighing, then it contains the odd egg and that egg is heavy. Weigh three of those four eggs. If they balance, then the fourth egg is the heavy one. If they don't balance, then the egg in the lower pan is the heavy one.

TRIPLE PAN BALANCE, PART 2

Puzzle: In the preceding puzzle, you can find an odd egg with two weighings. Among how many eggs could you find an odd egg with three weighings? How?

You can find an odd egg among up to 63 eggs with three weighings.

First place 16 eggs on each of the pans, leave 15 eggs on the table, and consider the following cases.

1. If the pans balance, then the 15 eggs on the table contain the odd egg. Use the solution to the preceding puzzle to find it.
2. If one of the pans is higher than the others, then it contains the odd egg and that egg is light. From that group of eggs, place four eggs in each of the pans, leave four eggs on the table, and consider the following cases.

   a. If the pans balance, then the four eggs on the table contain the light egg. Place three of them in the pans. If they balance, then the fourth egg is the light one. If they don't balance, then the high pan contains the light egg.

b. If the pans don't balance, then the high pan contains the light egg. Weigh three of that pan's eggs as in step 2a.

3. If one of the pans is lower than the others, then it contains the odd egg and that egg is heavy. Reverse the logic of step 2 to find the heavy egg.

BAZAAR WEIGHTS, PART 1

Puzzle: Suppose you have a gummy bear shop in a bazaar. Tradition requires you to use an ancient, rusty double pan balance to measure gummy bears to the nearest ounce. You do this by placing pieces of metal with known weights on the pans along with the gummies.

What is the fewest number of weights that you need to measure any quantity of gummy bears between 1 and 120 ounces?

The obvious answer is to use weights that are powers of 2: 1, 2, 4, 8, ..., 64. Then you can add weights to make up any number of ounces between 1 and 127.

With that approach, a number's binary representation tells you which weights to use. If you read the bits from right to left, the bits correspond to the weights 1, 2, 4, and so forth.

For example, 120 ounces is 1111000 in binary, so you should use the 8, 16, 32, and 64 ounce weights.

The trickiest part of this puzzle is realizing that you can place weights on either or both sides of the balance. For example, to weigh 3 ounces of gummy bears, you could place the gummies plus a 1 ounce weight on one side and a 4 ounce weight on the other side.

When you place a weight in the pan opposite the gummy bears, you are adding to the total weight of the gummies. When you place a weight in the same pan as the gummy bears, you are subtracting weight from the gummies' total. In the preceding example, you add 4 ounces and subtract 1 to get a total of 3.

To weigh any amount with the fewest weights, those weights should be powers of 3: 1, 3, 9, 27, 81. Figure 9–1 shows the amounts you need to place in the left and right pans to measure amounts between 1 and 13 ounces. With more weights you can weigh heavier loads similarly.

Total Ounces	Left Weights	Right Weights
1		1
2	1	3
3		3
4		3, 1
5	1, 3	9
6	3	9
7	3	9, 1
8	1	9
9		9
10		9, 1
11	1	9, 3
12		9, 3
13		9, 3, 1

Figure 9–1: Weighing between 1 and 13 ounces with 1–ounce, 3–ounce, and 9–ounce weights.

In general if you have weights that are powers of three and the largest weight is W, then you can measure any weight between 1 and the total of all of your weights. For example, Figure 9–1 uses weights 1, 3, and 9 to create totals between 1 and 1+3+9=13.

BAZAAR WEIGHTS, PART 2

Puzzle: Prove that weights that are powers of 3 let you measure weights between 1 ounce and the sum of the weights.

Unless the job candidate is a mathematician, you should probably allow a fairly intuitive proof to this puzzle instead of requiring a rigorous one. The proof isn't too confusing if you use induction. (If you don't remember how induction works, see Chapter 6.)

The claim is, if you have weights 1, 3, 9, ..., 3^N that are powers of 3, then you can measure all weights between 1 and the sum $1+3+9+...+3^N$.

For the base case, look at Figure 9–1 again. It shows how you can measure weights that satisfy the claim for N=0, 1, or 2. (So the biggest weights are 1, 3, and 9 respectively.)

Now suppose the claim holds for N=K. To finish the proof, we need to show that it holds for N=K+1.

By using the smaller weights up to 3^K, you can measure all weights between 1 and the sum of those weights. Call that sum S_K.

If you place the new weight 3^{K+1} in the right pan, you can use combinations of the smaller weights in both pans to essentially subtract values between 1 and S_K from 3^{K+1}. That lets you measure all weights between S_K+1 and $3^{K+1}-1$.

Similarly you can use combinations of the smaller weights to essentially add values to the new weight and measure values between than $3^{K+1}+1$ and the sum of all of the weights. Call that sum S_{K+1}.

Naturally you can place the new weight in the right pan and use none of the smaller weights to measure 3^{K+1} exactly.

This shows that you can measure all of the values between 1 and S_{K+1}, which is what we needed to show.

Figure 9–2 shows the idea on a number line.

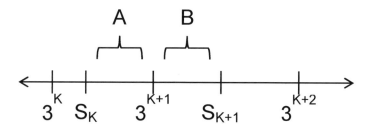

Figure 9–2: Smaller weights let you make new values smaller and larger than the weight 3^{K+1}.

If the sum of the weights up to 3^K is S_K, then you use combinations of those weights subtracted from 3^{K+1} to measure values in region A.

Similarly you use combinations of the smaller weights added to 3^{K+1} to measure values in region B.

For a concrete example, suppose you know how to use the weights 1, 3, and 9, and now you're adding the new weight 27. Then S_K is 1+3+9=13 and region A includes values 14 through 26. For example, you can measure the value 17 by placing weights 1 and 9 in the left pan (with 17 ounces of gummy bears) and the new 27 ounce weight in the right pan.

Region B includes values 28 through 1+3+9+27=40. For example, you can measure the value 35 by placing 35 ounces of gummy bears and the 1–ounce weight in the left pan and the 27–ounce and 9–ounce weights in the right pan.

BAZAAR WEIGHTS, PART 3

Puzzle: Suppose you're using weights as in the preceding puzzle but you have weights that are powers of 2: 1, 2, 4, 8, and so forth. You can use the binary representation of the weight that you need to measure to figure out which weights to use, but before you start you don't know how much the gummy bears weigh so you can't make that calculation mathematically.

Explain an algorithm that you could actually use to learn how much the gummy bears weigh.

This is pretty easy for weights that are powers of 2. Place the gummies in the left pan. Then add to the right pan the largest weight that doesn't make the right pan heavier than the left. Repeat until the pans balance and you're done.

For example, suppose you have 11 ounces of gummies in the left pan. You first put the 1–ounce weight in the right pan. It's not heavier than the gummies, so you remove it and try the 2–ounce weight. It's still not heavier so you remove it and try the 4–ounce weight. You continue trying weights until you discover that the 16–ounce is heavier than the gummies. Then you remove that weight and replace it with the next smaller weight, which is the 8–ounce weight.

Now you start over trying the 1–ounce weight, the 2–ounce weight, and so forth. You'll soon find that the 4–ounce weight plus the 8–ounce weight is heavier than the gummies, so you remove the 4–ounce weight and replace it with the next smaller weight, which is the 2–ounce weight.

When you start over again, you'll find that the 1–ounce weight makes the pans balance and you know that the gummies weigh 1+2+8=11 ounces.

In practice you would soon get a feel for how heavy the gummies are and you probably could guess pretty closely what weights you need to use. Then you would just need to make some small adjustments to make the pans balance.

You could also use some math. Depending on the type of gummy, there are probably around 10 or 12 gummies per ounce. (Unless you're selling those huge 5–pound gummies.)

BAZAAR WEIGHTS, PART 4

> **Puzzle:** Suppose you're using weights that are powers of 3 to weigh gummy bears. Explain an algorithm that you could actually use to learn how much the gummy bears weigh.

This is a lot harder than it is if the weights are powers of 2. Start by placing the gummies in the left pan. Then repeat the following steps until the pans balance.

1. Find the smallest weight that you can add to the lighter pan to make that pan heavier. (Or if they balance, you're done.) Call this weight W.
2. Now remove weight W from the lighter pan and add all of the weights smaller than W to the lighter pan. There are two possibilities.

   a. Suppose weight W is heavy enough to tip the scales but all of the lighter weights together are not. To balance the scales, we need to place weight W in the lighter pan and then use the smaller weights to "subtract" weight from it by placing them on the other side. Remove the lighter weights, place weight W in the lighter pan, and then repeat starting at Step 1.

   b. Suppose all of the lighter weights together can tip the scales. To balance the scales, we don't need weight W. Instead we can use a combination of the smaller weights to add weight to the lighter pan. Place the largest weight that is smaller than weight W in the lighter pan and then repeat starting at Step 1.

For example, suppose you want to measure 75 ounces of gummy bears. You start by placing the gummies in the left pan.

The smallest weight that would tip the balance weighs 81 ounces. The sum of the smaller weights $1+3+9+27=40$ is not enough to tip the scales, so we add weight 81 to the lighter pan, which is on the right.

Now we look for the smallest weight that can tip the scales back the other way. Because we checked the 81–ounce weight last, we can start the new search with the next smaller weight, which is the 27–ounce weight.

The pans currently weigh 75 ounces and 81 ounces respectively, so the 27–ounce weight can tip the scales. The 9–ounce weight can, too, and the 3 –ounce weight cannot, so we pick the 9–ounce weight.

The sum of the weights smaller than 9 is $1+3=4$. That's not enough to tip the scales, so we add the 9–ounce weight to the lighter pan, which is currently on the left.

Again we look for the smallest weight that can tip the scales. The pans now weigh 75+9=84 ounces and 81 ounces, so the 3 ounce weight makes the pans balance if you put it in the right pan and we are done.

To find the weight of the gummies, add the weights in the right pan and subtract the weights in the left pan to get 81+3–9=75 as desired.

OSTRICH QUEEN

Puzzle: When Queen Oona is on her deathbed, she decrees that there shall be a Grand Ostrich Race in three weeks' time. Her five children will enter three birds each in the races and the winner will inherit the throne.

Prince Auk has 25 racing ostriches and he needs to identify the three fastest. He has five jockeys so he can race up to five birds at a time. Unfortunately an ostrich can only race once per week without risk of injury, and even once per week is pushing it.

How can Prince Auk determine which three of his ostriches are the fastest in time for the Grand Ostrich Race?

This isn't exactly a weighing puzzle, but some of the ideas are similar. In this case you use races instead of scales to compare groups of ostriches.

First number the ostriches 1 through 25 and race them in groups of five. The following list shows the races on Day 1.

Group A:	1	2	3	4	5
Group B:	6	7	8	9	10
Group C:	11	12	13	14	15
Group D:	16	17	18	19	20
Group E:	21	22	23	24	25

Prince Auk can eliminate the two slowest birds in each of those five races because they've all been beaten by three faster ostriches. Suppose the defeated ostriches are those with the highest numbers in each race. (If they aren't the highest numbered, just renumber the birds after the race so they are.)

The following list shows the birds remaining after the first race.

Group A:	1	2	3
Group B:	6	7	8
Group C:	11	12	13
Group D:	16	17	18
Group E:	21	22	23

Birds 1, 6, 11, 16, and 21 are the fastest in their groups, but that doesn't indicate how they compare to each other. For example every bird in Group A might be slower than all of the birds in Group B.

For the 6th race, pit the fastest ostriches from each of the first five races against each other. Those are birds 1, 6, 11, 16, and 21. Suppose bird 1 comes in first, bird 6 comes in second, and bird 11 comes in third in this 6th race.

Birds 16 and 21 were beaten by all three of the others in the 6th race so they are definitely not among the three fastest overall and the prince can eliminate them.

Birds 16 and 21 were also the fastest birds in their groups, so the prince can eliminate the slower birds in their groups.

Bird 11 came in 3rd in the 6th race. That means the other birds in its group (birds 12 and 13) are slower than birds 11, 6, and 1, so the prince can eliminate them.

Similarly Bird 6 came in 2nd in the 6th race so bird 8 is slower than birds 1, 6, and 7 and it can be eliminated.

The following list shows the remaining birds after the 6th race.

Group A:	1	2	3
Group B:	6	7	
Group C:	11		
Group D:			
Group E:			

It would be nice to race the six remaining ostriches against each other, but Prince Auk only has five jockeys so that's not possible. Fortunately there's a trick here that narrows the field. Ostrich 1 has raced against all of the group winners so we know it is the fastest in the flock.

All the prince needs to do now is race the other five birds (2, 3, 6, 7, and 11) against each other. The two fastest of them plus ostrich 1 are the prince's three fastest birds.

The prince has run seven races, five at the beginning of week 1, one at the beginning of week 2, and one at the beginning of week 3, so the three finalists are rested and ready to run in the Grand Ostrich Race after 3 weeks. (At the race his sister Princess Buitre drugs the other ostriches so she wins and begins her rule of tyranny.)

SUMMARY

When you're working with pan balances, remember that you can still learn something about objects if they are in neither pan. You can also use known weights, either standard weights or objects that you know have the "standard" weight, to counterbalance objects with unknown weights.

PROGRAMMING EXERCISES

1. Write a program that simulates the "Counterfeit Coin" puzzle. The user should enter the weights of the eight coins. The program should then pretend to make the necessary weighings to find the counterfeit coin. The program should use the user–entered weights only to simulate the weighings. (In other words, don't cheat.) When it's done, the program should display a list of the weighings it made and their results, along with the counterfeit coin.
2. Write testing code that tests the code you wrote for Exercise 1. It should call the weighing code with each of the coins as the counterfeit and verify that the code picks the correct coin.
3. Repeat Exercise 1 for the "Counterfeit Egg" puzzle.
4. Repeat Exercise 2 for the program that you wrote for Exercise 3.
5. Write a program that simulates a double pan balance and weights that are powers of 2: 1, 2, 4, … When the user enters a target weight, the program should determine which weights to use to balance the target weight.
6. Repeat Exercise 5 but using weights that are powers of 3: 1, 3, 9, 27, …

10

Tricky Times and Subtle Speeds

These puzzles include clock puzzles and stories that involve speeds and distances covered. It's often useful to remember the distance formula D=S×T where D is distance, S is speed, and T is time. For example, if you run 10 miles per hour for 15 minutes, then you've run for 1/4 hour so you cover a total of 10×1/4=2.5 miles.

Some puzzles also use average speed calculations. Even if your speed isn't constant, if you cover distance D during time T, then your average speed is S=D/T.

COUNTING MATCHING MINUTES

> **Puzzle:** How many times per day do the hour and minute hands of a clock point in the same direction?

The hands point in the same direction at noon, a bit after 1:00, a bit after 2:00, and so forth, so the obvious but incorrect answer is 24 times per day. Let's look at the times a bit more closely.

For example, consider the time a bit after 1:00. At 1:00 the hour hand points at the 1. When the minute hand points at the 1, it's 1:05. During the 5 minutes it took the minute hand to get to the 1, the hour hand moved a bit more, so the minute hand doesn't actually catch the hour hand until a bit after 1:05.

Similarly the other times when the hands point in the same direction are a bit after 2:10, a bit after 3:15, a bit after 4:20, and so on up to a bit after 11:55.

As times goes on, the "bit after" grows larger. Consider the time a bit after 11:55. At 11:55 the hour hand is almost on the 12. It takes the minute hand a full 5 minutes to catch up, so the time "a bit after 11:55" is actually 12:00.

Now you can make a complete list of the times when the hands point in the same direction: a bit after 1:05, a bit after 2:10, ..., a bit after 10:50, and 12:00. That makes a total of 11 times in a 12–hour period or 22 times per day.

MATCHING MINUTES

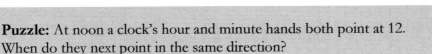

> **Puzzle:** At noon a clock's hour and minute hands both point at 12. When do they next point in the same direction?

There are several ways you can solve this puzzle. The following two sections explain a hard but obvious strategy and an easy but less obvious strategy.

Hard Strategy

The hard but obvious strategy is to use algebra.

Let H be the time in hours after noon when the two hands point in the same direction. The minute hand moves 360 degrees per hour, so at time H the number of degrees that the minute hand has moved is:

$$minute\_hand\_degrees = 360 \times H \bmod 360$$

We know that a bit more than one hour has passed, so applying the modulus operator subtracts 360 from the total giving:

$$minute\_hand\_degrees = 360 \times H - 360$$

The hour hand moves 360/12=30 degrees per hour, so at time H the number of degrees that the hour hand has moved is:

$$hour\_hand\_degrees = 30 \times H \bmod 360$$

The hour hand has not moved around the full circle yet, so we can drop the modulus operator.

$$hour\_hand\_degrees = 30 \times H$$

Setting these two equations equal gives the following equation.

$$360 \times H - 360 = 30 \times H$$

If you solve this equation for H, you'll find H=12/11.

This means the hour and minute hands point in exactly the same direction 12/11 hours after noon. Converting this into hours, minutes, and seconds gives you 1:05:27.2727

Easy Strategy

For the easy but less obvious strategy, note that the hour and minute hands point in the same direction 11 times in 12 hours. That means the next time the hands point in the same direction must be 1/11th of the way around the clock's face or at 60/11 minutes after the hour. Converting this into minutes and seconds gives you the time when this occurs: 1:05:27.2727...

Figure 10–1 shows the approximate times when the hour and minute hands point in the same direction.

Time	Time
12:00:00	6:32:43
1:05:27	7:38:10
2:10:54	8:43:38
3:16:21	9:49:05
4:21:49	10:54:32
5:27:16	12:00:00

Figure 10–1: Approximate times when a clock's hour and minute hands point in the same direction.

Figure 10–1 also makes it easy to see that there are 11 times per 12–hour period when the hour and minute hands point in the same direction.

COUNTING OPPOSITE HOURS

Puzzle: How many times per day do a clock's hour and minute hands point in exactly opposite directions?

This is similar to the "Counting Matching Minutes" puzzle and it has a similar solution.

The hands point in opposite directions a bit after 12:30, a bit after 1:35, a bit after 2:40, and so on, so the obvious but incorrect answer is 24 times per day.

As in the earlier puzzle, the "bit after" grows as the hours pass so the 11th time the hands point in opposite directions is a bit after 12:30 again.

Now you can make a complete list of the times when the hands point in opposite directions: a bit after 12:30, a bit after 1:35, ..., a bit after 10:20, and a bit after 11:25. That makes a total of 11 times in a 12–hour period or 22 times per day.

OPPOSITE HOURS

Puzzle: At noon a clock's hour and minute hands both point at 12. When is the first time after noon that they point in exactly opposite directions?

As in the "Matching Minutes" puzzle, there is an obvious but hard strategy and a less obvious but easy strategy for solving this puzzle. The following two sections describe both methods.

Hard Strategy

The obvious but hard way to solve the puzzle is again to use algebra.

Let H be the time in hours after noon when the two hands point in opposite directions. The minute hand moves 360 degrees per hour, so at time H the number of degrees that the minute hand has moved is:

$$\text{minute\_hand\_degrees} = 360 \times H$$

The hour hand moves 30 degrees per hour, so at time H the number of degrees that the hour hand has moved is:

$$\text{hour\_hand\_degrees} = 30 \times H$$

We know that the minute hand has moved 180 degrees farther than the hour hand, so we can combine those two equations to get the following.

$$360 \times H = 30 \times H + 180$$

Now if you solve this equation for H, you get H=18/33.

Converting this into hours, minutes, and seconds gives you 12:32:43.6363...

Easy Strategy

The less obvious but easier strategy for solving this puzzle relies on an observation to the one used to solve the "Matching Minutes" puzzle.

First note that the hour and minute hands point in opposite directions 11 times in 12 hours. That means the interval between those events must be 12/11 hours.

That's all you needed to solve the earlier puzzle because the hour and minute hands point in the same direction at 12:00. In this puzzle, however, the hands don't point in opposite directions at 12:00, so you can't simply say that the next time they do so is at 12:00 plus 12/11 hours.

Fortunately there is a well–defined time where the hands do point in opposite directions: 6:00. The times between 12:00 and 6:00 where the hands point in opposite directions are a bit after 12:30, a bit after 1:35, a bit after 2:40, a bit after 3:45, a bit after 4:50, and a bit after 5:55.

The last time, a bit after 5:55, is actually 6:00, so there are 5 times between 12:00 and 6:00 when the hands point in opposite directions. That means the first time after 12:00 when that happens is 6:00 minus 5×12/11 hours, which is 12:32:43.6363...

Figure 10–2 shows the approximate times when the hour and minute hands point in opposite directions.

Time
12:32:43
1:38:10
2:43:38
3:49:05
4:54:32
6:00:00

Time
7:05:27
8:10:54
9:16:21
10:21:49
11:27:16
12:32:43

Figure 10–2: Approximate times when a clock's hour and minute hands point in opposite directions.

Figure 10–2 also makes it easy to see that there are 11 times per 12–hour period when the hour and minute hands point in opposite directions.

FOOTRACE

> **Puzzle:** Boris and Doris are on their high school track team. On long races Boris runs a consistent 7–minute mile and Doris runs a consistent 6–minute mile. If they run five miles on a quarter–mile track, how many times will Doris pass Boris?

There are a couple of ways you can approach this problem. For example, you can calculate exactly when Doris passes Boris each time.

Probably the easiest approach is to focus on the total time. Doris takes $5 \times 6 = 30$ minutes to run five miles or 20 laps around the track. During that same 30 minutes, Boris can run $30/7 \approx 4.3$ miles or a bit more than 17 laps.

Doris runs three more laps than Boris so she passes him three times. If she were then to wait at the finish line for Boris to complete the race, he would pass her three times before he was done.

CLOCK TRIFECTA

> **Puzzle:** At noon a clock's hour, minute, and second hands all point at 12. When is the first time after noon when all three hands point in the same direction?

The solution to the "Matching Minutes" puzzle showed that the hour and minute hands point in the same direction every 12/11 hours.

To make the discussion a little simpler, let's talk about the number of elevenths that the hands move around the clock. In that case the hour hand moves 1 eleventh of the way around the clock during one 12/11 hour interval.

The second hand moves 3600 times as fast as the hour hand, so during one interval it moves $3600/11 = 327 + 3/11$ times around the clock's face. If you discard the integer number of laps around the clock, the second hand ends up pointing 3 elevenths of the way around the clock face.

After N intervals of 12/11 hours, the hour hand is positioned $N \times 1$ elevenths of the way around the clock and the second hand is positioned $N \times 3$ elevenths of the way around the clock. To see when the hour an minute hands point in the same direction, we can see when $N \times 1$ mod 11 and $N \times 3$ mod 11 are the same.

Figure 10–3 shows the multiples of 1 and 3 modulo 11 for different values of N.

N	N×1 mod 11	N×3 mod 11
0	0	0
1	1	3
2	2	6
3	3	9
4	4	1
5	5	4
6	6	7
7	7	10
8	8	2
9	9	5
10	10	8
11	0	0

Figure 10–3: Positions of the hour and second hands in 11ths of the clock face.

Figure 10–3 shows that the hour and second hands don't point in the same direction again until 11 intervals have passed. At that point, both of the hands are pointing 0 elevenths of the way around the clock face so they are both pointing at 12 and the time is 12:00.

That means the first time after noon when all three hands point in the same direction is 12:00 midnight.

Variation: How many times per day do a clock's hour, minute, and second hands all point in the same direction?

If you think that all three hands point in the same direction once per hour, then you might incorrectly conclude that they do so 24 times per day.

If you understand the reasoning used in the "Matching Minutes" puzzles, then you may incorrectly think that all three hands point in the same direction 22 times per day.

In fact, as the preceding discussion shows, all three hands only point in the same direction at noon and midnight. That means the correct answer is that all three hands point in the same direction only two times per day.

TRACKBIRD

> **Puzzle:** Suppose at exactly 8:00 AM a train leaves New York City headed for Philadelphia at 25 mph. At the same time, a trackbird (an exotic kind of bird that prefers to fly along train tracks) leaves from the same spot and flies along the track at 50 mph.
>
> When it reaches the station in Philadelphia, the trackbird immediately turns around and flies back. When it reaches the train (which has been traveling for a while), the trackbird immediately reverses again. The trackbird continues to fly back and forth between the train and the station in Philadelphia until the train arrives at the station.
>
> If the track is 100 miles long, how many miles does the trackbird fly before the train arrives?

On the first leg (or wing) of its journey, the trackbird flies 100 miles to reach Philadelphia. You can then use some fairly non–trivial mathematics to calculate the distance it flies to go back to meet the train. Then you can calculate the distance it travels back to Philadelphia, back to the train, and so forth.

Eventually you'll get an infinite series of shorter and shorter distances. Then with some moderately advanced mathematics you can calculate the sum to get an answer.

Fortunately there's a much easier solution that applies to all of the "train and bird" (or "bus and dragonfly," or whatever) puzzles. First calculate the total time for the story to come to an end. Because the trackbird has been flying the whole time, the distance it covers is the total time multiplied by its speed.

In this example, the train travels at 25 mph and covers 100 miles, so it takes 4 hours. The trackbird flies at 50 mph, so in 4 hours it travels 200 miles. That's all there is to it!

Another way to look at it is that the trackbird flies twice as fast as the train so it coves twice the distance.

TWO TRAINS AND A BIRD, PART 1

Puzzle: Suppose a train leaves New York City headed for Philadelphia at 25 mph. At the same time, a second train leaves Philadelphia headed for New York City at 25 mph on the same track.

Also at the same time a trackbird leaves the first train and flies at 50 mph along the track toward the second train. When it reaches the second train, the trackbird immediately reverses course and flies back to the first train. The trackbird continues flying back and forth between the two trains until they collide.

If the trains start 100 miles apart, how many miles did the trackbird fly before the collision? (The trackbird flies above the trains so it isn't hurt by the collision. Any people on or near the trains are another matter entirely.)

As in the preceding puzzle, all that matters is the total elapsed time and the trackbird's speed. The two trains collide after each has traveled 50 miles, 2 hours into their journeys. The trackbird flies at 50 mph, so in 2 hours it flies 2×50=100 miles.

TWO TRAINS AND A BIRD, PART 2

Puzzle: Consider the preceding puzzle but this time suppose one train travels 20 mpg, the other travels 30 mph, and the trackbird flies 50 mph. How far does the trackbird fly?

Again all that matters is the total elapsed time and the trackbird's speed.

The trains start 100 miles apart. Their speeds add up to 20+30=50, so they are closing the distance at a net of 50 mph. That means they collide in 2 hours and the trackbird travels 2×50=100 miles just as before.

TWO TRAINS TO NEW YORK

Puzzle: Suppose a local train and an express train both leave Philadelphia at the same time on parallel tracks headed for a station 100 miles away in New York City. The local averages 25 mph and the express averages 40 mph.

When the two trains start, a trackbird also leaves the front of the local and flies at 50 mph toward the front of the express. When it reaches the express (the first time it will be pretty much instantaneous) the trackbird immediately turns around and flies back to the local. The trackbird continues ricocheting back and forth between the two trains until both trains have arrived in New York.

How far does the trackbird fly before it stops to roost in New York?

Hopefully you're getting the hang of it by now. All that matters is the total elapsed time and the trackbird's speed.

The trackbird starts flying when both trains start and it stops when the local reaches New York. The local averages 25 mph so it takes 4 hours to get to New York. During that time the trackbird flies $4\times50=200$ miles.

Notice that the speed of the express train is irrelevant. Its speed determines the exact path followed by the trackbird, but as long as the express is faster than the local the total distance traveled by the trackbird is determined by the local's speed.

TORTOISE AND HARE IN TRAINING

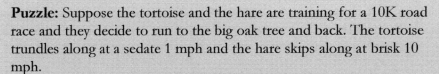

Puzzle: Suppose the tortoise and the hare are training for a 10K road race and they decide to run to the big oak tree and back. The tortoise trundles along at a sedate 1 mph and the hare skips along at brisk 10 mph.

To get a good workout, the hare decides to modify the way he runs. When he reaches the tree, he turns around and runs back to the tortoise. Later, when he reaches the tortoise, he turns again and runs back to the tree.

He continues bouncing back and forth between the tree and the tortoise until the tortoise reaches the tree. At that point he heads back to the gym. He then repeats his technique, bouncing back and forth between the tortoise and the gym this time, until the tortoise returns to the gym. (Then they both hit the sauna before heading home.)

How far does the rabbit run?

This problem is tricky because it doesn't seem to contain enough information. In fact it doesn't, but that doesn't mean you can't come up with a meaningful answer.

Suppose you're the interviewer and the candidate says, "I don't have enough information. How far away is the tree?" In that case, respond with, "Let's see what you can tell me without knowing that."

Suppose you're the candidate: When the interview says, "Let's see what you can tell me without knowing that," you need to do something. You could work with generalities, or you could define a variable D to represent the distance.

As in the bird and train puzzles, the only things that matter are the elapsed time and the speed of the animal that we're measuring, in this case the hare.

Suppose D is the distance to the tree in miles. Then the tortoise returns to the gym in $2\times D/1=2\times D$ hours. During that time, the hare can run $(2\times D)\times 10=20\times D$ miles.

More concisely and intuitively, the hare runs 10 times faster than the tortoise, so he runs 10 times as far.

THREE BIRDS

Puzzle: Suppose three birds leave their home in New York to be nestmates at the University of Pennsylvania in Philadelphia. The first flies 20 mph, the second flies 40 mph, and the third flies 50 mph.

Any time that the second or third bird reaches the new nest or reaches one of the other birds, it immediately reverses direction. They end up ricocheting back and forth between each other and the campus nest until they all arrive at the new nest where they stop and order pizza.

If the dorm nest is 100 miles from the old nest, what is the total distance traveled by all three birds?

If you think about it, this situation is remarkably complex, with the fastest bird bouncing back and forth between the second bird and the dorm nest, and the second bird ricocheting madly between the fastest and slowest birds.

Fortunately all that matters is the total elapsed time and the speed of the birds whose distances we want to know.

The whole frenetic performance ends when the slowest bird reaches the new dorm nest. At 20 mph that takes $100/20=5$ hours.

Now you can calculate the distances traveled by all of the birds. The slowest bird flies 5×20=100 miles, the second bird flies 5×40=200 miles, and the fastest bird flies 5×50=250 miles. The total distance traveled by all three birds is therefore 100+200+250=550 miles.

> **Note:** I use New York and Philadelphia a lot in these puzzles because they are 100 miles apart. You can use other cities if you like, but the calculations may be more complicated if, for example, you use Sacramento and Fresno, which are 158 miles apart.
>
> If you want to make things really complicated, you can also use less friendly speeds. For example, the birds could fly at 17 mph, 63.7 kph, and 54.2 cubits per microfortnight.

GONE FISHING

> **Puzzle:** Suppose you rent a boat with a small electric motor next to a river delta. You spend the next 30 minutes traveling one mile up the slow, lazy river, and there you stop to fish for a while. After three hours of not catching anything, you head back downstream, taking 10 minutes to return to your starting point.
>
> Assuming there's no current in the lake, how long will it take you to go one mile on the lake?

It took 30 minutes to go one mile against the river's current and 10 minutes to go one mile with the river's current, so it's tempting to average the two and say it will take (30+10)/2=20 minutes to go one mile with no current.

Because that's such an obvious answer, you can probably guess that it's wrong. The problem is that you're traveling with the current for less time than you're traveling against the current. In some sense if you average the times you're giving too much credit to the speed against the current so the resulting time is too long.

The following sections describe two different strategies that you can use to solve this problem correctly.

Algebraic Strategy

Let M be the speed given to the boat by the motor and let C be the current's speed. Now you can use the times to travel upstream and downstream to create two equations with M and C as unknowns.

$$1 \text{ mile} = 30 \text{ minutes} \times (M - C)$$

$$1 \text{ mile} = 10 \text{ minutes} \times (M + C)$$

Simply solve these two equations for M and C.

$$M = \frac{1}{15} \text{ miles per minute} = 4 \text{ mph}$$

$$C = \frac{1}{30} \text{ miles per minute} = 2 \text{ mph}$$

If M=4 mph, then it should take 15 minutes to go one mile on the lake without current.

Averaging Strategy

Although you cannot average the times you spent going upstream and downstream, you can average the *speeds* you achieved on those trips.

To see why, let D be the distance traveled, let M is the speed given by the motor, and let C be the current's speed. Then the speed upstream is M–C and the speed downstream is M+C.

The following equation shows the average of the two speeds.

$$\text{Average speed} = \frac{(M - C) + (M + C)}{2} = \frac{2 \times M}{2} = M$$

So if you average the speeds, the result is M. After you know M, you can calculate the time needed to travel one mile on the lake.

For this example the speed upstream is one mile per 30 minutes or 2 mph. The speed downstream is one mile per 10 minutes or 6 mph.

Then the average speed is (2+6)/2=4 mph, so it should take 15 minutes to go one mile on the lake without current.

SIXTY–THREE DOLLARS

Puzzle: Suppose your eccentric roommate uses an unusual spending pattern to pay for his lunch. He spends $1 on lunch on the first of the month, $2 on the second, $3 on the third, and so forth. (Lunches early in the month tend to be just apples and carrots, while lunches late in the month may include steak or lobster.)

First, how much does your roommate spend on lunches in a year?

One day he wakes you up at 4:00 AM and says, "I spent a total of $63 on lunches in the last five consecutive days." On what date did he reveal this critical piece of information?

First, to calculate the amount of money your roommate spends in a year, it helps to know the following formula.

$$1 + 2 + 3 + \cdots + N = \frac{N \times (N + 1)}{2}$$

This is an important formula and it's not hard to remember, so you should memorize it.

Next, the months that contain 30 days are April, June, September, and November. For each of those four months, your roommate spends 1+2+3+...+30=$465.

The months that contain 31 days are January, March, May, July, August, October, and December. For those seven months, your roommate spends 1+2+3+...+31=$496.

February contains 28 days most years and 29 days during leap years, so your roommate spends either 1+2+3+...+28=$406 or 1+2+3+...+29=$435.

Adding up all of the months, your roommate spends 4×$465+7×$496+$406=$5,738 during most years and 4×$465+7×$496+$435=$5,767 during leap years.

Next, you need to figure out what the date is when your roommate spends $63 in five consecutive days. To do this, you need to consider several cases depending on whether the days are all in the same month.

Suppose X is the date of the first lunch. For example, if the first lunch occurred on the 12th of a month, then X is 12. The following cases look at the number of the consecutive days that occur in the same month.

> **Case 1: The days are all in the same month.** Then if you add up all of the dates you get X+(X+1)+(X+2)+(X+3)+(X+4)=63. Rearranging a bit gives you 5×X+10=63 so X=63/5. That value isn't an integer so this case cannot occur.
>
> **Case 2: The last day is in the following month.** Then if you add up all of the dates you get X+(X+1)+(X+2)+(X+3)+1=63. Rearranging gives you 4×X+7=63 so X=56/4=14. In that case the dates are 14, 15, 16, 17, and 1. This time X is an integer, but no month ends after only 17 days so this case

cannot occur.

Case 3: The last two days are in the following month. Then if you add up all of the dates you get X+(X+1)+(X+2)+1+2=63. Rearranging gives you 3×X+6=63 so X=57/3=19. In that case the dates are 19, 20, 21, 1, and 2. Again X is an integer but no month ends after only 21 days so this case cannot occur.

Case 4: The last three days are in the following month. Then if you add up all of the dates you get X+(X+1)+1+2+3=63. Rearranging gives you 2×X+7=63 so X=56/2=28. In that case the dates are 28, 29, 1, 2, and 3. The only time this happens is during a leap year and the first date is February 28.

Case 5: The last four days are in the following month. Then if you add up all of the dates you get X+1+2+3+4=63. Rearranging gives you X+10=63 so X=53. No month has 53 days so this case cannot occur.

The only case that works is Case 4 where the first date is February 28 and the last date is March 3. Your roommate woke you up on the morning after the last date, so he woke you at 4:00 AM on March 4. Presumably you threw a pillow at him and went back to sleep.

When you're working on calendar puzzles, it helps to know how many days are in each month. The following poem gives one way to remember.

Thirty days have September, April, June, and November.

When short February's done, all the rest have 31.

February has 28 days in most years and 29 in leap years.

The following list shows the rules for leap years:

1. If the year is divisible by 4, then it is a leap year (and a summer Olympics year), unless ...

2. ... the year is also divisible by 100, in which case is *not* a leap year (but it's still a summer Olympics year), unless ...

3. ... the year is also divisible by 400, in which case *is* a leap year after all (and still a summer Olympics year).

SUMMARY

The puzzles in this chapter include clock, speed, distance, and calendar puzzles. For clock puzzles, you often need to use modular arithmetic.

You can solve many speed and distance puzzles if you just remember one simple rule: Distance=Speed×Time. It doesn't matter how complicated an object's path is. If it moves at a constant speed throughout a given time, then the distance it travels is simply Speed×Time.

To solve calendar puzzles, memorize the number of days in each month. Often those puzzles require you to consider months individually or to examine many special cases. Just plug through them until you've covered them all and you should be okay.

PROGRAMMING EXERCISES

1. Make a graphical clock that displays hour, minute, and second hands showing the current time.
2. Make a graphical clock that displays all of the times when the hour and minute hands point in the same directions. Also display the second hand and verify that it doesn't point in the same direction as the other two hands except at 12:00.
3. Repeat Exercise 2 but display the times when the hour and minute hands point in opposite directions.
4. Make a graphical program that simulates the "Trackbird" puzzle. For simplicity you can draw the train as a rectangle and the bird as a small circle. The program should keep track of the total distance the bird flies and display it when it is done.
5. Repeat Exercise 4 for the "Two Trains and a Bird, Part 1" puzzle.
6. Repeat Exercise 4 for the "Two Trains and a Bird, Part 2" puzzle.
7. Repeat Exercise 4 for the "Three Birds" puzzle.
8. Write a program that converts between cubits per microfortnight, miles per hour, and kilometers per hour.

11

Lucid Logic

These puzzles require you to make logical deductions in fanciful situations. They assume that all of the parties involved have perfect logic–solving skills. For example, prison guards may be despicable cads, but they can always solve any logic puzzle perfectly, at least as long as you can explain how they should do it.

LIARS AND TRUTH–TELLERS

> **Puzzle:** Suppose you've been imprisoned and your sadistic jailer leads you to two doors. Behind one lies the cafeteria and a lunch of moldy bread. Behind the other is a day's worth of solitary confinement and hunger.
>
> Two more sadistic jailers (they have a big union) guard the doors. One of them always tells the truth and the other always lies.
>
> What single question can you ask one of the door guardians to figure out which door leads to lunch?

When you ask a guard a question, the answer will contain either a true statement or a false statement. That won't help you if you don't know which it is.

The key to this puzzle is to force an answer that contains both truth and falsehood. For example, you could ask Guard 1, "If I ask the other guard which door leads to the cafeteria, what would he say?"

If you've asked the truth teller, he will correctly report the other guard's lie. If you've asked the liar, he will incorrectly report the other guard's truth. In either case, the correct answer is told truthfully once and lied about once so the result will be incorrect. Now you can simply go through the other door.

To verify that result, let's walk through the possibilities in more detail.

Suppose Guard 1 is the truth–teller. In that case Guard 2 is the liar, so Guard 2 would point to solitary confinement if he were asked. Because Guard 1 is the truth–teller, he correctly points to the same door that Guard 2 would have pointed to, which is solitary confinement.

Now suppose Guard 1 is the liar. Then Guard 2 is the truth–teller, so he would point to the cafeteria if asked. Because Guard 1 is the liar, he points to the door that Guard 2 would *not* have pointed to, which again is solitary confinement.

In either case the guard you ask points toward solitary confinement and you can simply go through the other door.

Variation: What single question can you ask to make a guard point toward the cafeteria?

In the preceding solution, you asked about the cafeteria and the guard pointed to solitary confinement. Simply ask about solitary confinement instead. For example, you could ask, "If I ask the other guard which door leads to solitary confinement, what would he say?"

LIAR OR TRUTH–TELLER

Puzzle: Suppose your sadistic jailer leads you to doors leading to the cafeteria and to solitary confinement as in the "Liars and Truth–Tellers" puzzle. This time, however, there is only one guard and you don't know whether he's a liar or a truth–teller.

What single question can you ask of that guard to figure out which door leads to lunch?

You don't actually need to have two guards present to invoke the concept of the "other kind of guard." For example, you could ask the question, "If I ask the other kind of guard (where the two kinds are liars and truth–tellers) which door leads to the cafeteria, what would he say?"

If the guard is a liar, then the "other kind" of guard would be a truth–teller and would therefore point to the cafeteria door. The liar will then switch the answer and point to solitary confinement.

If the guard is a truth–teller, then the "other kind" of guard would be a liar and would therefore point to solitary confinement. The truth–teller will then report the result correctly and point to solitary confinement.

In either case, you should open the door that's not pointed to by the guard.

PILLOWS OR PAIN

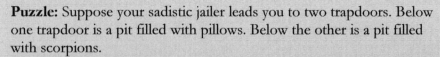

> **Puzzle:** Suppose your sadistic jailer leads you to two trapdoors. Below one trapdoor is a pit filled with pillows. Below the other is a pit filled with scorpions.
>
> Beside the trapdoors are three more sadistic jailers. Two always lie and one always tells the truth. You can ask a single question of one of the three. Then you will be forced to stand on a trapdoor while it opens and you face your fate.
>
> What single question can you ask to pick the safe trapdoor?

This puzzle is a generalization of the "Liars and Truth–Tellers" puzzle and it has a similar solution. You need to ask a question that gives you an answer that contains a known amount of truth and falsehood. If you include all three guards in the question, then the result will include two lies that will cancel each other out leaving the truth.

For example, you could ask Guard 1, "If I ask Guard 2, 'What would Guard 3 say if I ask him where the pillows are,' what would you say?" This is a pretty confusing question to come up with from scratch. It's a bit more understandable if you have just analyzed the "Liars and Truth–Tellers" puzzle.

Let's look at the possibilities.

1. **Guard 1 is the truth–teller:** If you ask Guard 3 where the pillows are, he will lie and point to the scorpions. Guard 2 is also a liar so he will change that answer and claim that Guard 3 would point to the pillows. Guard 1 is the truth–teller, so he will correctly report this result by pointing to the pillows.
2. **Guard 2 is the truth–teller:** If you ask Guard 3 where the pillows are, he will lie and point to the scorpions. Guard 2 is the truth–teller so he will report this correctly and point to the scorpions. Guard 1 is a liar, so he will change that answer and point to the pillows.
3. **Guard 3 is the truth–teller:** If you ask Guard 3 where the pillows are, he will truthfully point to the pillows. Guard 2 is a liar so he will change the answer and point to the scorpions. Guard 1 is also a liar so he will change *that* answer and point to the pillows.

No matter which guard is the truth–teller, Guard 1 always points to the trapdoor above the pillows.

TALE OF THREE APPS

Puzzle: Not long ago my coworker Maki (who is a genius at solving logic puzzles) was at a company team–building exercise and was locked in a dungeon with 3 apps that her company's IT department had written. One app always makes correct statements, one app had a confusing specification so it always makes incorrect statements, and one app was just plain badly written so it alternates between correct and incorrect statements.

Each app has a "Call Wallah" button and a help screen. Maki knew that if she tapped the button on the correct app, the company chai wallah would open the door and give her a tasty chai and a scone. If she tapped the wrong app, the IT director would answer and drone at her for hours about the new company password rules. Obviously it was crucial to pick the right button!

The apps' help screens said the following.

App 1: You may ask us one question and then you must tap a button.

App 2: The first app is lying. You can ask three questions.

App 3: No, you definitely only get one question. Definitely.

With the solution to the "Pillows or Pain" puzzle still fresh in her mind, Maki typed into App 1 the question, "What would App 2 say if I asked it, 'Is App 3's help screen correct?'"

In answer to this confusing query, App 1 tersely replied, "Yes."

Next Maki typed into App 1 the question, "Does all of this really build better teams?"

App 1 didn't reply so she tried Apps 2 and 3, which also gave no response.

When none of the apps replied, Maki immediately knew which app was which and tapped the correct button. (She then had to wait for 10 minutes while the scones finished baking because the chai wallah didn't expect her to solve the puzzle so quickly.)

How did Maki know which app was which?

Because none of the apps answered Maki's second question, it must have been true that she was allowed only one question. That means App 2's help screen was incorrect when it said she could ask three questions so it must either be the incorrect app or the alternating app.

The help screens for App 1 and App 3 both said that Maki could ask only one question so they were both correct. That means neither of them was the incorrect app, so the incorrect app must be App 2.

Figure 11–1 summarizes the 2 possible cases.

	App 1	App 2	App 3
Case 1	Correct	Incorrect	Alternates
Case 2	Alternates	Incorrect	Correct

Figure 11–1: The two possible cases.

We still don't know whether App 1 or App 3 is the alternator, but whichever of them it is made a correct statement on its help screen. Therefore the alternating app will give an incorrect statement when it is next asked a question.

Now recall Maki's question where she asked App 1, "What would App 2 say if I asked it, 'Is App 3's help screen correct?'" App 3's help screen was in fact correct. Because App 2 makes incorrect statements, it would incorrectly say, "No, App 3's help screen was wrong." App 2 would make this same reply to the question whether we're in Case 1 or in Case 2.

Now consider Case 1. App 1 makes correct statements so it would report App 2's answer faithfully and say, "No."

Next consider Case 2. App 1 alternates and is prepared to make an incorrect statement. In this case it reports App 2's reply incorrectly and says, "Yes."

That gives Maki the solution. If App 1 answers, "No," then we know we're in Case 1. If App 1 answers, "Yes," then we know we're in Case 2.

When Maki asked the question, App 1 replied, "Yes," so she knew it was Case 2, she tapped the button on App 3, and enjoyed a well–earned snack.

DAILY LIARS

Puzzle: John and Joan are twins who lie on specific days of the week. John lies on Fridays, Saturdays, and Sundays. Joan lies on Tuesdays, Wednesdays, and Thursdays.

On what day of the week would they both say, "I will lie tomorrow?"

The trick here is to notice that there are two reasons why either of the twins might make this statement. Either the twin is telling the truth today and will lie tomorrow, or the twin is lying today and will tell the truth tomorrow.

Probably the easiest way to solve this puzzle is to make a schedule of when each twin lies. Figure 11–2 shows the schedule. The instances when each twin says he or she will lie tomorrow are highlighted in bold.

Day	Today John Tells	John Says Tomorrow He Will Tell	Today Joan Tells	Joan Says Tomorrow She Will Tell
Monday	Truth	Truth	Truth	**Lies**
Tuesday	Truth	Truth	Lies	Truth
Wednesday	Truth	Truth	Lies	Truth
Thursday	Truth	**Lies**	Lies	**Lies**
Friday	Lies	Truth	Truth	Truth
Saturday	Lies	Truth	Truth	Truth
Sunday	Lies	**Lies**	Truth	Truth

Figure 11–2: John and Joan tell lies on specific days of the week.

You can see in Figure 11–2 that the only day of the week when both John and Joan say they will lie tomorrow is Thursday.

KNIGHT, KNAVE, OR COMMONER

Puzzle: King Julian's daughter, Princess Abby, has reached marrying age (13) and she has three possible suitors: a knight, a knave, and a commoner. She wouldn't mind marrying the knight (who's rich) or the knave (because it will make King Julian furious), but she doesn't want to marry the commoner (because they're so, well, common).

Unfortunately she doesn't know which suitor is which. All she knows is that the knight always tells the truth, the knave always lies, and the commoner can do either as the occasion seems to require.

King Julian allows her to ask each of the suitors one question and then she must choose. What questions can she ask to guarantee that she picks the knight or the knave?

Abby can ask all three suitors the same question, "Are you a commoner?" The knight will say "no," the knave will say "yes," and the commoner will say either "yes" or "no." No matter what the commoner says, his answer will agree with one of the other two.

If Abby picks the person whose answer is different from the other two answers, then she knows she won't pick the commoner.

TRUTH ABOUT TRUTH

Puzzle: Suppose your plane crash lands in the remote Ambiguous Archipelago. The strange thing about the archipelago is that its islands are inhabited by two tribes. The members of one tribe always tell the truth and the members of the other tribe always lie.

As you're walking through the jungle, looking for a payphone, you come to three natives who say the following.

    Native 1: Lorem ipsum dolor sit amet.

    Native 2: He just said that he belongs to the liar's tribe.

    Native 3: No, Native 2 is lying.

Which native should you ask for directions to the payphone?

Because you don't speak the local language, you don't know what Native 1 said. He might have said something about his village, the weather, or the color of your shirt. Whatever he said, however, you know that he didn't say that he was a liar. If he was a truth–teller, he wouldn't say that because it would be false. If he was a liar, he wouldn't say that because it would be the truth.

Then when Native 2 says that Native 1 claimed to be from the liar's tribe, you know that

Native 2 must be lying.

Native 3 correctly then says that Native 2 is lying. Natives who live in the liar's tribe always lie, so Native 3 cannot be a liar and therefore must be a truth–teller.

That means you should ask Native 3 for directions. Native 2 would lie. Native 1 may be a liar or a truth–teller, but he doesn't seem to speak English anyway.

LOGICAL MISMATCH

> **Puzzle:** Suppose your plane lands on an island containing liars and truth–tellers (as so often seems to be the case). As you stagger from your plane's wreckage, two natives walk up and one says, "If I'm a truth–teller, then so is he."
>
> Can you tell whether these two can be trusted to lead you to safety?

This puzzle is tricky because of a difference in the ways that English and logic handle implications of the form "If A then B."

For example, suppose I said, "If I hit you with this bat, then your head will hurt." If I don't hit you with the bat, then when you consider the statement as plain English, all bets are off. I'm not telling you that your head will hurt and I'm not telling you that it won't. Who knows? Maybe you already have a headache from working through so many logic puzzles.

In logic, however, an implication is true *if it is not false*. An implication is false only if the antecedent (the "if" condition) is true and the consequent (the "then" condition) is false. In this example, the statement is false only if I *do* hit you with the bat and your head *does not* hurt. Maybe I missed and hit you in the shoulder. Logically speaking, the statement is true under all conditions except if I hit you and your head doesn't hurt. That means it is true in all three of the following situations.

1. I hit you and your head hurts.
2. I don't hit you and your head hurts.
3. I don't hit you and your head does not hurt.

Now let's go back to the original problem. Suppose the original statement, "If I'm a truth–teller, then so is he," is false. In that case, the first native must be a liar because he made this false statement. The only way the implication can be false is if the antecedent is true and the consequent is false. But the antecedent is false because we know the speaker is a liar, so the implication is true. That leads to a contradiction, so our original assumption that the statement was false is wrong.

Now assume that the statement is true. In that case, the first native is a truth–teller because he made a true statement. Then because the antecedent is true, and because we're assuming that the statement is true, then the consequent must also be true. That means the second native must also be a truth–teller.

Assuming that the statement is false leads to a contradiction and assuming that it's true does not, so the statement must be true and both of the natives must be truth–tellers. That means you can trust them to lead you to safety, although they may ask for a gratuity first.

WAFFLING POLITICIANS

Puzzle: Your town was hit by a tornado, so now it is swarming with politicians pretending to be useful. You go to an emergency aid station and find yourself surrounded by 19 useless politicians and one emergency manager who may actually be useful. Unfortunately they're all wearing overalls and hard hats so you can't tell who is who.

The emergency manager always tells the truth. The politicians always alternate between telling the truth and lying. You can ask two questions of anyone in the room. You can ask the same person both questions, or you can ask two different people one question each.

What two questions should you ask to identify the emergency manager?

First ask someone, "Are you a politician?" There are two cases depending on the answer you get.

If that person says "yes," then you know it's not the emergency manager because he tells the truth and would say "no." This must be a politician and he just answered truthfully, so his next answer will be a lie. For the second question ask, "Who is *not* the emergency manager?" The politician must lie so he'll point out the emergency manager to you.

If the person you asked the first question says "no," then you know this person is either the emergency manager or a politician who just lied. In either case, that person will tell the truth when you ask the next question. For the second question ask, "Who is the emergency manager?" Now the person will truthfully point out the emergency manager.

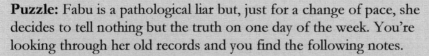

FABU THE LIAR

Puzzle: Fabu is a pathological liar but, just for a change of pace, she decides to tell nothing but the truth on one day of the week. You're looking through her old records and you find the following notes.

Day 1: I lie on Mondays and Tuesdays.

Day 2: Today is Thursday, Saturday, or Sunday.

Day 3: I lie on Wednesdays and Fridays.

On which day of the week does Fabu tell the truth?

Suppose Statement 1 is true and the other statements are false. Then Day 1 must *not* be a Monday or Tuesday. Now consider the other days of the week that Day 1 might be and show that each leads to a contradiction.

Wednesday: If Day 1 is Wednesday, then Day 2 is Thursday. Then Statement 2 would be true and we're assuming that it's false, so we have a contradiction.

Thursday: If Day 1 is Thursday, then Statement 3 would be true and we're assuming that it's false, so we have a contradiction.

Friday: If Day 1 is Friday, then Day 2 is Saturday. That would make Statement 2 true and we're assuming that it's false, so we have a contradiction.

Saturday: If Day 1 is Saturday, then Day 2 is Sunday. But that would make Statement 2 true and we're assuming it's false, so we have a contradiction.

Sunday: If Day 1 is Sunday, then Statement 3 true and we're assuming that it's false, so we have a contradiction.

All of the cases lead to a contradiction, so our original supposition that Statement 1 was true must be incorrect. In that case, Statement 1 must be false.

Statement 1 says Fabu lies on Mondays and Tuesdays. Because we now know that this statement is false, Fabu must tell the truth on either Mondays or Tuesdays.

We also now know that Statement 3 must be true. If it were false, then Fabu would have to tell the truth on ether Wednesdays or Fridays, but we now know that she tells the truth on either Mondays or Tuesdays.

That contradiction means Statement 3 must be true. Because Fabu tells the truth on either Mondays or Tuesdays, Day 3 must be one of those days. Consider the two cases.

Monday: If Day 3 is a Monday, then Day 2 is a Sunday. That would make Statement 2 true and we're assuming that it's false, so we have a contradiction.

Tuesday: If Day 3 is a Tuesday, then Day 2 is a Monday and Day 1 is a Sunday. If you carefully review the 3 statements, you'll find that they are consistent with those days.

Therefore Fabu tells the truth on Tuesdays and Day 1 is a Sunday.

HARDEST LOGIC PUZZLE EVER!

This puzzle is a variation of one invented by philosopher/logician Raymond Smullyan. Later, it was made more complex by others including philosopher/logician George Boolos, not to be confused with philosopher/logician George Boole of Boolean algebra fame. (This background may tell you something about the hobbies of philosopher/logicians.) For general information about these people and others related to the puzzle, see WikiPedia. To see George Boolos's solution to this puzzle, see `www.thebigquestions.com/boolos.pdf`.

> **Puzzle:** Suppose you're at a programming convention, hoping to hire some new top–notch software development ninjas, and you fall into a rough crowd. During a heated debate about the proper placement of burndown charts on Scrumboards, you're captured and hauled in front of the capos of three gangs of software engineers. The three capos understand English, but they refuse to speak it. (Because that wouldn't be 1337 enough.)
>
> The gangs are called Truthspeakers, Liars, and Chances. As you can probably guess, a Truthspeaker always tells the truth, a Liar always lies, and a Chance always answers randomly. Unfortunately you don't know which capo controls which gang.
>
> To make matters worse, the engineers have their own private argot. You know that their words for "yes" and "no" are "bardeen" and "shockley," but you don't know which is which. (The only other word you know is "brattain," which means "wombat," but that's not important for this puzzle.)
>
> A requirements analyst who still speaks some English tells you that you may ask three yes/no questions to try to figure out which capo controls which gang.
>
> What questions do you ask?

You can debate about whether this is really the world's hardest logic puzzle, but it is definitely very hard. It might make an interesting topic for a group discussion, but it's certainly too hard to ask in an interview. (Unless, perhaps, you're hiring a philosopher/logician.)

In any case, the puzzle is complicated enough that each of the three questions that you're going to ask deserves its own section.

Question 1

The goal of question 1 is to identify one of the capos that you know isn't a Chance. To do that, you need to get true information out of a capo who is a Truthspeaker or a Liar.

To get true information out of either a Truthspeaker or a Liar, you can ask about *asking* instead of actually asking. (You may want to reread that sentence a few times.) For example, consider the small question, "Is 7 prime?" If you ask this question, a Truthspeaker and a Liar will give you different answers.

Now consider the meta–question, "If I ask you whether 7 is prime, will you say, 'Yes?'"

If you ask a Truthspeaker the meta–question, he will want to say "yes" to the sub–question because 7 is prime. Because he tells the truth, he will then truthfully say "yes" to the meta–question.

If you ask a Liar the meta–question, he will want to say "no" to the sub–question because he can't admit that 7 is prime. Because he always lies, he will then lie about *that* answer and say "yes" to the meta–question.

So whether you ask a Truthspeaker or a Liar the meta–question, you get the correct answer, "Yes."

Now you might like to use this technique to ask one of the capos whether some other capo is a Truthspeaker. For example, you could ask Capo 1 if Capo 2 is a Truthspeaker. Unfortunately there are two problems with that approach. First, you don't know which word means "yes" and which word means "no." Second, if Capo 1 leads the Chance gang, then the answer you get is meaningless.

Instead of trying to find a Truthspeaker, you can try to identify a capo who does not lead Chance. To do that, consider the sub–question, "Is Capo 2 a Chance?" and then ask Capo 1 the meta–question, "If I ask you whether Capo 2 is a Chance, will you say, 'Yes?'"

The first three columns in Figure 11–3 show the possible combinations of capo identities. Column 4 shows the English answer Capo 1 will give to the sub–question. Column 5 shows the answer Capo 1 will give to the meta–question.

Capo 1	Capo 2	Capo 3	Sub–Answer	Meta–Answer
Truthspeaker	Liar	Chance	No	No
Truthspeaker	Chance	Liar	Yes	Yes
Liar	Truthspeaker	Chance	Yes	No
Liar	Chance	Truthspeaker	No	Yes
Chance	Truthspeaker	Liar	?	?
Chance	Liar	Truthspeaker	?	?

Figure 11–3: Possible combinations when asking Capo 1 about Capo 2.

In Figure 11–3 you can see that Capo 1 gives you the correct answers to the meta–question as long as he's a Truthspeaker or a Liar. Unfortunately you still don't know the words for "yes" and "no," and you don't learn anything if Capo 1 is a Chance.

Now you change the meta–question to the following official Question 1.

> **Question 1:** Ask Capo 1, "If I ask you whether Capo 2 is a Chance, will you say, 'bardeen?'"

Suppose "bardeen" means "yes." If Capo 1 isn't a Chance and he wants to say "yes (Capo 2 is a Chance)," then he says "bardeen." If Capo 1 isn't a Chance and he wants to say "no (Capo 2 isn't a Chance)," then he says "shockley." So in either of these cases, "bardeen" means Capo 2 is a Chance and "shockley" means Capo 2 is not a Chance.

Now suppose "bardeen" means "no." If Capo 1 isn't a Chance and he wants to say "yes (Capo 2 is a Chance)," then he says "shockley." If Capo 1 isn't a Chance and he wants to say "no (Capo 2 isn't a Chance)," then he says "bardeen." So in either of these cases, "bardeen" still means Capo 2 is a Chance and "shockley" still means Capo 2 is not a Chance.

Whether "bardeen" means "yes" or "no," the answer "bardeen" means Capo 2 is a Chance and the answer "shockley" means Capo 2 is not a Chance.

After you ask Question 1, you know whether Capo 2 is a Chance so you know which of Capo 2 and Capo 3 is *not* a Chance.

The one remaining problem (for now) is that Capo 1 might be a Chance. In that case the answer you get indicates that either Capo 2 or Capo 3 is *not* a Chance. But you really don't care which one you assign to that role as long as he's not a Chance. If Capo 1 is the Chance, then you can use either of the others as the designated non–Chance.

Question 2

Now things become a bit easier. At this point, you have identified a non–Chance Capo. Now ask the following question.

> **Question 2:** Ask the non–Chance capo, "If I ask you whether you are a Truthspeaker, will you say, 'bardeen?'"

Because the non–Chance Capo isn't a Chance, if he answers "bardeen," then he is a Truthspeaker. If he answers "shockley," then he's a Liar.

To see why, you can run through all of the possibilities as we did in the previous section. Whether he's a Truthspeaker or Liar, he will try to say "yes" to the sub–question. The Truthspeaker will succeed and the Liar will switch his answer for the meta–question to "no." So either way he will try to report the truth.

If "bardeen" means "yes," then an answer of "bardeen" means Truthspeaker and an answer of "shockley" means a Liar.

If "bardeen" means "no," then the Truthspeaker says "no," which is "bardeen." The Liar says "yes," which is "shockley." Again "bardeen" still means Truthspeaker and "shockley" still means Liar.

Question 3

At this point you know whether the non–Chance capo is a Truthspeaker or a Liar. Ask the following question.

> **Question 3:** Ask the non–Chance capo, "If I ask you whether Capo 1 is Chance, will you say, 'bardeen?'"

As before, an answer of "bardeen" means "yes" and an answer of "shockley" means "no" regardless of whether the non–Chance capo is a Truthspeaker or a Liar.

Now you know which gang is led by the non–Chance capo (who is not Capo 1). You also know whether Capo 1 is Chance. By using the process of elimination you can figure out the final capo's gang.

Now that you know who leads the Truthspeakers, you can negotiate to hire your software development ninjas.

I warned you that this was a tough puzzle!

SUMMARY

These kinds of logic puzzles can be somewhat convoluted and may require even more convoluted reasoning to solve. If you can, try making a table of the possible combinations of liars and truth–tellers.

Also think about meta–questions (questions about questions) that can include both lies and truth in a way that gives you a consistent answer.

PROGRAMMING EXERCISES

These exercises are particularly tricky, at least partly because so few programmers need to perform these kinds of Boolean calculations regularly.

1. Make a program that solves the "Daily Liars" puzzle. The user should be able to click on the days that John and Joan lie. It should then display a table similar to the one in Figure 11–2. It should highlight the entries where they each say, "I will lie tomorrow," and it should indicate the days (if any) when they both say that.

2. Write a program that simulates the "Knight, Knave, or Commoner" puzzle. Have the program display three person icons and make it randomly pick which represents the knight, knave, and commoner. They should all look the same so the user can't tell which is which. Each should also have two buttons. The first should say, "Are you a commoner?" When the user clicks it, the program should answer as the person who owns the button would. The second button should say, "Pick Me." When the user clicks it to set the princess's choice of suitor, the program should reveal who is who. (Perhaps with amusing images of a knight, knave, and commoner. Use your imagination.)

3. Make a program to simulate the "Waffling Politicians" puzzle. Make 20 buttons that say "Are you a politician?" Make the program randomly decide which represent the 19 politicians and whether they are ready to tell the truth. When the user clicks a button, it should answer appropriately and change its caption to either, "Who is not the emergency manager" or "Who is the emergency manager" as appropriate. When the user clicks it, highlight the correct button.

4. Make a program to solve the "Fabu the Liar" puzzle. Use nested loops similar to the following.

```
For Each day1_day in Monday to Sunday
    For Each truth_day in Monday to Sunday
        . . .
    Next truth_day
Next day1_day
```

Inside the loops, make Boolean variables such as `lies_on_mondays` to indicate whether Fabu lies on that day for the current value of `truth_day`. Next use those values to make variables such as `day1_statement` to represent the three statements in Fabu's records. Then make variables such as `day1_valid` to indicate whether the statement for Day 1 is valid. Finally, if all three of the statements are valid, display the current value of `day1_day` and `truth_day`.

5. Modify the program you wrote for Exercise 4 to handle the following statements.

> **Day 1:** I lie on Mondays and Thursdays.
>
> **Day 2:** I tell the truth on Fridays or Sundays.
>
> **Day 3:** Today is not Monday or Saturday.

6. Write a program to simulate the "Hardest Logic Puzzle Ever!" It should randomly assign "bardeen" and "shockley" to mean "Yes" and "No," and it should randomly assign the three capos to the Truthspeakers, Liars, and Chances. Add buttons to represent the three questions.

   a. **Question 1:** Create a button to ask Capo 1 the question, "If I ask you whether Capo 2 is a Chance, will you say, 'bardeen?'" When the user clicks it, the program should display the answer (bardeen or shockley) and indicate which of Capo 2 or Capo 3 is *not* a Chance.

   b. **Question 2:** Create a button that asks the non–Chance capo, "If I ask you whether you are a Truthspeaker, will you say, 'bardeen?'" The program should indicate whether that capo is a Truthspeaker or a Liar.

   c. **Question 3:** Create a button that asks the non–Chance capo, "If I ask you whether Capo 1 is Chance, will you say, 'bardeen?'" Now the program should indicate which capos lead which gangs. It should also verify that it is correct.

12 Roundabout Reasoning

These are logic puzzles with a specific kind of structure that involves a fairly large number of people. To solve these puzzles, you start with a small number of people, ideally one or two, and see what they can deduce about each other. You then add another person and see how that changes things. You continue adding more people until you eventually know everything about everyone.

FIVE PIRATES

Puzzle: Five pirates return from a raid with 32 gold coins and they need to decide how to divide the booty. According to the Revered Pirate Code, the captain must propose a method for dividing the treasure and then the pirates vote on it. If at least half of the pirates agree with the proposal, it is adopted.

If the captain can't get at least half of the pirates (including himself) to agree to his proposal, the pirates mutiny and force the captain to walk the plank. The most senior remaining pirate then becomes captain and the whole thing starts over. Obviously if a pirate can get more treasure after a mutiny than he can without one, he will try to force a mutiny.

What proposal can the captain make that guarantees that he survives and receives as many of the 32 gold coins as possible?

For convenience, number the pirates 1 through 5 where 1 is the most senior pirate (the captain) and 5 is the least senior pirate (the cabin boy).

To divide the booty, the captain says he will take 30 coins and give 1 coin to each of the third– and fifth–most senior pirates. The other two get the captain's thanks and hearty handshakes. Here's how the captain explains why this division of spoils works.

Suppose there were only two pirates. Then the captain can get half of the votes by voting for his own plan, so he simply takes all 32 coins and there's no room for argument.

Next suppose there are three pirates. The captain needs to enlist one other pirate to help him win the vote. He takes 31 coins and gives one coin to Pirate 3. If Pirate 3 votes against the plan, the captain will be replaced by Pirate 2. Then there would be only two pirates, so the new captain would take all of the coins as described in the preceding paragraph and the new Pirate 2 (who was Pirate 3 before the mutiny) gets nothing. In that case, Pirate 3 is better off voting for the original captain's plan so he at least gets one coin.

Now suppose there are four pirates. The captain takes 31 coins and gives one to Pirate 3. If Pirate 3 votes against the plan, the captain is overthrown and Pirate 3 becomes the new Pirate 2. As the previous paragraph showed, Pirate 2 gets nothing, so Pirate 3 is better off voting for the original captain's plan so he remains Pirate 3 and at least gets one coin.

At this point, you probably have the hang of it and can carry the argument through the final step. If there are five pirates, the captain takes 30 coins and gives one coin to each of Pirate 3 and Pirate 5. If either of them votes against the plan, then the captain is replaced and Pirates 3 and 5 become Pirates 2 and 4. As the preceding paragraph shows, if there are only four pirates, then Pirates 2 and 4 get nothing. Therefore Pirates 3 and 5 are better off voting for the original distribution so they at least get one coin each.

After the captain finishes this confusing but convincing explanation, the pirates all agree that this is the only possible solution and they all celebrate. While they're all passed out drunk, the cabin boy steals everything and runs away, but that happens after the puzzle is finished.

SIX PIRATES

Puzzle: The five pirates from the "Five Pirates" puzzle are joined by a new recruit who's good with knives. (He can juggle them in a scary way.) Together the six raid a settlement of monks. Unfortunately the monks have taken vows of poverty so the pirates don't find any money. They do, however, find a parrot who can squawk, "Pieces of eight!"

Obviously they can't divide the parrot without killing it. After a few minutes of discussion, they decide that the parrot wouldn't make much of a meal, so they decide that one of them should keep it as booty.

When they return to the ship, the pirates are in a foul mood (pun intended) so their priorities have changed. Now if a pirate can get the same amount of loot whether the booty division plan is approved or not, he will vote against the plan so that he can experience the schadenfreude of watching the current captain die.

How can the captain propose to divide the booty to save his own hide?

For convenience, number the pirates 1 through 6 where 1 is the most senior (the captain) and 6 is the least senior (the new knife juggler). To save himself, the captain can offer the parrot to any one of pirates 2, 4, or 6. He then explains his decision as follows.

Suppose there are two pirates. The captain can vote for his own plan so he simply keeps the parrot.

Next, suppose there are three pirates. If the captain keeps the parrot, the other pirates will mutiny. If he gives the parrot to Pirate 2, Pirate 2 will force a mutiny so he can become the captain of a two–pirate crew and keep the parrot anyway. That means the captain must give the parrot to Pirate 3. If a mutiny occurs, Pirate 3 becomes Pirate 2 in a two–pirate crew so he'll get nothing. Therefore Pirate 3 votes in favor of the captain's plan and Pirate 3 gets the parrot.

Now suppose there are four pirates. In this case the captain gives the parrot to Pirate 3. If Pirate 3 votes against the plan, the crew mutinies and Pirate 3 becomes the new Pirate 2 in a three–pirate crew. The preceding paragraph shows that he would get nothing, so he supports the captain's plan and accepts the parrot.

Suppose there are five pirates. No matter to whom the captain offers the parrot, the other three crewmembers will get nothing so they mutiny. No matter what the captain does, he's going to die, so he musters his dignity, grabs the parrot, and runs off the plank. Now the remaining four pirates are back to the preceding four–pirate case, although the parrot's gone.

Because there is no viable solution for a five–pirate crew, you might think there can't be a solution for larger crews. Surprisingly there is a solution for a six–pirate crew.

Suppose there are six pirates. Pirate 2 has a strong vested interest in seeing the captain's plan succeed. If the plan fails, then Pirate 2 becomes the new captain of a five–person crew and, we know from the previous paragraph, that the captain of a five–person crew always dies. Therefore Pirate 2 will vote for the captain's plan no matter what it is.

If the captain gives the parrot to Pirate 5, then after two mutinies the old Pirate 5 becomes Pirate 3 in a four–pirate crew and in that case he gets the parrot. This means the original captain cannot offer the parrot to Pirate 5 or there will be a bloodbath.

The captain can offer the parrot to any of Pirates 3, 4, or 6 because none of them would get anything in a reorganized four–pirate crew operating under new management.

So the captain, Pirate 2, and whichever of Pirates 3, 4, or 6 is offered the parrot will vote in favor of the plan and the captain has a majority.

MANY PIRATES

Puzzle: What happens with the "Six Pirates" puzzle for larger crews?

With seven pirates, Pirate 2 know that he will survive if there's a mutiny and the crew is reduced to six, so he will vote against the captain's plan. The captain can bribe one pirate with the parrot, but his vote plus that one won't be enough to save him, so a mutiny is inevitable.

With eight pirates, if the plan isn't accepted, then Pirate 2 will become the captain of a crew of seven if there's a mutiny. To avoid that, Pirate 2 would support the plan, but his vote plus the captain's plus one more bought at the price of the parrot won't be enough so, again, mutiny is inevitable.

Similarly with nine pirates, mutiny is inevitable. The captain, Pirate 2, Pirate 3, and one other pirate who is bribed with the parrot all vote for the plan, but it's still not enough votes to prevent a mutiny.

With a crew of 10, things change again. If the plan fails, successive mutinies will whittle the crew down until it reaches the next stable configuration which consists of six pirates. In that case, Pirates 1 through 4 would all be killed. Their votes plus one purchased with the parrot give a total of five votes in favor of the plan, so they can prevent a mutiny.

Crews with 11 through 17 members suffer repeated mutinies until the crew becomes stable again when it contains 10 pirates.

Things change again with a crew of 18. If the plan fails, Pirates 1 through 8 are all at risk. Those eight plus one bribed with the parrot gives the captain nine votes, which is enough to prevent a mutiny.

In general, after the trivial crew containing two members, a crew is stable if it includes 2^N+2 pirates for some integer $N \geq 0$. Figure 12–1 shows the first few values of N and the corresponding stable crew sizes.

N	0	1	2	3	4	5	6
2^n+2	3	4	6	10	18	34	66

Figure 12–1: Stable crew sizes.

After dealing with the "Five Pirates" and "Six Pirates" puzzles, the surviving pirates should contact the Pirate's Union and see if they can change the booty division rules.

100 HATS

Puzzle: At a certain prison the convicts work 40 hours per week in the blazing sun. In an attempt to motivate the prisoners to work longer hours, the sadistic guards propose a game. If the prisoners do well, they'll work fewer hours. If they do badly, they'll work more.

The guards place 100 prisoners in a line all facing the same direction. They then put a red hat or a blue hat on each prisoner. Each prisoner can see the hats of those in front of him, but he can't see his own hat or the hats of the people behind him.

Now the game begins. Starting at the back of the line, each prisoner must guess whether he's wearing a red hat or a blue hat. Whenever a prisoner guesses correctly, the prisoners get to deduct 1 hour from their new 100–hour work week breaking rocks.

For the first few weeks, the prisoners guess randomly and they work around 50 hours per week (to the delight of the guards). What strategy can the prisoners use to minimize the number of hours they must work?

When the prisoners guess randomly, they're right about half of the time so they end up working around 50 hours per week.

Another strategy would be for every even–numbered prisoner to name the color of the hat in front of him. Then the odd–numbered prisoners would repeat the last color they heard. This way the prisoners are guaranteed to be right at least half of the time. The even–numbered prisoners may also be right sometimes.

An even better approach uses parity. (Yes, it's actually software–related!) The first prisoner at the very back of the line counts the number of red and blue hats that he sees in front of him. Because there are 99 prisoners in front of him, one of those counts is even and the other is odd. He then announces the color that has an odd count. Suppose that color is red. Now all of the other prisoners know that there are an odd number of red hats, not counting the first prisoner's hat.

Prisoner 2 counts the red hats that he sees. If he sees an even number, he knows that his hat must be red. If he sees an odd number, he knows that his hat must be blue.

Each later prisoner uses the answers of the previous prisoners to keep track of whether there is an odd or even number of red hats remaining, and then he reports his color accordingly. If the number of red hats remaining has the same odd/even parity as the number of red hats that a prisoner sees, then he knows he has a blue hat. If the number of red hats remaining has different odd/even parity as the number of red hats that a prisoner sees, then he knows he has a red hat.

Using this strategy, the first prisoner has a 0.5 probability of correctly guessing his hat color and all of the other prisoners are always correct. On average the prisoners work only 1/2 hour per week in the scorching sun. (The guards then make them work the other 99.5 hours in dank dungeons instead of the scorching sun. They are sadistic, after all.)

99 HATS

Puzzle: After a few weeks with the prisoners using the strategy described in the "100 Hats" puzzle, the prison is falling behind on its outdoor work. The warden is mad at the guards because the pool needs cleaning, the tennis courts need repainting, and the polo field needs mowing.

Eventually one of the prisoners tells the guards how the prisoners are beating the system in exchange for a contraband pack of Pokémon cards. To disrupt the prisoners' strategy, the guards throw the stoolie into solitary confinement. (He doesn't really mind because he has a lot of Pokémon cards to go through.)

Now that there are only 99 prisoners in the lineup, the number of red and blue hats that the first prisoner sees are always either both even or both odd. That means the first prisoner can't use his guess to tell the other prisoners which color has an odd number of hats and therefore the previous strategy won't work.

For a few weeks the prisoners return to their random guessing strategy and start to catch up on their outdoor chores. Then, just as they're about to finish building the new pergola, the prisoners start guessing correctly again and work slows to a crawl.

What is the prisoners' new strategy?

The first prisoner can no longer single out the color with the odd number of hats, but the prisoners can still use the odd/even parity idea.

The key is to use the first prisoner's color choice to give the other prisoners some piece of information other than the color with the odd number of hats. For example, the prisoners can focus on red hats. The first prisoner can count the red hats and say "red" if the count is even and "blue" if the count is odd.

Now each later prisoner can keep track of whether there should be an even or odd number of red hats remaining. For example, if a prisoner knows that an odd number of red hats should remain (including his own hat), and he sees an even number of red hats in front of him in line, then he knows that his hat is red.

The new strategy allows the prisoners to again work for only zero or one hour per week. The pergola remains unfinished until the warden fires the guards and hires new ones who use old fashioned motivational techniques such as whips and threats of solitary confinement.

VACATIONING GENIE

Puzzle: The villagers are sick and tired of Dr. Fronkensteen's monsters, so they grab their pitchforks and torches and storm the castle. Unfortunately a stressed–out genie has rented the castle for the month via Airbnb. The genie is furious at having his nap disturbed and curses all of the villagers with muteness.

Because the genie really isn't a bad guy, he gives the villagers a way to lift the curse. He's placed imps on at least one of the villagers' heads. Each imp is undetectable to the person wearing it, but they are clearly visible to everyone else. If someone wearing an imp jumps in the castle's moat at midnight, the imp leaves.

Anyone who's not wearing an imp and who jumps into the moat gains an imp as punishment for acting illogical. Finally, to ensure that there's no cheating, anyone who tries to hint to someone else that they're wearing an imp will be cursed with blindness.

> When the villagers remove the last imp, the curse is lifted and the villagers can speak again. How can the villagers remove their imps?

Consider what happens if there's only one imp. In that case the imp–wearer sees no imps on the other villagers' heads. The genie said that there is at least one imp, so the imp–wearer can deduce that he must be wearing an imp. At midnight he jumps into the moat.

Meanwhile the non–wearers see the single imp. Any particular non–wearer can't tell if there is only the one imp that he sees or whether he also has an imp on his head. When the non–wearers see the wearer jump in the moat, they know that they don't also have imps and the curse has been lifted. (They also know the cursed has been lifted because they can talk again.)

Now suppose there are two imps. The imp–wearers can see only one imp on other villagers' heads, so they can't tell if there are one or two imps. If there was only one imp, then the person wearing it would jump into the moat at midnight. Because that doesn't happen at the first midnight, the imp–wearers now know that there must be two imps. At the second midnight, they both jump into the moat. As before the non–imp–wearers then know that the curse has been lifted.

Suppose there are three imps. The imp–wearers can see only two imps, so they know there are two or three imps. When no one jumps into the moat at the first or second midnight, they know that there are three imps. At the third midnight, all three of them jump into the moat and the curse is lifted.

In general, if there are N imps, then the imp–wearers know there are N–1 or N imps, and the non–wearers know there are N or N+1 imps. After N–1 midnights pass with no one jumping into the moat, the imp–wearers know that there are N imps and they all jump into the moat at the Nth midnight. The non–wearers then know that there were only N imps and the curse has been lifted.

In fact the genie cursed enough people so the villagers remove their imps on the day the genie finishes his vacation and goes home to his bottle. He just wanted some peace and quiet.

MISSING IMP

> **Puzzle:** In the "Vacationing Genie" puzzle, the genie says that he has placed at least one imp on some villager's head. What if he doesn't make that condition?

If there is at least one imp, then everything happens as before and the villagers eventually remove the curse.

If there are no imps, then each of the villagers sees no imps and realizes that there must be either zero or one imps. In that case, every villager should jump into the moat at midnight. Because none of the villagers was actually wearing an imp, they all now acquire imps as punishment for acting illogical.

Now each villager can see that all of the other villagers are wearing imps, so they know that jumping into the moat didn't work. From that they can conclude that they actually started with zero imps. That means they are all now wearing imps, so they should all jump into the moat again at the second midnight to remove the curse.

Adding and then removing the imps is technically necessary anyway because the curse is removed only when the last imp is removed. If there are never any imps, then they can't be removed.

CHEATERS

Puzzle: A particular village has a ruthless way of dealing with cheaters. If a wife discovers that her husband has been cheating on her, she kills him in his sleep.

The villagers are shameless gossips so, if any man is cheating, every man and woman in the village knows about it except for that man's wife. (Because no one has the heart to break the news to her. They'll kill each other without a qualm but they won't tattle if it means hurting the wife's feelings.)

One day a life insurance salesman comes to town, sells life insurance policies to everyone, and then spends a few hours gossiping. He quickly learns that that *every* husband is cheating on his wife, and he asks, "So you all know that someone is cheating, right?"

What happens to the village?

This puzzle is somewhat similar to the "Vacation Genie" puzzle and it has a similar outcome.

If there's a single cheating husband, then every woman knows it except the one married to him. That woman doesn't know about anyone cheating, so the news that at least one husband is cheating tells her that it's her husband! The night after the insurance salesman leaves, she kills her husband in his sleep.

Now suppose there are two cheating husbands. Each of their wives knows about the other cheating husband but not about her own, so she knows there are either one or two cheaters. When neither of those wives kills her husband on the first night, they both know that here are two cheaters so they kill their husbands on the second night.

Meanwhile the wives of the non–cheaters know about both of the cheaters so they know there are either two or three cheaters. When the cheaters' wives kill them during the second night, the other wives know that there were only two cheaters and justice has been served.

More generally, suppose there are N cheaters. Then initially the N cheated–upon wives don't know if there are N or N–1 cheaters. When no one dies after N–1 nights, they know that there are N cheaters so they kill their husbands on the Nth night. Meanwhile the non–cheated–upon wives know there are either N or N+1 cheaters. When the N cheaters are killed during night N, they know that there were only N cheaters.

So the final answer is, if the village contains N cheaters, they are all killed on night N. In this story, every husband is cheating so they're all killed. (Perhaps this is how the Amazonian tribe got started.) (After the village is wiped out, the insurance salesman is fired for selling so many policies that paid off so quickly.)

> **Follow–up:** In practice the cheating husbands see where this is all headed so they flee from the village before night N. What if the husbands don't gossip so they don't know who's cheating?

A cheater may not know who else is cheating, but he knows that *he* is. In the worst case, he is the only one and his wife will kill him during the first night! All of the cheaters must flee from the village before the first night falls or they risk death.

BLOODBATH DELAYED

> **Puzzle:** In the "Cheaters" puzzle, the pesky insurance salesman started the village bloodbath by pointing out that there was at least one cheater. But because every husband was cheating, every villager already knew that at least one husband was cheating.
>
> Why didn't the bloodbath occur sooner?

This is a tricky question. Everyone knew that someone was cheating so the fatal cascade of logic could start at any moment. Until it starts, however, the villagers can't tell the cascade's stage at any given moment. Each villager knows that there are either N or N–1 cheaters, but they don't know whether the N nights with no deaths have passed yet because they don't know when to start counting. Basically they need a clock.

The insurance salesman essentially said, "Start counting nights now," and the result was inevitable.

BLOODBATH ACCELERATED

Puzzle: In the "Cheaters" puzzle, the insurance salesman started the logical cascade by pointing out that there was at least one cheater.

Suppose the village contained at least 10 couples. What would happen if he has instead asked, "So you all know that at least 10 husbands are cheating, right?"

In that case, the villagers could skip the first 10 steps.

If there are exactly 10 cheaters, then the wives of the cheaters would know about 9 cheaters. Because they now know there are 10 cheaters, each knows that her husband is one of them so each kills her husband during the first night.

The rest of the solution to the original "Cheaters" puzzle still works so, if there are N cheaters, they are all killed on night N–10.

AUTOGRAPH HUNTER

Puzzle: Suppose you're attending Comic Con and you've been invited to a reception to promote a new movie. When you arrive, you're given a nametag and a list of everyone who is present.

You know that the movie's Big Star is somewhere on the list, but you don't recognize any of the names. Everyone else in the room is a huge fan of the Star, and some of the fans know each other, but the Star doesn't know any of the fans.

You don't want to admit that you've never heard of the Star in this room full of rabid fans (they might tear you to pieces), but you're determined to get an autograph anyway, so you devise the following strategy.

You're going to wander around nibbling on free hors d'oeuvres and asking people the question, "Do you know [name]?" where you pick [name] from the list of attendees. You'll insert names from the list until you figure out who the Star is.

What is the minimum number of questions that you need to ask to identify the Star?

Suppose you ask Alice Anderson. "Do you know Zippy Zeltsmith?" If Alice answers "no," then you know that Zippy isn't the Star because everyone in the room except you knows the Star. If Alice answers "yes," then you know that Alice isn't the Star because the Star doesn't know any of the fans.

In either case, you learn that someone, either Zippy or Alice, isn't the Star. Cross that name off of the attendee list and continue asking the question until there's only one name left. That person is the Star. If there are N fans at the reception, you'll need to ask the question N times.

Follow–up: What if you ask someone, "Do you know Bob Baker?" and that person says, "That's me!"

Because everyone is wearing nametags, you can be careful not to ask people if they know themselves.

Follow–up: Does it matter who you ask the questions?

Suppose you have already know that Quynh isn't the Star so you have crossed her name off of the list, and you ask her, "Do you know Tiffany?" If Quynh says "yes," then you know that Quynh is not the Star, but you already knew that so you wasted a question.

To avoid wasting questions, you should only ask people whose names are not crossed off.

Follow–up: How many questions could you ask a single person?

You can ask someone whether they know other people as long as their name isn't crossed off. If you get lucky and start by asking the Star, then you could ask the Star about every other person present. (The Star may find that odd, but I suspect most stars are used to fans asking weird questions.)

FRAT PARTY

Puzzle: Suppose you attend a frat party and three of your friends (Anya, Bob, and Patty) fall asleep after drinking too much. While they sleep, the house prankster uses a marker to draw smiley faces on their foreheads.

When the three wake up, they look at each other and start laughing. After a few seconds Patty (who's a philosophy major) stops laughing. Why?

Suppose Patty didn't have a smiley face on her forehead. Then Anya would see Bob with a smiley face and Patty without. Because Bob is laughing, Anya knows that she (Anya) must have a smiley face on her forehead, too. In that case, Anya would stop laughing.

Similarly Bob should shortly stop laughing.

Because neither Anya nor Bob stopped laughing, Patty knows that she must also be wearing a smiley face.

THREE COLORED HATS

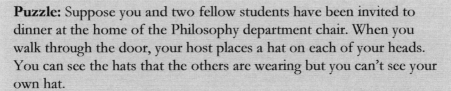

Puzzle: Suppose you and two fellow students have been invited to dinner at the home of the Philosophy department chair. When you walk through the door, your host places a hat on each of your heads. You can see the hats that the others are wearing but you can't see your own hat.

Your host then says, "You're each wearing a red hat or a blue hat, and I promise there's at least one of each color. Now we'll play a little game. During each round, you must say either 'Pass' or 'I know my hat color.' When all three of you think you know your hat colors, you'll reveal your guesses. If you're right, dinner will begin. If you're wrong, YOU GET NO DESSERT!" He pauses for an evil chuckle, strikes a dramatic pose, and says, "Let the game begin!"

How do you decide what colors the hats are?

If there are three hats and there they include hats of both colors, then two hats must have the same color. Suppose there are two red hats and one blue hat.

The dinner guest who is wearing the blue hat sees two red hats. Because the host said there was at least one hat of each color, this person knows that he must be wearing a blue hat. During Round 1, he says, "I know my hat color."

The red hat wearers each see a red hat and a blue hat so they can't tell what color they are wearing. During Round 1, they both say, "Pass."

After Round 1 the red hat wearers know that the person wearing the blue hat figured out his color. He could only do that if he saw two hats with the same color. Because one of the hats that the blue hat wearer can see is red, the other hat must also be red. That lets the red hat wearers deduce that they are wearing red hats.

During Round 2 they all say, "I know my hat color." They are all correct so dinner is served. (Then you get to learn whether your host remembered that Laura is a vegetarian and Oliver is lactose intolerant.)

> **Follow–up:** What happens if the host forgets to tell you that there's at least one hat of each color?

In that case anyone who sees two hats of the same color cannot deduce that he has a hat of the other color. For example, the three of you can't tell the difference between red/red/red and red/red/blue. In fact, you also can't tell the difference between blue/blue/blue and blue/blue/red. Those are the only four possible combinations of hat colors, so you're basically doomed.

In that case, you may as well guess randomly to get a $1/2^3 = 1/8$ probability of getting dessert.

FOUR COLORED HATS

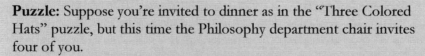

> **Puzzle:** Suppose you're invited to dinner as in the "Three Colored Hats" puzzle, but this time the Philosophy department chair invites four of you.
>
> How do you decide what colors the hats are?

You know that the hats can't all have the same color because the chair said that both colors were present. That means there are two cases: there's one hat of one color and three hats of the other color, or there are two hats of each color.

Case 1

First consider Case 1 where there's one hat of one color and three hats of the other color. Suppose there's one red hat and three blue hats. Then the person with the red hat sees three blue hats, so he can deduce that he has a red hat. In Round 1, he says "I know my hat color," and the others pass.

You'll see when you read about Case 2 that the only way someone can figure out his hat color in Round 1 is if there is one hat of one color and three hats of the other color. Because the red hat wearer figured out his hat color in Round 1, the blue hat wearers know that they all have the other hat color.

In Round 2 everyone says, "I know my hat color," and dinner is served.

Case 2

Now consider Case 2 where there are two red hats and two blue hats. Each person sees two hats of one color and one hat of the other color. From that they can't tell whether this is Case 1 or Case 2, so in Round 1 all four people pass.

If it was Case 1, then in Round 1 the person with the odd–colored hat would have been able to deduce his color. That didn't happen, so after Round 1 all of the guests know that they're in Case 2.

Each guest sees one hat of one color and two hats of the other color. Because it's Case 2, each guest can deduce that he has the same color as the unmatched hat. For example, if you see two red hats and one blue hat, then you have a blue hat.

Now in Round 2 all of the guests say, "I know my hat color," and your host serves the soup.

FOUR HATS WITH THREE COLORS

> **Puzzle:** Suppose you're invited to dinner as in the "Four Colored Hats" puzzle, but this time your host says there is at least one red hat, one blue hat, and one green hat.
>
> How do you decide what colors the hats are?

This is similar to the two–color case with three hats. If there are three colors and all of them are present, then two of the guests see one hat of one color and two hats of another color. In Round 1 they know that they must have the missing color.

For example, suppose there are two red hats, one blue hat, and one green hat. Initially the blue hat wearer sees two red hats and one green hat. He sees no blue hats, so he knows he has a blue hat. Similarly the green hat wearer knows he has a green hat.

In Round 2 the red hat wearers know that the green and blue hat wearers knew their colors, so they can deduce that their hats have the other color: red. In Round 2 everyone knows his hat color.

FIVE COLORED HATS

Puzzle: Suppose you're invited to dinner as in the "Three Colored Hats" puzzle, but this time the Philosophy department chair invites five of you.

How do you decide what colors the hats are?

As in the "Four Colored Hats" puzzle, there are two cases. This time in Case 1 there's one hat of one color and four hats of the other color. In Case 2, there are two hats of one color and three hats of the other color.

Case 1

First consider case 1 where there's one hat of one color and four hats of the other color. Suppose there's one red hat and four blue hats. Then the person with the red hat sees four blue hats, so he can deduce that he has a red hat. In Round 1, he says "I know my hat color," and the others pass.

The only way someone can figure out his hat color in Round 1 is if there is one hat of one color and four hats of the other color. Because the red hat wearer figured out his hat color in Round 1, the blue hat wearers now know that they all have the other hat color.

In Round 2 everyone says, "I know my hat color," and you all head for the dining room.

Case 2

Now consider Case 2 where there are two hats of one color and three hats of the other color. Suppose there are two red hats and three blue hats. The blue hat wearers each see two red hats and two blue hats so they immediately know they're in Case 2, but they don't know which color they have. The red hat wearers see one red hat and three blue hats, so they don't know if they're in Case 1 or 2. At this point no one can guess his color, so everyone passes in Round 1.

After Round 1 the red hat wearers know that it's not Case 1. Because they can each see three blue hats, they know that they must have red hats. (If one of them had a blue hat, he would know that it was Case 1, but he knows that it's not.) During Round 2 the red hat wearers say, "I know my hat color."

Meanwhile the blue hat wearers still can't tell which color they have. During Round 2 they say, "Pass."

During Round 2, the red hat wearers know their color, so you know there must be two of them. The blue hat wearers can then conclude that they must all have the other color. During Round 3 everyone says, "I know my hat color," and you can start eating.

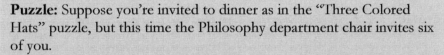

SIX COLORED HATS

> **Puzzle:** Suppose you're invited to dinner as in the "Three Colored Hats" puzzle, but this time the Philosophy department chair invites six of you.
>
> How do you decide what colors the hats are?

As in the previous "N Colored Hats" puzzles, you can consider the possible arrangements of colors. This time there are three cases. In Case 1 there is one hat of one color and five hats of the other color. In Case 2 there are two hats of one color and four hats of the other color. In Case 3 there are three hats of each color.

Case 1

First consider Case 1 where there is one hat of one color and five hats of the other color. As in the other puzzles, the person with the odd–colored hat can deduce his color in Round 1. Then the others know that they must all have the other color in Round 2.

Case 2

Next consider Case 2 where there are two hats of one color and four hats of the other color. Let's assume there are two red hats and four blue hats. The blue hat wearers each see two red hats and three blue hats, so they know that it's either Case 2 or Case 3.

The red hat wearers see one red hat and four blue hats, so they know that it's either Case 1 or Case 2. At this point no one knows enough to guess his hat color so everyone passes in Round 1.

No one knew his hat color in Round 1, so in Round 2 the red hat wearers know now that it's not Case 1. That means it must be Case 2, so the red hat wearers know their colors in Round 2. The blue hat wearers are still unsure so they pass.

The red hat wearers knew their color in Round 2, so now the blue hat wearers know that this is Case 2. Because the rad hat wearers knew their color in Round 2, the blue hat wearers know that they must have the other color, blue.

That means in Round 3 everyone knows his hat color.

Case 3

Finally consider Case 3 where there are three hats of each color. Every person sees two hats of one color and three hats of the other color, so they all know that it's either Case 2 or Case 3. They can't tell which, so they all pass in Round 1.

If this was Case 2, then the logic for Case 2 says that two of the guests would know their hat colors in Round 2. They would know their colors because they could see one hat of one color and four hats of the other color. That isn't true in Case 3 where they all see two hats of one color and three hats of the other color, so no one has enough information to deduce his hat color and everyone passes in Round 2.

Finally, because everyone passed in Round 2, everyone now knows that this is Case 3. Everyone can see two hats of one color and three hats of the other color, so they know that they have the same color as the two hats. For example, if you see two red hats and three blue hats, then you have a red hat. Bon appétit!

FOUR ANGELS

> **Puzzle:** Suppose four apprentice angels are perched in a Christmas tree. They know that between them they are wearing two silver halos and two gold halos, although they don't know the colors of their own halos.
>
> They can generally look down and see the halos of those below them, but because the halos are fairly small (they're only apprentice angels after all) when they look up they can't see the halos on the angels above them.
>
> Angel A is near the top of the tree so he can see the halos worn by Angels B and C. Angel B is next highest so he can see Angel C's halo.

> Angel D is tucked away below the lower branches rummaging through the presents near the trunk so no one can see his halo.
>
> Now the angels are told that any of them who figures out his own halo color will be advanced to the next level in the celestial bureaucracy: Probationary Angel. Which angels can deduce their halo colors?

There are two cases.

In Case 1, the halos worn by Angels B and C have the same color. In that case Angel A sees two halos of the same color, so he knows that he must have the other color and he says so. When you read about Case 2, you'll see that Angel A couldn't have known his color unless Angels B and C had the same color and Angel A had the other color. Now Angels B and C know that they have the color that A doesn't have, and Angel D knows that he has the same color as Angel A. They all announce their colors and are all promoted to Probationary Angel.

In Case 2, Angels B and C have halos of different colors. In that case, Angel A cannot determine his halo color. After a few moments of Angel A not saying anything, the other angels know that B and C must have different colors. Angel B can see the halo worn by Angel C, so he knows that he must have the other color and he announces it. Angel C knows that he has the color that B doesn't have, so then he announces his color.

At this point Angels A and D are stuck. They know that one of them has a silver halo and the other has a gold halo, but they can't tell who has which.

If it's going to be a fair test, then it had better be Case 1.

SUMMARY

Jumping to the final solution to these puzzles is pretty much impossible if you haven't seen a particular puzzle before. Instead of trying to start at the end, think of the puzzle as a form of induction. Start with a base case with only one or two people. Then work your way up through larger and larger problem sizes until you can see the general case and the final solution.

PROGRAMMING EXERCISES

Unfortunately most of the puzzles in this chapter are quite difficult to implement as programs. For example, the "Five Pirates" puzzle seems like an ideal opportunity to try all possible combinations of bribes to see which ones work. Unfortunately just enumerating the combinations ordered by the captain's preference is difficult. The puzzle is solvable, but probably not during an interview. You might like to give it a try in your spare time or you could work on it together with the candidate.

Meanwhile you could ask the candidate to solve some of the simpler exercises described here or to suggest outlines of solutions.

1. Write a program that simulates the "100 Hats" puzzle. It should first randomly assign the hats. The first prisoner should count the red and blue hats that he sees and make an appropriate guess. As the program progresses, it should keep track of the red and blue hats guessed so far and then make each prisoner guess appropriately. The program should finish by listing each prisoner's hat color and guess.

2. Repeat Exercise 1 for the "99 Hats" puzzle.

3. Write a program that simulates the "Autograph Hunter" puzzle. It should randomly pick the Star and then display a list of the people present. The user should then click on two people to ask the first whether he or she knows the second. The program should then indicate the person who should be crossed off of the list, perhaps by surrounding that person's name with parentheses. When there's only one person left, the program should tell you who the Star is and display the number of questions you asked.

4. Write a program that simulates the "Three Colored Hats" puzzle. The program should randomly assign the hats. During Round 1, the person who sees two hats of the same color should say, "I know my hat color," and the other two should pass. During Round 2, the other two should know their hat colors and they should all announce them.

5. Repeat Exercise 4 for the "Four Colored Hats" puzzle.

6. Repeat Exercise 4 for the "Four Hats with Three Colors" puzzle.

13

Creative Counting

These puzzles have solutions that involve counting. Several use binary representations of numbers to map combinations of results to numbered objects. A 1 in the binary representation may represent including an object in the result and a 0 in the representation may represent leaving an object out of the solution.

Other puzzles involve dividing a bar into pieces that can add up in certain ways, toggling doors open and closed, and enumerating squares or other shapes in a picture. Some may not seem like numeric puzzles, but they all involve counting in some fashion.

WINE–LOVING KING

Puzzle: An evil wine–loving king has a wine cellar containing 1,000 bottles of the finest vintages. One day the king learns that the equally evil neighboring queen has poisoned one of the bottles. The poison is extremely potent so even the tiniest drop is lethal.

Valuing the wine more than the prisoners in his dungeon, the king decides to simply give a drop from each bottle to a prisoner until the prisoner eventually dies. Unfortunately the king's physician explains that the poison only takes affect four weeks after it is drunk and the king wants to serve the non–poisoned wine at his gala in five weeks.

The king would give drop to 1,000 different prisoners, but he only has 200 in the dungeon. As the king is making plans to round up another 800 prisoners, the court alchemist thinks of a plan that can identify the poisoned bottle in four weeks while risking no more than 10 of the prisoners. What was the alchemist's plan?

The king essentially needs to "count" the 1,000 bottles of wine with no more than 10 prisoners. He can do that by using a binary numbering system.

The alchemist obtains 10 large empty beakers and numbers them 1 through 10. He then numbers the wine bottles 1 through 1,000 in binary. Next he looks at each bottle's binary representation and places a drop of wine in the beakers corresponding to the binary bits that are 1.

For example, consider wine bottle number 317. The binary representation of 317 is 0100111101. The second bit is a 1 so he places a drop of that wine in beaker number 2. Similarly bit numbers 5, 6, 7, 8, and 10 are 1, so also he places drops in the corresponding beakers.

When the alchemist finishes mixing samples of all of the wines, prisoners numbered 1 through 10 drink the contents of beakers 1 through 10.

After four weeks, the alchemist uses the prisoners to build a binary number. If a prisoner is dead, his bit is a 1. If a prisoner is alive, his bit is a 0. For example, suppose prisoners 1, 2, 5, 7, 9, and 10 have died. Then the new binary number is 1100101011. That number is 811 in decimal, so wine bottle number 811 is the one that is poisoned.

Follow-up: Explain why this works.

The binary representation gives you a unique way to identify each bottle's number. For example, 317 is the only number between 1 and 1,000 that has 1s in the pattern 0100111101, so it's the only bottle that corresponds to that exact pattern of dead prisoners.

Follow-up: What bottle numbers would kill the fewest prisoners?

Any bottle with a single 1 in its binary representation would kill only a single prisoner. Those are bottles 1, 2, 4, 8, 16, 32, 64, 128, 256, and 512. Therefore the 10 bottles with those numbers would kill only a single prisoner.

Follow-up: What bottle numbers would kill the most prisoners?

A number with 10 binary digits that are all 1s would be at least 1,023, which is outside of the range 1 to 1,000, so those numbers are too big. The numbers with nine digits that are 1s and one digit that is 0 and that lie within the range 1 to 1,000 are 0111111111 (511), 1011111111 (895), 1110111111 (959), and 1111011111 (991). Therefore the four bottles with those numbers would kill nine prisoners.

Follow–up: Is there any way to kill 0 prisoners?

If you number the wine bottles 0 through 999 then, if bottle number 0 is poisoned, no prisoners would be killed.

GOLD STANDARD

Puzzle: Suppose you've hired an alchemist to do miscellaneous chores around the house for the next week. He will mow the lawn, clean the gutters, scoop the kitty litter, and so forth. Being an alchemist, he insists on being paid in gold after each day's work.

You have a single gold bar scored with marks that divide the bar into seven equal pieces, and you can break the bar at any of the marks. What is the fewest number of breaks you can make to be able to pay the alchemist exactly what you owe him at the end of each day?

This is a simple binary counting puzzle. The only trick is that the alchemist can give you change each day. For example, you could pay him 5 segments and he can give you back 2 in change if he has them. (If the candidate gets stuck, you may need to point this out.)

If you create pieces that are powers of 2 times 1/7, then you can use them to make any number up to the full total of sevenths that you have available.

Obviously you need to break 1/7th off to pay the alchemist at the end of Day 1.

For Day 2, you could break off another 7th, but you get the fewest breaks if you create the widest variety of sizes. For the second day, break off a 2/7th piece, give it to the alchemist, and he can give you the 1/7th piece in change.

For Day 3, you can return the 1/7th piece.

For Day 4, you could again break off another 1/7th piece, but you're better off making a new 4/7 piece. Give him the 4/7th piece and he can return the other pieces to you in change.

So the pieces are 1/7th, 2/7th, and 4/7th. The following list shows the pieces you need to give to the alchemist at the end of each day.

Day 1: 1/7th
Day 2: 2/7th
Day 3: 1/7th + 2/7th
Day 4: 4/7th
Day 5: 1/7th + 4/7th
Day 6: 2/7th + 4/7th
Day 7: 1/7th + 2/7th + 4/7th

Follow–up: If you wanted to hire the alchemist for more than seven days, what would be the natural way to break up the gold bar and how many days would he need to work to earn the whole bar?

The initial puzzle uses seven days because seven is one less than a power of two. In this case, $2^3-1=7$. When you give the alchemist all of the bar's pieces, that corresponds to the binary value $111=7$.

The next power of two would be 4 and you would have $2^4-1=15$. You would cut the bar into the pieces 1/15th, 2/15th, 4/15th, 8/15th. Now you can pay him for any number of days between 1 and 15, and he would need to work for 15 days to earn the whole bar.

TOGGLING DOORS

Puzzle: Suppose you're an oompa loompa and you're assigned to guard a hallway with 100 doors at night in Willy Wonka's candy factory. The nights are really boring, so you invent a game to keep yourself busy. You close all of the doors and then you begin the game.

You return to your desk to check for messages (there are none) and then you saunter down the hallway toggling every door. If a door is open, you close it. If a door is closed, you open it. (The first time down the hallway they're all closed, so you open them all.)

Next you return to your desk (still no messages) and wander down the hallway again, this time toggling every 2nd door.

In the following rounds, you return to your desk and then meander down the hallway toggling every 3rd door, every 4th door, every 5th door, and so forth until you toggle every 100th door.

When you finish the game, which doors are open?

You can tell whether a door will be opened or closed by looking at the door number's divisors. Suppose a door's number N has D as a divisor. Then when you walk down the hallway toggling every Dth door, you will toggle door N.

For example, consider door number 12. When you toggle every 4th door, you will toggle door 12 because 4 divides evenly into 12.

If N has an even number of unique divisors, then you will have toggled door N an even number of times so the door will be closed at the end. If N has an odd number of unique divisors, then you will have toggled it an odd number of times and it will be open when you're done.

For example, consider door number 48. The following list shows the divisors of the number 48.

1×48
2×24
3×16
4×12
6×8

Then the unique divisors are: 1, 2, 3, 4, 6, 8, 12, 16, 24, and 48. There are 10 unique divisors, so you end up toggling this door an even number of times and it will be closed at the end of the game.

Divisors come in pairs, so you may wonder how a number can have an odd number of divisors. That happens when a divisor appears twice, and that happens for numbers that are perfect squares.

For example, the following list shows the divisors of the number 81.

1×81
3×27
9x9

The divisor 9 appears twice, so the unique divisors of 81 are 1, 3, 9, 27, and 81. There are only five unique divisors and five is odd, so door number 81 will be open when the game is over.

The perfect squares between 1 and 100 are 1, 4, 9, 16, 25, 36, 49, 64, 81, and 100 so those are the open doors.

One variation of this puzzle has you toggle 100 lights on and off instead of opening and closing doors.

Another variation asks you how many doors are open and closed (or how many lights are on and off) at the end. If doors 1, 4, 9, 16, 25, 36, 49, 64, 81, and 100 are open, that's 10 doors so 90 doors will be closed.

In the morning Willy Wonka sees the open doors. Being an extremely clever fellow, he quickly figures out what you were doing all night. The next night he assigns you to a hallway with 1,000 doors.

SNAIL IN THE WELL

> **Puzzle:** A snail falls into a well that's 30 feet deep. Each day he climbs three feet up the wall. Each night he slides back two feet. How many days does it take the snail to climb out of the well?

The snail progresses a net of 1 foot per day, so the obvious but incorrect answer is 30 days.

In fact, after 27 days the snail has gone 27 feet. Then on day 28 he climbs 3 more feet and reaches the edge of the well. Because he's out of the well, he doesn't slide back that night.

> This problem is similar to the *fencepost problem*, which is common in programming. Consider a fence consisting of rails and posts. The rails connect the posts. In the fencepost problem, something corresponds to posts and something else corresponds to the rails. There is one more post than rail, so counting one when you should be counting the other creates an off–by–one error that may seem intuitively correct and is therefore hard to spot.
>
> For example, suppose you want to look at the items in an array starting at position 10 and ending at position 17. You might think you're looking at 17–10=7 items, but that doesn't count the items at both ends of the range. You're really considering 17–10+1=8 items.
>
> More generally in a fencepost problem, an operation works in one way most of the time, but it behaves differently at its end conditions. In the "Snail in the Well" problem the snail's net progress is 1 foot per day except at the end when it escapes from the well.

COUNTING SQUARES

Puzzle: How many squares are there in Figure 13–1?

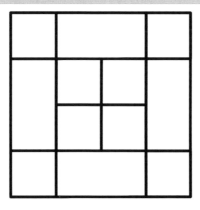

Figure 13–1: Count the squares.

If you just try to count squares as you see them, you'll probably become confused at some point and lose track of which squares you've already counted.

The best approach is to methodically count the squares of different sizes. The following list shows the number of squares of various sizes in the figure.

Small 1×1:	8
Medium 2×2:	5
Large 3×3:	4
Extra Large 4×4:	1
Total:	18

Figure 13–2 shows each of the 18 squares highlighted.

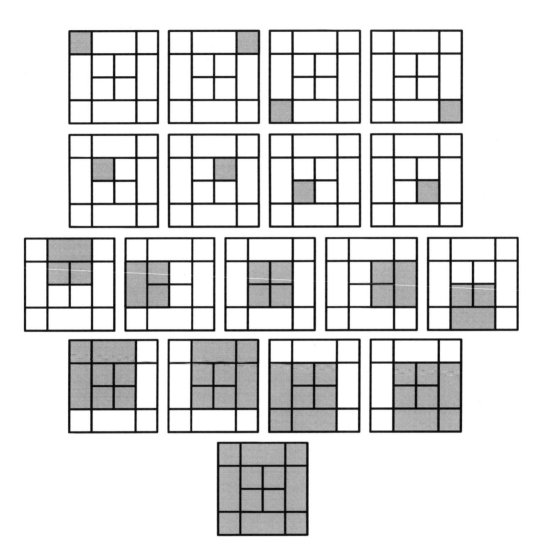

Figure 13–2: The squares in the Figure 13–1.

Being methodical and looking for squares of one size at a time makes it easier to count them correctly.

COUNTING SQUARES, REDUX

Puzzle: How many squares are there in Figure 13–3?

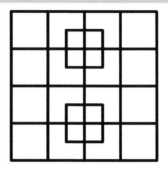

Figure 13–3: Count the squares in this figure.

As in the preceding puzzle, if you just count the squares as you see them, you'll probably become confused at some point and lose track of which squares you've already counted. The best approach is to methodically count the squares of different sizes. The following list shows the number of squares of various sizes in the figure.

Tiny 1/2×1/2:	8
Small 1×1:	18
Medium 2×2:	9
Large 3×3:	4
Extra Large 4×4:	1
Total:	40

Figures 13–4, 13–5, and 13–6 show the tiny, small, and medium squares in Figure 13–3, respectively. Figure 13–7 shows the large and extra–large squares.

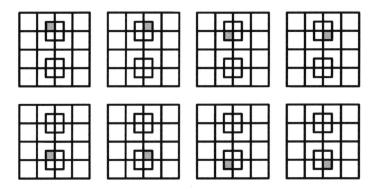

Figure 13–4: Tiny squares in the Figure 13–3.

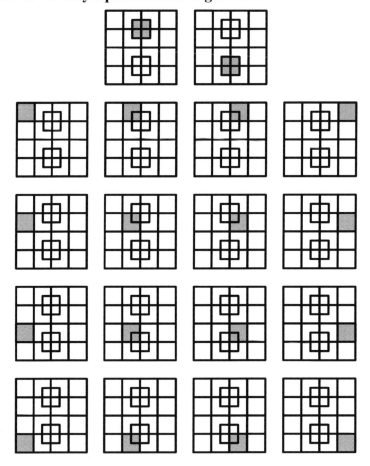

Figure 13–5: Small squares in the Figure 13–3.

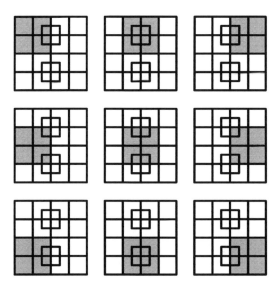

Figure 13–6: Medium squares in the Figure 13–3.

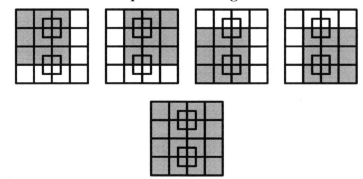

Figure 13–7: Large and extra–large squares in the Figure 13–3.

As in the preceding problem, being methodical and looking for squares of one size at a time makes it easier to count the squares.

SQUARES IN A GRID

Puzzle: How many squares are there in an N×N grid?

In a 1×1 grid, there's clearly only one square.

In a 2×2 grid, there is one large 2×2 square and four small 1×1 squares for a total of five.

In a 3×3 grid, there is one large 3×3 square, four medium 2×2 squares, and nine small 1×1 squares for a total of 14.

Now consider the more general case of an N×N grid. There is only one large N×N square.

The next smaller square has side lengths N–1 so there are two places where you can position it horizontally and two places where you can position it vertically. That means there are four possible places you can position an (N–1)×(N–1) square. Figure 13–8 shows the four possible positions.

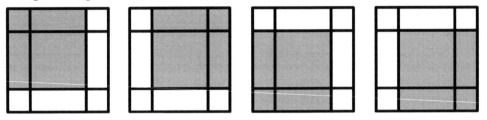

Figure 13–8: Four positions where you can place an (N–1)×(N–1) square.

The next smaller square has side lengths N–2 so there are three places you can position it horizontally and three places you can position it vertically. That means there are nine possible places you can position an (N–2)×(N–2) square.

Figure 13–9 shows the number of positions for squares of various sizes in an N×N grid.

Square Size	# Positions
N×N	1
(N–1)×(N–1)	4
(N–2)×(N–2)	9
(N–3)×(N–3)	14
(N–K)×(N–K)	$(K+1)^2$
⋮	
1×1	N^2

Figure 13–9: The number of positions where you can put a square of various sizes in an N×N grid.

Adding up the numbers of positions in Figure 13–9 gives $1+4+9+...+N^2$ or $1^2+4^2+9^2+...+N^2$. You can use the following identity to simplify this a bit (although most candidates won't know this).

$$\sum_{i=1}^{N} i^2 = \frac{N \times (N + 1) \times (2 \times N + 1)}{6} = \frac{N^2}{2} + \frac{N^3}{3} + \frac{N}{6}$$

Figure 13–10 shows the number of possible squares for various square grid sizes.

Grid Size	# Squares
1×1	1
2×2	5
3×3	14
4×4	30
5×5	55
6×6	91
7×7	140
8×8	204
9×9	285
10×10	385

Figure 13–10: The number of squares in N×N grids.

You can use induction to prove the previous formula, but most candidates will have enough trouble showing that the number of squares is $1^2+2^2+3^2+...+N^2$ (unless you're hiring a mathematician).

RECTANGLES IN A GRID

Puzzle: How many rectangles are there in a rectangular N×M grid?

The easiest way to solve this puzzle is to use binomial coefficients. The following formula shows how to calculate binomial coefficients.

$$\binom{N}{K} = \frac{N!}{K! \, (N - K)!}$$

The value $\binom{N}{K}$ is usually pronounced "N choose K" and it represents the number of ways you can make K choices from a set of N items. For example, suppose you have four letters A,B, C, and D, and you want to pick two of them. The following equation shows the number of ways you can do that.

$$\binom{4}{2} = \frac{4!}{2!\,(4-2)!} = \frac{24}{2 \times 2} = 6$$

The six possible selections are AB, AC, AD, BC, BD, and CD.

Note that selections such as these ignore duplicates that are in different orders. For example, AB and BA are considered the same so only AB is shown in the previous list.

To define a rectangle in an M×N rectangular grid, you can pick the locations of its edges inside the grid.

First consider the left and right edges. If the grid sits at the origin, then the possible locations for the left and right edges have X coordinates 0, 1, 2, ..., M. You need to pick two X coordinates, one for the left edge and one for the right edge, and there are a total of M+1 possible locations for those edges, so there are $\binom{M+1}{2}$ ways that you can pick the edges.

Similarly there are $\binom{N+1}{2}$ ways that you can pick the rectangle's top and bottom edges.

The total number of possible rectangles is the number of choices for the left/right edges multiplied by the number of choices for the top/bottom edges. The following equation gives the total number of combinations.

$$\binom{M+1}{2}\binom{N+1}{2} =$$
$$\left(\frac{(M+1)!}{2!\,(M+1-2)!}\right)\left(\frac{(N+1)!}{2!\,(N+1-2)!}\right) =$$
$$\left(\frac{(M+1)!}{2!\,(M-1)!}\right)\left(\frac{(N+1)!}{2!\,(N-1)!}\right)$$

Notice that (M+1)!=(M+1)×M×(M−1)!, so the preceding equation simplifies to the following.

$$\frac{M \times (M+1) \times N \times (N+1)}{4}$$

Figure 13–11 shows the number of rectangles for a few sample grid sizes.

Grid Size	# Rectangles
1x1	1
2x1	3
2x2	9
3x1	6
3x2	18
3x3	36
4x1	10
4x2	30
4x3	60
4x4	100
5x1	15
5x2	45
5x3	90
5x4	150
5x5	225

Figure 13–11: The number of rectangles in M×N grids.

Note that the number of rectangles in an M×N grid is the same as the number in an N×M grid.

A candidate who isn't familiar with binomial coefficients will probably be unable to solve this puzzle. (So you should memorize the formula for calculating them.)

PRISON LIGHTS, PART 1

Puzzle: The warden meets 32 new prisoners as they arrive and gives the following speech.

"Today you will spend the afternoon in this room, which we call the Light Room. This evening you will be isolated in cells in another building. From those cells you can neither see this room nor communicate with each other.

"Every day I will pick one of you at random and bring you back to the Light Room, where you can turn the lights on or off if you like. You can see that the lights are on now. No one will change the lights' setting between your visits.

"At any point any one of you can say, 'We have all visited the Light Room.' If that person is right, you'll all go free. If that person is wrong, we'll start the game over."

What strategy can the prisoners adopt to guarantee that they only need to play the game once?

First the prisoners should elect a leader. This is the only person who is allowed to say, "We have all visited the Light Room."

Whenever any prisoner other than the leader visits the light room, he should do the following.

- If this prisoner has turned off the lights before, he should do nothing.
- If the lights are currently off, he should do nothing.
- If this prisoner has not turned off the lights before and the lights are currently on, he should turn them off.

When the leader visits the Light Room, he should check the state of the lights. If the lights are on, then he knows that no prisoner has visited the Light Room since the last time he turned the lights on. In this case the leader does nothing.

If the lights are off, then the leader knows that some new prisoner has visited the Light Room since he last turned the lights on. He keeps count of the number of prisoners who have visited the Light Room. When the count reaches 31, he knows that every prisoner has visited the Light Room so he announces, "We have all visited the Light Room."

If the count hasn't reached 31 yet, the leader turns the lights on and returns to his cell.

Follow–up: Why does the leader only count to 31 instead of 32?

The leader is the 32nd prisoner.

Follow–up: What is the minimum sentence that the prisoners might serve before being freed?

The quickest way for the prisoners to go free is if every non–leader visits the Light Room in turn and the leader visits in between each of those trips. That would require 31+31=62 trips. One prisoner makes the trip each day, so the minimum possible sentence is 62 days.

> **Follow–up:** What if the lights are initially off when the warden meets with the prisoners?

In that case the prisoners can reverse their strategy. The non–leaders should turn the lights on and only the leader is allowed to turn the lights off.

PRISON LIGHTS, PART 2

> **Puzzle:** Consider the preceding puzzle "Prison Lights, Part 1" and suppose the warden picks the prisoners to visit the Light Room in numeric order. First prisoner 1 visits, then prisoner 2 visits, and so on, repeating the sequence as necessary. The prisoners think they are picked at random so they can't simply leave after 32 days.
>
> How long will the prisoners stay in prison?

The answer depends on which prisoner is picked to be the leader.

First suppose prisoner 32 is picked as the leader. Each time all of the prisoners pass through the Light Room, the lowest numbered prisoner who hasn't yet turned off the lights will do so. Later in that cycle the leader (prisoner 32) will count that prisoner and turn the lights on. The whole process will take 31 cycles for every non–leader to turn off the lights and each cycle takes 32 days, so the prisoners will be released after 31×32=992 days.

Next suppose prisoner 1 is picked as the leader. In this case each cycle through the prisoners lets one more prisoner turn off the lights. This time, however, the leader doesn't count that prisoner until the beginning of the next cycle. That means the prisoners need 31 cycles for all of the prisoners to turn off the lights and then 1 more day for the leader to count the final prisoner. That makes a total of 993 days.

Now suppose prisoner N is picked as the leader where 1<N<32. During the first cycle, prisoner 1 turns off the lights and later the leader turns them on again. That takes N trips to the Light Room.

After that, every 32 prisoner cycle includes one prisoner who hasn't turned off the lights yet and then returns to the leader. That means during each such cycle 1 new prisoner turns off the lights and then the leader counts that prisoner. Prisoner 1 already turned off the lights, so the prisoners need 30 more cycles to count the remaining prisoners.

That makes the total number of trips $N+30\times32=N+960$. (Note that is agrees with the earlier result if $N=32$.)

> **Follow–up:** What choice of leader gives the prisoners the shortest sentence?

The smallest value you can get with the formula $N+960$ where $1<N<32$ is when $N=2$. Then the prisoners are released after $2+960=962$ days. The prisoners get the shortest sentence if the leader is prisoner 2.

PRISON LIGHTS, PART 3

> **Puzzle:** Consider the preceding puzzle "Prison Lights, Part 2" but suppose the Light Room isn't the room where the prisoners originally meet so they don't know whether the lights are initially on or off. What strategy should the prisoners use now?

Suppose the prisoners use the previous strategy. When the leader sees that the lights are off for the 31st time, one of two things must have happened. Either the lights were initially on and all 31 non–leaders have turned them off, or the lights were initially off and only 30 non–leaders have turned them off. That would be bad because the leader needs to be certain that all 31 non–leaders have turned off the lights.

The prisoners can use a similar strategy but instead of turning off the lights only once, each non–leader should turn off the lights twice. Whenever any prisoner other than the leader visits the light room, he should do the following.

- If this prisoner has turned off the lights twice before, he should do nothing.
- If the lights are currently off, he should do nothing.
- If this prisoner has not turned off the lights twice before and the lights are currently on, he should turn them off.

Now when the leader sees the lights off for the 62nd time, one of two things must have happened. First, suppose the lights were initially on. Then the non–leaders have turned them off 62 times. In that case all 31 non–leaders must have turned off the lights twice so everyone has visited the Light Room.

Second, suppose the lights were initially off. Then the non–leaders have turned them off 61 times. In that case 30 of the non–leaders have turned off the lights twice and the 31st non–leader turned off the lights only once. All 31 non–leaders must have turned off the lights at least once, so everyone has visited the Light Room.

> **Follow–up:** What is the minimum sentence that the prisoners might serve before being freed?

The leader needs to visit the Light Room 62 times. The quickest way for that to happen is if the leader visits the room first and the lights are initially off. Then the leader needs to visit 61 more times, with a non–leader turning off the lights in between each of those visits. That requires 122 more trips for a total of 123 trips and a 123 day sentence.

PRESSING THE FLESH

> **Puzzle:** At the wrap party for your latest blockbuster movie, everyone shook hands with everyone else. There were 66 handshakes in total. How many people were at the party?

The following sections describe two different strategies for solving this puzzle.

Binomial Coefficients

The easiest way to solve this puzzle is to use binomial coefficients. See the solution to the "Rectangles in a Grid" puzzle for a description of binomial coefficients.

A handshake occurs for every distinct pair of people at the party. If there are N people at the party, then the number of ways you can pick pairs of people is given by $\binom{N}{2}$. With some trial and error you can find that $\binom{12}{2} = 66$ so there were 12 people at the party.

Counting Handshakes

Another way to calculate the number of handshakes is to add up the number of handshakes that each person performs. The first person shakes hands with N–1 people. The second person then must shake hands with N–2 other people. The third person shakes hands with N–3 people, and so on until the last person has already shaken hands with everyone else. The total number of handshakes is:

$$(N-1) + (N-2) + (N-3) + \ldots + 0$$

There are N terms in the equation, so you can rearrange it a bit to get the following.

$$N^2 - (1 + 2 + 3 + \ldots + N) =$$

$$N^2 - \frac{N \times (N-1)}{2} =$$

$$\frac{N^2 - N}{2}$$

You can set this equal to 66 and solve for N, or you can use a little trial and error to find that N=12.

SPLITTING HAIRS

Puzzle: What is the probability that at least two people in New York City have exactly the same number of hairs on their heads (not counting bald people)?

This may seem like a ridiculous question about probability, but it's actually about the pigeonhole principle. The pigeonhole principle says, if you have N items and you divide them into M groups, and N>M, then at least one group must contain more than one item. For example, if you have a group of 10 mailboxes (sometimes called pigeonholes) and you need to place 11 letters in them, then at least one mailbox must contain more than one letter.

New York City has about 8.4 million residents, most of whom are not bald. As an extremely conservative estimate, suppose at least 5 million New Yorkers are not bald.

On average humans have around 100,000 hairs on their heads. The number varies widely, so let's be conservative again and say most people have no more than 200,000 hairs on their heads.

Now imagine that you have a giant pigeonhole setup with 200,000 entries and you place the people of New York in the box that corresponds to the number of hairs that they have. Because we need to put more than 5 million people in the 200,000 boxes, at least some of those 200,000 boxes must contain more than one person.

In fact if the 5 million people were divided evenly into the 200,000 boxes, each box would contain 25 people. That means there is at least one group of at least 25 people with the same number of hairs on their heads. Most likely there are thousands of such groups. (I suppose you could start a Meetup group to connect with the others in your group.)

COUNTING TEACHERS

> **Puzzle:** How many pre–kindergarten through 12th grade teachers are there in New York City?

At first glance this may seem like a ridiculous question. (Actually most interview puzzles are ridiculous questions so why should this one be different?) You need to realize that the interviewer really just wants to see you make some estimates and do some back–of–the–envelope calculations and doesn't really care what the answer is. The idea is to come up with something like the Drake equation for teachers.

> **Note:** The Drake equation estimates the number of intelligent civilizations in the galaxy by using guesses for values such as the rate of star formation in the galaxy and the number of planets per star that could support life. For more information, see
> `en.wikipedia.org/wiki/Drake_equation`.

The interviewer probably doesn't expect you to pull out your smart phone and start looking up values. Instead you should make some simplifying assumptions and guesses.

First, how many people are there in the Big Apple? Let's call that value P for "people." My semi-wild guess is that P is around 9 million.

Next what fraction of the people are pre–K through grade 12 students? We can calculate this as a fraction of the people who are the right age. The grades pre–K through 12 includes 14 years of school. If we let L be life expectancy (around 80 years) then the fraction of people who are the right age to be students is roughly $14/L$.

By putting those numbers together we can estimate of the number of students.

$$\#Students = P \times 14/L$$

Now let's figure out how many teachers those students would need. Let's call the average number of students per class C for "class size." A typical class might have 25 students.

However, teachers don't all teach every minute of the day. They need time off to eat lunch, catch up on grading, and generally maintain their sanity. Let's call the fraction of the day that a teacher is actually teaching T for "teaching fraction." This might be around 0.7.

We can combine C and T to get the number of student–days that one teacher can provide.

$$\text{\#Student days per Teacher} = C \times T$$

Now we can combine those two equations to calculate the number of teachers needed.

$$\text{\#Teachers} = [\text{\#Students}]/[\text{\#Student days per Teacher}]$$

$$= [P \times 14/L]/[C \times T] = \frac{P \times 14}{L \times C \times T}$$

If we plug in my guesses, we get:

$$\text{\#Teachers} = \frac{9{,}000{,}000 \times 14}{80 \times 25 \times 0.7} = 90{,}000$$

The actual number of teachers at the end of 2015 was 92,624 (see `schools.nyc.gov/AboutUs/schools/data/stats`), which is pretty close to the estimate. Any value within a factor of 2 is pretty good.

In fact my estimate isn't quite as good as it seems. The 92,624 number only includes public teachers, and around 19 or 20 percent of the students in New York City attend private schools, so the true number of teachers is larger.

Variations on this puzzle ask candidates to estimate all sorts of weird values such as the number of piano tuners in Seattle, the price you would charge to clean every chimney in Detroit, or the number of cigarettes smoked each month in India. Those may be more amusing, but I prefer the number of teachers because it's easy to look up the true number.

To solve this kind of puzzle, use an organized approach and make the best guesses that you can. If you can think of a second way to estimate the result, do so and see if the results agree.

As an interviewer, you might tell the candidate the true number and then ask where the error lies. If you're the candidate, you should be able to indicate which guesses seem the most suspicious.

SINGLE–ELIMINATION

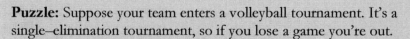

> **Puzzle:** Suppose your team enters a volleyball tournament. It's a single–elimination tournament, so if you lose a game you're out.
>
> If there are 30 teams, how many games must be played to pick the winner?

This puzzle can be confusing if you start thinking about challenge brackets and which teams play against each other. It's particularly tricky because the number of teams isn't a power of two, so you can't have nice, symmetric challenge brackets. Some teams will need to have byes to make everything work out.

Fortunately there's a simpler way to look at the problem. Each game eliminates one team from the tournament. Because you need to whittle the field down to a single team, you need to eliminate 29 teams. Therefore there must be 29 games.

DOUBLE–ELIMINATION

Puzzle: Suppose your team wins the tournament in the "Single–Elimination" puzzle and now you're going to regionals. This time it's a double–elimination tournament. If you lose a game, you go into a consolation bracket where you play other teams that have lost a game. If you lose a second time, you're out.

At the end, the champion of the consolation bracket plays against the champion of the winner's bracket until one of those teams has two losses.

If there are 30 teams, how many games must be played to pick the grand champion?

You can almost solve this puzzle by using the same strategy used to solve the "Single–Elimination" puzzle. You need to eliminate 29 teams and they must each lose twice to be eliminated, so the teams must play $2 \times 29 = 58$ games.

However, there is a catch. During the playoffs between the champions of the consolation and winners brackets, the winners champion might lose a game. In that case the two teams need to play again. After that rematch, one of the two teams will have two losses and will be eliminated.

That means the total number of games is either 58 or 59 if that last playoff game is needed.

Another way to think of this is that all of the eliminated teams lose twice and the grand champion team loses either zero or one time.

SUMMARY

If a puzzle involves including some objects and excluding others, you may be able to solve it by mapping objects to digits in a binary representation of a number. That's how to solve the "Wine–Loving King" puzzle.

In the "Gold Standard" puzzle, you need to divide a gold bar into pieces and then use the pieces to count from one to seven. This is somewhat reminiscent of the "Bazaar Weights" puzzles in Chapter 9, although in the "Gold Standard" you don't have two balance pans where you can place weights.

For other counting puzzles, watch out for fencepost problems and count carefully.

PROGRAMMING EXERCISES

1. Write a program to help with the "Wine–Loving King" puzzle. It should take as an input a wine bottle number and then tell you which flasks should contain drops from that bottle. It should also let you use checkboxes to indicate the prisoners who have died and from that it should tell you which wine bottle was poisoned.

2. Write a program that simulates the "Toggling Doors" puzzle. It should run through an array representing the doors and mark them as opened or closed. When it's finished, the program should verify that the correct doors are open and closed.

3. Write an animated version of the program you wrote for Exercise 2. It should display the doors graphically. Let the user adjust the speed of the animation so it can go slowly enough for you to see the doors opening and closing.

4. Write an animated program that displays the squares in an N×N grid one after another. Make it count the squares it displays and verify that agrees with the formula shown in the solution to the "Squares in a Grid" puzzle.

5. Repeat Exercise 4 for the rectangles in an N×M grid. Verify that the number of rectangles agrees with the formula shown in the solution to the "Rectangles in a Grid" puzzle.

6. Write a program that lists all of the handshakes for the "Pressing the Flesh" puzzle. Let the user enter the number of people at the party.

14

Jarring Journeys

These puzzles involve journeys. The solutions to some use a handy path–counting technique similar to some of the shortest path algorithms described in my book *Essential Algorithms: A Practical Approach to Computer Algorithms* (Rod Stephens, John Wiley & Sons, 2013). Those techniques are useful in many kinds of route–finding programs.

Other puzzles require you to extend the range of a group of travelers who have limited resources. To solve those puzzles you need to look for creative ways to conserve resources or cache them along the route for later use.

WALKING TO WORK

Puzzle: Your place of work is four blocks east and three blocks south of where you live. To make your morning walk more interesting, you take a different route to work each day. You can turn on any street as long as you're always moving east or south. (Moving west or north would make the walk take longer.)

How many days can you walk to work without repeating the exact same path?

A good way to solve this puzzle is to draw a picture of the street grid. Then label each intersection with the number of paths you can take from your house to that intersection.

Start by labeling the upper left corner where your house is with a 1 because there's only one way you can go from your house to your house: just sit there.

Now find unlabeled intersections whose neighbors to the west and north are already labeled. Suppose an unlabeled intersection is east of an intersection labeled A and south of an intersection labeled B. You can use paths via either of those intersections to get to the new intersection, so there are A+B possible paths to the new intersection. Label the new intersection with the sum of A+B.

Repeat those steps until you've labeled the lower right intersection where your work is. Its label tells you how many paths there are from your house to your work.

Figure 14–1 shows the steps you follow to complete the drawing.

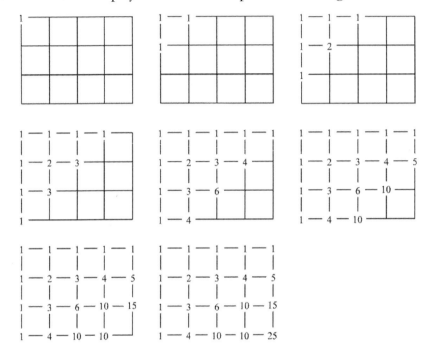

Figure 14–1: The number of paths from the upper left intersection to the other intersections in a street network.

The label on the intersection at the lower right in Figure 14–1 is 35 so there are 35 possible paths from home to work.

For extra credit, note that the values in the grid form part of Pascal's triangle. That means you can use binomial coefficients to calculate the values directly, although it's a bit tricky because the rows in Pascal's triangles correspond to diagonals in the grid. Figure 14–2 shows the grid with the first few rows of Pascal's triangle indicated by gray arrows.

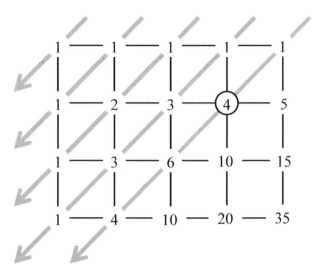

Figure 14–2: Rows in Pascal's triangle correspond to diagonals in the street grid.

The value in column C row R of Pascal's triangle is given by the binomial coefficient $\binom{R}{C}$ where you start numbering both R and C from 0. For example, the circled entry in Figure 14–2 is at row (diagonal) 4 column 1 so its value is $\binom{4}{1} = 4$.

Follow–up: How many unique paths are there from your work back to your house?

Any path from home to work is also a reversed path from work to home, so there are 35 unique paths home.

Follow–up: Suppose you don't want to follow the same path twice in either direction between home and work. How many possible round trips can you make?

You can only use half of the paths in each direction. Because there are 35 unique paths in total, you can make 35/2=17 round trips. Then the next time you go to work, you will use up the last unique path and you'll be stuck at work. You'll have to reuse a path or live at work from now on.

Follow–up: How many paths are there if there's construction on one of the streets so the grid looks like Figure 14–3?

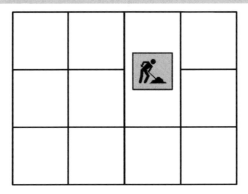

Figure 14–3: This grid is missing a street segment.

It's easy enough to repeat the previous steps to make a diagram showing the total number of paths through the grid. For each intersection add the values of the intersections to the north and west, ignoring an intersection if it isn't connected by a street segment. Figure 14–4 shows the new picture.

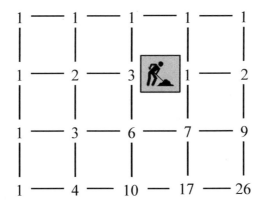

Figure 14–4: There are 26 paths from the upper left corner to the lower right corner.

Figure 14–4 shows that there are 26 paths from home to work if that particular street is blocked by construction.

PATHS THROUGH A CUBE, PART 1

Puzzle: Suppose you're a sparrow living inside a mall that's basically shaped like a large 3×3×3 cube. Sort of like a hollow Rubik's cube filled with tween clothing shoppes and shoe stores. Figure 14–5 shows the mall from the outside.

Your nest is in one of the corner sub–cubes and the food court is in the opposite corner sub–cube. How many different paths can you take through the sub–cubes while flying from your nest to the food court?

Figure 14–5: A sparrow living inside a 3×3×3 cube.

This is similar to the "Walking to Work" puzzle except in three dimensions. You can use the same technique to solve the problem, although it is harder to visualize.

One way to make visualization easier is to split the larger cube into three layers. You still need to keep track of which sub–cubes are connected to which others, but at least you can write numbers of paths on the layers.

Each sub–cube's value should be the total of the values in the sub–cubes:

- To the left of the sub–cube on the same layer
- Behind the sub–cube into the page on the same layer
- Above the sub–cube on the layer above

Figure 14–6 shows the numbers of paths to each of the sub–cubes.

Figure 14–6: The number of paths from the top/back/left sub–cube to the other sub–cubes.

Figure 14–6 shows that there are 90 paths from the nest to the food court.

PATHS THROUGH A CUBE, PART 2

Puzzle: Suppose you're a sparrow living inside a mall as in the puzzle "Paths through a Cube, Part 1," but the mall management has planted a huge tree in the bottom center sub–cube. You can easily fly around the trunk, but the tree has too many leaves for you to easily fly through in the very center sub–cube. (In other words, the center cube in the middle layer is blocked.)

Now how many paths are there from your nest to the food court?

You can solve this puzzle in the same way you solved the puzzle "Paths through a Cube, Part 1." Figure 14–7 shows the new path counts.

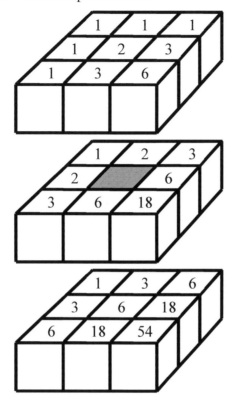

Figure 14–7: The number of paths from the top/back/left sub–cube to the other sub–cubes if the center cube is blocked.

Figure 14–7 shows that there are 54 paths from the nest to the food court if the center cube is blocked.

Now you might consider moving your nest into the tree. You'll have fewer paths to the food court (only six), but it'll be a quicker trip and the nest will probably be safer than it is now behind the air vent above Old Navy.

AMELIA EARHART RETURNS

Puzzle: After a lengthy stay on Galduta Island in the South Pacific, Amelia Earhart (with the help of Angus MacGyver) finally manages to piece together a large fleet of airplanes made out of palm leaves, coconuts, and seashells. The planes are modeled on Amelia's Lockheed Model 10 Electra (similar to the plane shown in Figure 14–8), and now she's determined to use them to fly around the world.

The planes can only take off and land at Galduta Island. They also use a special fuel (made from secret ingredients such as fermented betel nut, ground crab shells, and pulverized mango skins) that is only available on the island.

Unfortunately the planes can only hold enough fuel to make it halfway around the world. The one ray of hope is that one plane can transfer some of its fuel to another plane in flight. (Assume that takes no time.)

How many planes (with pilots) and tanks of fuel does Amelia need to successfully circumnavigate the world? (And no, she can't take all of a pilot's fuel and leave him to crash somewhere over the Atlantic Ocean.)

The solution to this puzzle is very hard to visualize. While writing this book, I tried several different kinds of explanation including a verbose description (pretty long), a brief description (lacking detail), pictures (*very* long), and a table (concise but hard to understand). Maybe someday printed books will allow animation and make this a lot easier to visualize, but for now I've settled on the brief description and the table.

Figure 14-8: A Lockheed model 10a.

The solution is a bit easier to understand if you think about fuel in twelfths of the distance around the world. Let's call the amount of fuel needed to go one twelfth of the way around the world an "oodle." The planes can go halfway around the world on a single tank, so the tanks hold six oodles of fuel.

Let's also call the amount of time needed to burn one oodle of fuel a "tick." Because of the way we defined an oodle, a tick is one twelfth of the time needed to circle the world.

Amelia uses three planes piloted by herself, MacGyver, and a passerby named Felix Moncla. (Everyone on Galduta Island has trained to use the makeshift airplanes.)

All three planes start off heading in the same direction carrying full tanks of fuel. After two ticks, Felix transfers two oodles of fuel to MacGyver. Now Amelia has four oodles of fuel, MacGyver has six oodles of fuel, and Felix has only two oodles of fuel.

Felix barely has enough fuel to return to the island, so that's what he does. He grabs a sandwich, takes three oodles of fuel, and heads back out again.

At three ticks from the start, MacGyver transfers three oodles of fuel to Amelia. Now Amelia has a full tank and MacGyver has only two oodles of fuel. That's not enough to return to the island, but MacGyver turns around and heads back anyway, hoping that Felix hasn't forgotten about him.

At five ticks from the start, MacGyver is out of fuel. Fortunately Felix appears just in the nick of time and transfers one oodle of fuel to MacGyver. MacGyver and Felix both return to the island to refuel. At six ticks from the start, they head out again, this time going the opposite direction around the world.

At eight ticks from the start, Felix transfers two oodles of fuel to MacGyver, giving MacGyver a full tank and Felix only two oodles of fuel. Felix returns to the island.

At nine ticks from the start, Amelia's engine is starting to sputter when suddenly MacGyver appears from the other direction! MacGyver transfers three oodles of fuel to Amelia so she has three oodles of fuel, which is just enough to finish the trip around the world.

Unfortunately MacGyver has only two oodles of fuel left. That's not enough to return to the island, but MacGyver turns around anyway and hopes Felix hasn't stopped for a nap.

Meanwhile Felix reached the island, grabbed three oodles of fuel, and headed back out.

At 11 ticks MacGyver's plane is running on fumes. Felix appears and transfers one oodle of fuel to MacGyver. Now all three planes have one oodle of fuel left and they all arrive triumphantly at Galduta Island exactly 12 ticks after they started the strangest circumnavigation in history.

The table in Figure 14–9 shows the location and fuel status of each of the 3 planes throughout the whole trip. The notation C→B means plane C (Felix) transfers fuel to plane B (MacGyver). The notation C+3 means plane C picks up three oodles of fuel at the island.

Ticks	A (Amelia)		B (MacGyver)		C (Felix)	
	Loc	Fuel	Loc	Fuel	Loc	Fuel
0	0	6	0	6	0	6
1	1	5	1	5	1	5
2	2	4	2	4	2	4
C→B	2	4	2	6	2	2
3	3	3	3	5	1	1
B→A	3	6	3	2	1	1
4	4	5	2	1	0	0
C+3	4	5	2	1	0	3
5	5	4	1	0	1	2
C→B	5	4	1	1	1	1
6	6	3	0	0	0	0
B+6, C+6	6	3	0	6	0	6
7	7	2	11	5	11	5
8	8	1	10	4	10	4
C→B	8	1	10	6	10	2
9	9	0	9	5	11	1
B→A	9	3	9	2	11	1
10	10	2	10	1	0	0
C+3	10	2	10	1	0	3
11	11	1	11	0	11	2
C→B	11	1	11	1	11	1
12	0	0	0	0	0	0

Figure 14–9: Plane positions during the round–the–world trip.

All three planes start with six oodles of fuel for a total of 18 oodles between them. The notations C+3, B+6, C+6, and C+3 mean the planes pick up an additional 18 oodles of fuel. That means the total amount of fuel used is 18+18=36 oodles. That makes sense because all three planes are flying nonstop for the entire 12 ticks, so they should use

3×12=36 oodles of fuel. (Remember the distance puzzles back in Chapter 10? One of the keys to those puzzles was to think about how far a bird can fly in a certain time. The same applies here.)

In total Amelia only needs three planes and 36 oodles of fuel (three circumnavigations worth).

> **Follow–up:** Which pilot flew the greatest distance?

All three pilots fly the entire time so they all fly the same distance. They all flew far enough to circle the world if only they had all been going in the right direction the whole time.

DESERT PLANE CRASH, PART 1

> **Puzzle:** Suppose your plane, which was carrying 10 people and a cargo of food rations, crash lands in the Sahara desert, 160 miles from the nearest phone. You try to call for help, but all of your cellphones' batteries are dead from playing Pokémon Go.
>
> A single person can carry up to four days' worth of rations (the jars of caviar and bottles of champagne are quite heavy) and can walk at most 20 miles per day.
>
> What is the smallest party that can enable someone to reach civilization and send back help to those who stay at the plane?

The key here is to realize that some people can carry rations that others will use later. As long as the carrier doesn't use up more food than he can carry, he can help the others in the expedition. The following list describes the steps you can take to get someone to a phone.

Start: A party of four people (suppose they're Carol, Darryl, Cheryl, and Carlos) starts out carrying four rations each for a total of 16 rations.

End of Day 1: 20 miles out. The four people each eat a ration, leaving 16–4=12 rations. The next morning Carol turns around empty–handed and heads back to the plane while the three others continue carrying four rations each. (Carol arrives at the plane at the end of Day 2 dusty and hungry.)

End of Day 2: 40 miles out. The three remaining people each eat a ration, leaving 12–3=9 rations. The next morning Darryl takes one ration and turns back while the two remaining people continue carrying four rations each. (Darryl eats his ration at the end of Day 3 and arrives at the plane at the end of Day 4.)

End of Day 3: 60 miles out. The two remaining people each eat a ration, leaving 8–2=6 rations. The next morning Cheryl takes two rations and turns back while Carlos continues carrying four rations. (Cheryl eats one ration at the end of Day 4 and one at the end of Day 5. She arrives at the plane at the end of Day 6 and drops exhausted in the shade of a wing.)

End of Day 4: 80 miles out. Carlos eats one of his rations leaving three rations.

End of Day 5: 100 miles out. Carlos eats another ration leaving two rations.

End of Day 6: 120 miles out. Carlos eats one of his rations leaving one ration.

End of Day 7: 140 miles out. Carlos eats his last ration.

End of Day 8: 160 miles out. Carlos arrives at civilization.

So after eight days Carlos notifies the authorities about the crash. A few hours later several helicopters arrive at the scene of the crash to find the other survivors relaxed and well–tanned. Meanwhile Carlos takes a long bath. (It's been a grueling and sweaty trek.)

Desert Plane Crash, Part 2

Puzzle: Unfortunately your plane has crashed again as in the puzzle "Desert Plane Crash, Part 1." (You really need to hire a better pilot.)

The bad news is that this time you and the pilot are the only passengers. You're also 180 miles from civilization.

The good news is that you and the pilot have been working out so you can each carry five rations at a time.

How can you reach civilization to get help this time?

The key idea this time is that you can leave rations in a cache to use later. The following list shows the steps that you can take.

Start: You and the pilot head out, each carrying five rations for a total of 10 rations.

End of Day 1: 20 miles out. You each eat one ration, leaving 10–2=8 rations, and you keep going.

End of Day 2: 40 miles out. You each eat one ration, leaving 8–2=6 rations. The next morning the pilot takes one ration and heads back to the plane while you continue with the remaining five rations. (The pilot eats his ration at the end of Day 3 and arrives at the plane at the end of Day 4.)

End of Day 3: 60 miles out. You eat one ration, leaving 5–1=4 rations. The next morning you leave two rations (hidden under a rock so wild animals with can openers and corkscrews don't find them) and head back to the plane carrying the two remaining rations.

End of Day 4: 40 miles out. You eat one of your rations, so you have one left.

End of Day 5: 20 miles out. You eat your last ration.

End of Day 6: 0 miles out. You arrive back at the plane. You take five rations and the pilot takes four. The next morning you both head back out.

End of Day 7: 20 miles out. You each eat one ration, leaving 9–2=7 rations, and you keep going.

End of Day 8: 40 miles out. You each eat one ration, leaving 7–2=5 rations. The pilot takes one ration and heads back to the plane again while you continue with the remaining four rations. (The pilot eats his ration at the end of Day 9 and arrives at the plane at the end of Day 10.)

End of Day 9: 60 miles out. You eat one ration, leaving 4–1=3. The next morning you take the two rations from under the rock so you have a total of five and continue.

End of Day 10: 80 miles out. You eat one ration, leaving four rations.

End of Day 13: 100 miles out. You eat one ration leaving three rations.

End of Day 14: 120 miles out. You eat one ration leaving two rations.

End of Day 15: 140 miles out. You eat one ration leaving one ration.

End of Day 16: 160 miles out. You eat your last ration.

End of Day 17: 180 miles out. You arrive at civilization.

So after 17 days you notify the authorities about the crash. They take a helicopter to rescue the pilot while you search Craigslist for a new pilot who doesn't crash so often.

BANANA–POWERED CAMEL

> **Puzzle:** Suppose you have 300 bananas at your plantation and you want to take then to market 100 miles away. Your sole mode of transportation is an evil–smelling, cranky, banana–powered camel that spits, bites, steps on your feet, and eats one banana per mile.
>
> If the camel can carry up to 100 bananas at a time, how many bananas can you get to market?

If you try the most obvious brute force approach, you'll run out of bananas. For example, suppose you load the camel with 100 bananas and start walking. After 100 miles you'll reach the market, but the camel will have eaten all of the bananas. With no bananas for the return trip, you'll have to sell your camel for cab fare. (At least the cab won't bite you and it will probably smell better.)

Instead load the camel with 100 bananas and walk 20 miles. That uses up 20 bananas, so you're left with 80. Leave 60 bananas there and use the remaining 20 to go back to your plantation.

Pick up the next load of 100 bananas and shuttle them to the 20–mile point. Again leave 60 and use 20 to get back to the plantation.

Take the last load of 100 bananas to the 20–mile point. You don't need to return to the plantation this time, so you can keep all of the 80 bananas left in the latest load. That gives you a total of 60+60+80=200 bananas.

Now do the same thing again, this time moving the bananas 33 miles to the 53–mile point. Take 100 bananas 33 miles, leave 34 bananas there, and use the remaining 33 bananas to return to the 20–mile point.

Pick up the second load of 100 bananas and carry them to the 53–mile point. That uses up 33 more bananas, so you have 67 bananas left from the second load and 34+67=101 bananas in total.

Eat one banana (you've earned it!), load the remaining 100 bananas on the camel, and finish the trip to market. From this point the market is 47 miles away so you're left with 53 bananas when you arrive. (If you move to the 53.33 mile mark during the second trip, you can arrive with 53.33 bananas, but no one is going to buy a third of a banana that's covered in camel slobber from you.)

DUBIOUS DIESEL

Puzzle: Suppose you're having lunch at a truck stop and a shady–looking character says he can give you 300 fuel cans holding 1 gallon of diesel each if you haul them away at 3:00 AM. Unfortunately the only vehicle you have that currently works is a noisy, beat–up, army surplus truck that only gets one mile per gallon. The truck's 50 gallon fuel tank is empty, so you're going to have to use the fuel in the cans to get anywhere.

If the truck's bed can hold 100 cans at a time and your garage is 100 miles away, how can you get the cans to your garage?

This problem is similar to the "Banana–Powered Camel" problem except the truck has a fuel tank. Instead of feeding the camel one banana per mile, you can pour 50 cans of diesel into the truck's tank at the start, essentially allowing the truck to carry 150 gallons at once.

First, use 50 cans to fill the truck's tank, load up 100 cans, and drive 50 miles until the tank is empty. Use 50 of the cans to refuel the truck, leave 50 cans behind, and return to the truck stop.

Use another 50 cans to fill the truck's tank, load the remaining 100 cans onto the truck, and drive to the 50 miles mark. At this point you have the 50 cans you left here during the first trip plus the 100 cans that the truck is currently carrying for a total of 150 cans.

Use 50 cans to fill the truck's tank again. Load the remaining 100 cans onto the truck and drive to your garage. You arrive with an empty tank and 100 cans of fuel.

In the morning the truck stop owner, and soon the police, are going to wonder about the 100 empty fuel cans lying on the ground at the truck stop and the 50 other empty cans halfway between the truck stop and your garage.

TROLL TOLL

> **Puzzle:** Suppose you work for the Archipelago Postal Service and you need to deliver three sacks containing 30 pineapples each to a village in the center of an island. Unfortunately the only path to the village has 30 bridges, under each of which sits a troll. Each troll demands one pineapple in payment for each sack that you are currently carrying.
>
> How many pineapples can you get to the village?

Because you're charged a toll on each sack and not on each pineapple, you should consolidate the sacks as quickly as possible. As you get rid of sacks, you lower the toll.

To consolidate the sacks, you should remove pineapples from one sack at a time until that sack is empty.

The first 10 trolls each demand three pineapples, which you take from the first sack. After that the first sack is empty so future trolls only charge you for two sacks.

The next 15 trolls each demand two pineapples, which you take from the second sack. After that the second sack is empty so future trolls only charge you for one sack.

Now the five final trolls charge you one pineapple each and you arrive at the village with 25 pineapples left.

The villagers are overjoyed to see you because they're cannibals and the pineapple you brought will go nicely with the roasted Archipelago Postal Service employee that you also brought.

CUPCAKES FOR GRANNY

> **Puzzle:** Suppose you want to bring cupcakes to your grandmother. Like all grandmothers, she lives across the river and through the woods in a forest infested with fantasy creatures. You need to cross five bridges to get to her house and, naturally, each of the bridges has a troll who demands a toll. Each troll takes half of the goods that you're carrying, in this case cupcakes.
>
> However, the trolls have grandmothers, too, so after taking their tolls they each kindheartedly give you back one cupcake so they don't leave you empty–handed.
>
> How many cupcakes do you need to start with to arrive at your grandmother's house with two cupcakes? (One for each of you.)

You only need to bring two cupcakes. Each troll takes half of them, which is one, and then returns one cupcake, leaving you with two again. You can cross any number of bridges and always keep your two cupcakes.

OGRE AT THE BRIDGE

> **Puzzle:** Suppose you're walking through the forest and you come to a bridge guarded by an ogre. The ogre says, "To cross this bridge, you must make a statement. If it's true, I'll strangle you and carry your body across. If it's false, I'll chop off your head and carry the pieces across."
>
> What statement can you make to cross safely?

If you say, "I will be decapitated," the ogre has a problem. If he chops off your head, then the statement was true and he should have strangled you. If he strangles you, then the statement was false and he should have chopped off your head. In theory the ogre can't make good on his threat so you're free to cross.

Or the ogre could strangle you and then decapitate your body. Your statement was true because you were decapitated, albeit after death, and the ogre strangled you as promised.

Alternatively you could hope that the ogre is confused by the word "decapitated" and you can cross the bridge while he's looking it up at dictionary.com. Personally, I would just turn around and take a different route through the forest.

TOLL CONTROL

Puzzle: Over summer break you decide to study the Jejune Pyramid in the Costoso Isles, and you need to get from your plane to the pyramid. The isles are connected by toll bridges that cost varying amounts. Figure 14–10 shows the arrangement of bridges and their tolls.

What is the smallest total toll that you can pay to get to the pyramid?

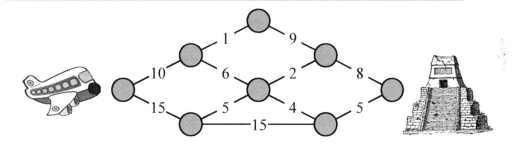

Figure 14–10: Tolls in the Costoso Isles.

This is basically a shortest path problem similar to those described in my book *Essential Algorithms* (Rod Stephens, John Wiley & Sons, 2013). You can solve it much as you can solve the path counting puzzles described earlier in this chapter.

First label the plane's isle 0. Next consider the bridges that connect labeled isles to unlabeled isles and calculate the tentative total costs to visit the unlabeled isles via those bridges. For example, suppose an isle is labeled 10 and a bridge with toll 4 leads from there to an unlabeled isle. Then the tentative cost to visit the unlabeled isle would be 10+4=14.

Find the unlabeled isle with the smallest tentative cost and label it with that cost. Repeat this process until all of the isles are labeled. Figure 14–11 shows the completely labeled map. The bridges used to reach each isle are highlighted in bold.

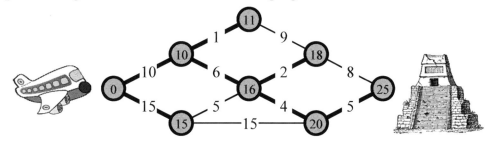

Figure 14–11: Tolls in the Costoso Isles.

From Figure 14–11 you can see that the least expensive path to the pyramid has total cost 25 and goes through the isles labeled 0, 10, 16, 20, and 25.

SUMMARY

Counting paths through a network is reasonably straightforward if you use shortest path techniques, but finding solutions to some of the other puzzles requires a certain amount of creativity.

To solve journey–extending puzzles such as "Amelia Earhart Returns" and the dessert–crossing puzzles, you can sometimes use haulers to carry supplies that will be used by other people later. This is helpful as long as a hauler can carry more supplies than he or she needs.

In a similar technique, you can cache supplies along the route for use during a later stage of the journey. This is very similar to the method that uses haulers except that you act as a hauler for yourself. You just carry the supplies at one time and then use them at another.

PROGRAMMING EXERCISES

1. Write a program to solve the "Walking to Work" puzzle. (Hints: Make a `Node` class that contains a list of predecessor nodes and a `NumPaths` property. Also give the class a `CountPaths` method that first recursively calls the node's predecessors' `CountPaths` methods and then uses the predecessors' path counts to set the current node's `NumPaths` property. Use the program to solve the "Walking to Work" puzzle.

2. Copy the program you wrote for Exercise 1 and modify it to calculate the number of paths as shown in Figure 14–4.

3. Copy the program you wrote for Exercise 1 and modify it to solve the "Paths through a Cube, Part 1" puzzle.

4. Copy the program you wrote for Exercise 1 and modify it to solve the "Paths through a Cube, Part 2" puzzle.

5. Write an animated program that shows the progress of the three planes in the "Amelia Earhart Returns" puzzle. For simplicity, you can represent the planes with simple shapes such as rectangles filled to show their fuel levels.

6. Write an animated program that shows the progress of the four people who participated in the rescue in the "Desert Plane Crash, Part 1" puzzle. For simplicity, you can represent the people with simple shapes such as rectangles filled to show the number of rations they are carrying.

15

Non–Intuitive Numbers

These puzzles have numeric solutions. Some have tricky solutions that require you to look at the problem in a certain way. Others have long algebraic solutions that may be straightforward but that are a lot of work.

FLOWER TEMPLES

> **Puzzle:** A monk wants to visit each of the three flower temples: the Lotus Temple, the Lily Temple, and the Dandelion temple. He must leave the same number of flowers at each temple or the guardian of the temple that got the fewest flowers will grow angry and attack.
>
> The temples cling precariously to a cliff on one side of a valley. At the base of the cliff is a mystical river that the monk must cross to reach each of the temples. When the monk crosses the river, it magically doubles the number of flowers that he is carrying.
>
> How many flowers must the monk carry into the valley and how many must he leave at each temple so he can leave empty–handed?

First let's work through an example to make sure the rules are clear and to see what happens. Suppose the monk starts with four flowers and leaves five flowers at each temple.

He crosses the river to visit the Lotus Temple, and the river doubles his four flowers to eight. Suppose he leaves five flowers at the Lotus Temple and then climbs back down the cliff with three flowers remaining.

Next he crosses the river again to visit the Lily Temple, and the river doubles his three flowers to six. He leaves five at the Lily Temple and climbs back down the cliff with one flower remaining.

The monk crosses the river a final time to visit the Dandelion Temple, and the river doubles his one flower to two. He leaves two flowers at the Dandelion Temple, but that's not the same number he left at the other two temples, so the Dandelion Temple guardian attacks and besets the monk with terrible hay fever.

That solution didn't work, so the monk cannot start with four flowers and leave five at each temple. You can use trial an error to find a solution, but that would take a while unless you're remarkably lucky.

Instead of just guessing, you can use algebra to solve the puzzle. Let X be the initial number of flowers the monk has and let Y be the number of flowers that the monk leaves at each temple.

When the monk visits the Lotus Temple, the river doubles his flowers to 2×X. He leaves Y flowers at the temple, so he leaves with 2×X–Y flowers.

When the monk visits the Lily Temple, the river doubles his flowers to 2×(2×X–Y). He leaves Y flowers at the temple, so he leaves with 2×(2×X–Y)–Y flowers. Rearranging a bit gives you 4×X–3×Y flowers.

When the monk visits the Dandelion Temple, the river doubles his flowers to 2×(4×X–3×Y). He leaves Y flowers at the temple, so he leaves with 2×(4×X–3×Y)–Y flowers. Rearranging that gives 8×X–7×Y flowers.

Because the monk wants to leave empty–handed, we know that his final number of flowers 8×X–7×Y must be equal to zero. That means the monk can use any integers for X and Y as long as they satisfy the following equation.

$$8 \times X - 7 \times Y = 0$$

If you solve this equation for X, you get:

$$X = \frac{7}{8}Y$$

The smallest values for X and Y that satisfy this equation are X=7 and Y=8, so the monk begins with seven flowers and leaves eight flowers at each temple. Let's quickly work through the story again to see that those numbers work.

Before the Lotus Temple, the river doubles the monk's seven flowers to 14. The monk leaves eight flowers at the temple and keeps six.

Before the Lily Temple, the river doubles the monk's six flowers to 12. The monk leaves eight flowers at the temple and keeps four.

Before the Dandelion Temple, the river doubles the monk's four flowers to eight. The monk leaves eight flowers at the temple and leaves empty–handed.

GEM SHRINES

> **Puzzle:** Having navigated the three flower temples, the monk must now visit the four gem shrines located in the Jade Fortress, Coral Palace, Pearl Pagoda, and Amber Apartment. The monk must leave the same number of gemstones at each shrine to appease their guardians.
>
> The shrines sit at the corners of a large square filled with crocodiles. Elevated walkways connect each of the shrines to a fountain in the center of the square.
>
> Before he visits each shrine, the monk must wash his hands in the fountain to cleanse himself of earthly influences. When he does that, the fountain magically doubles the number of gems he is carrying.
>
> How many gems must the monk start with and how many must he leave at each shrine so he can leave empty–handed? (His vow of poverty forbids him from leaving the square with any gems.)

This is similar to the "Flower Temples" puzzle and you can solve it in a similar way. Let X be the number of gems that the monk starts with and let Y be the number of gems he leaves at each shrine.

Before the monk visits the Jade Fortress, the fountain doubles his gems to 2×X. He leaves Y gems at the shrine and leaves with 2×X–Y gems.

Before the monk visits the Coral Palace, the fountain doubles his gems to 2×(2×X–Y). He leaves Y gems at the shrine and leaves with 2×(2×X–Y)–Y=4×X–3×Y gems.

Before the monk visits the Pearl Pagoda, the fountain doubles his gems to 2×(4×X–3×Y). He leaves Y gems at the shrine and leaves with 2×(4×X–3×Y)–Y=8×X–7×Y gems.

Before the monk visits the Amber Apartment, the fountain doubles his gems to 2×(8×X–7×Y). He leaves Y gems at the shrine and leaves with 2×(8×X–7×Y)–Y=16×X–15×Y gems.

Setting that equal to zero and solving for X gives the following equation.

$$16 \times X - 15 \times Y = 0$$

$$X = \frac{15}{16} \times Y$$

The smallest values for X and Y that satisfy this equation are X = 15 and Y = 16. Here's a quick walkthrough to check the result.

Before the monk visits the Jade Fortress, the fountain doubles the monk's 15 gems to 30. The monk leaves 16 gems at the shrine and keeps 14 gems.

Before the monk visits the Coral Palace, the fountain doubles the monk's 14 gems to 28. The monk leaves 16 gems at the shrine and keeps 12 gems.

Before the monk visits the Pearl Pagoda, the fountain doubles the monk's 12 gems to 24. The monk leaves 16 gems at the shrine and keeps 8 gems.

Finally, before the monk visits the Amber Apartment, the fountain doubles the monk's 8 gems to 16. The monk leaves 16 gems at the shrine and leaves empty–handed.

SISTERS' AGES

> **Puzzle:** Chloe and Zoe are sisters. On her birthday Chloe says, "Hey, you're three times as old as me!" Zoe thinks about this and replies, "And in 4 years, you'll be half as old as me!" Having worked out these mathematical epiphanies, they eat Chloe's birthday cake.
>
> How old are Chloe and Zoe?

This type of puzzle is easy to solve algebraically. Let C be Chloe's age and let Z be Zoe's age. The fact that Zoe is now three times as old as Chloe means Z=3×C. In four years Chloe will be half as old as Zoe so C+4=(Z+4)/2.

If you use your favorite algebraic technique to solve these two equations with two unknowns, you'll find that C=4 and Z=12. (Chloe is very advanced mathematically for a four–year–old.)

BROTHERS' AGES

> **Puzzle:** Jack and Zack are brothers. Jack is 3/4 as old as Zack, and four years ago Jack was 2/3 as old as Zack. How old are Jack and Zack?

Let J be Jack's age and let Z be Zack's age. The fact that Jack is 3/4 as old as Zack means J=3/4×Z. The fact that four years ago Jack was 2/3 as old as Zack means J−4=2/3×(Z−4). Solving these two equations with two unknowns gives J=12 and Z=16.

SIBLINGS' AGES

> **Puzzle:** Kenny tells Jenny, "Hah! You're only 2/3 as old as I am!" Jenny thinks about it and replies, "True, but at the end of the year I'll be 3/4 your age!" How old are Kenny and Jenny?

Let K be Kenny's age and let J be Jenny's age. When Kenny says, "You're only 2/3 as old as I am," we learn two things. First, Kenny is older. Second, J=2/3×K.

When Jenny talks about "at the end of this year," the only thing that could have changed is that one or both of them has had a birthday. Because Jenny's age is a larger fraction of Kenny's after this happens, either both of them have had their birthdays or Jenny has had a birthday and Kenny hasn't had one.

First, let's assume that both Jenny and Kenny have had their birthdays. Then the fact that Jenny will be 3/4 of Kenny's age means J+1=3/4×(K+1). If you solve the two equations J=2/3×K and J+1=3/4×(K+1), you'll find J=2 and K=3. While it's possible that a two–year–old and a three–year–old are smart enough to do the math, it seems unlikely.

Now let's assume Jenny has had her birthday and Kenny hasn't had his. Then the fact that Jenny will be 3/4 of Kenny's age means J+1=3/4×K. If you solve the two equations J=2/3×K and J+1=3/4×K, you'll find J=8 and K=12. That makes a lot more sense than them being two and three years old.

SCARY EQUATIONS, PART 1

> **Puzzle:** What is 1/2 of 2/3 of 3/4 of 4/5 of 5/6 of 6/7 of 7/8 of 8/9 of 9/10 of 10,000?

These sorts of problems look scary because they involve a lot of terms. Fortunately there's always some trick that greatly simplifies the problem. Before you start blindly multiplying and dividing numbers together, read the whole problem carefully and look for the trick.

In this example all of the numerators cancel with all of the denominators except 1/10. That only leaves 1/10×10,000, which equals 1,000.

SCARY EQUATIONS, PART 2

> **Puzzle:** What is 1/2 of 2/3 of 3/4 of 4/5 of 5/6 of ... 99/100?

This time all of the numerators cancel with all of the denominators except for 1/100, so the answer is 1/100.

SCARY EQUATIONS, PART 3

> **Puzzle:** Suppose A=1, B=2, and so on up to Z=26. Then what is the product (A–X)×(B–X)×(C–X)×...×(Z–X)?

The trick here is to realize that somewhere in this long list of products is the term (X–X). That term has the value 0, so no matter how many other terms you multiply with that one the result is 0.

SCARY EQUATIONS, PART 4

> **Puzzle:** Suppose A=1, B=2, and so on to Z=26. Then what is the sum (A–X)+(B–X)+(C–X)+...+(Z–X)?

First you should look for a simple trick. In this equation, the terms don't cancel and everything isn't multiplied by 0, so you actually have to perform the calculation.

If you replace the letters with the numbers they represent, you get the following.

$$(1 - 24) + (2 - 24) + (3 - 24) + \cdots + (26 - 24)$$

You can rearrange this a bit to get the following.

$$(1 + 2 + 3 + \cdots + 26) - 26 \times 24$$

The sum 1+2+3+...+N equals $\frac{N \times (N+1)}{2}$ (you should memorize that equation) so the previous equation becomes:

$$\frac{26 \times 27}{2} - 26 \times 24 = 351 - 624 = -273$$

BROKEN EGGS

Puzzle: A farmer is taking her eggs to market when she hits a pothole and every egg is broken. When she calls her insurance agent, he asks her how many eggs she had.

Although she was careful to insure her eggs, she forgot to count them. However she remembers something odd about some egg arrangements she made the previous day out of sheer boredom. When she arranged the eggs in groups of 2, 3, 4, 5, or 6, there was always 1 egg left over, but when she arranged the eggs in groups of 7, there were no eggs left over. What is the minimum number of eggs she might have had?

Let E be the number of eggs. When the eggs were arranged in groups of 2, there was 1 egg left over. That means the number of eggs was odd or, more mathematically, $E \bmod 2 \equiv 1$.

Another way to look at it is that $(E-1) \bmod 2 \equiv 0$. In other words, 2 divides evenly into the value E–1 or E–1 is a multiple of 2.

Similarly the fact that there was one egg left over when the eggs were arranged in groups of 3, 4, 5, and 6 means that E–1 is a multiple of all of the numbers 2, 3, 4, 5, and 6.

The least common multiple of 2, 3, 4, 5, and 6 is $2 \times 2 \times 3 \times 5 = 60$, so the value E–1 must be a multiple of 60.

The final condition is that there were no left over eggs when they were arranged in groups of 7. That means $E \bmod 7 \equiv 0$.

Now all you need to do to find a solution is examine multiples of 60 as candidates for E–1, calculate E, and see if $E \bmod 7 \equiv 0$. Figure 15–1 shows some values of E–1, E, and E mod 7.

E–1	E	E mod 7
60	61	5
120	121	2
180	181	6
240	241	3
300	301	0

Figure 15–1: Possible numbers of eggs.

Figure 15–1 shows that the minimum number of eggs that the farmer could have had was 301.

Note that E mod 7 ≡ 0 if E=301+K×60×7=301+K×420 for any integer K. For example, E could be 721, 1141, 1561, 1981, 2401, and so forth.

FOOLISH ELVES

Puzzle: What digits do the letters represent in the following equation?

```
  ELF
 +ELF
 ————
 FOOL
```

This kind of puzzle has several names including cryptarithm, cryptarithmatic, and verbal arithmetic. In these puzzles each letter represents a digit, two letters cannot represent the same digit, and values such as ELF cannot begin with a leading zero. The goal is to figure out which letters represent which digits.

The best cryptarithms have unique solutions and use words that make some sort of sense, as in ELF+ELF=FOOL.

The following cryptarithm, which is probably the most famous, was published by mathematician Henry Dudeney in the July 1924 issue of *The Strand Magazine*.

```
  SEND
 +MORE
 —————
 MONEY
```

This is a tough puzzle that would be hard for most candidates to solve during an interview.

To solve the "Foolish Elves" puzzle, notice that the F in the result must come from carrying over from the thousands place. The largest amount that you can carry over when adding two digits is 1, so F must be 1. Replacing the Fs with 1s gives the following.

```
  EL1
 +EL1
 ————
 1OOL
```

If you look at the ones column, you can easily see that L must be 1+1=2.

```
  E21
 +E21
 ————
 1OO2
```

Looking at the tens column you can see that O must be 2+2=4.

```
  E21
+ E21
-----
 1442
```

Now look at the hundreds column. The only digit that you can add to itself to get 14 is 7 so E must be 7.

```
  721
+ 721
-----
 1442
```

SLEEPY TIME

Puzzle: What digits do the letters represent in the following equation?

```
  SHHH
-    S
------
   ZZZ
```

The only way to get rid of the S in the top number's thousands digit is if S is 1 and the hundreds column needs to borrow a 1. Setting S to 1 gives the following.

```
  1HHH
-    1
------
   ZZZ
```

We need the hundreds digit to borrow a 1, so H must be 0.

```
  1000
-    1
------
   ZZZ
```

Now you can simply subtract to find Z.

```
  1000
-    1
------
   999
```

THE DUCHESS'S WILL

Puzzle: After trying for years to figure out a way to take it with her, the duchess finally shuffles off the mortal coil. Her debts almost exactly cancel out the assets of her estate with one notable exception: her collection of valuable gold coins. For those, she has left the following rather bizarre instructions in a video will.

"To my faithful butler, Alfonse, I leave one gold coin.

"I leave 1/5 of the remaining coins to my eldest daughter, Adaliah.

"Then to my butler, Alfred, who's been so dedicated these 72 years, I leave one gold coin.

"Next I leave 1/5 of the remaining coins to my second daughter, Bashemath.

"To my loyal butler, Andrew, I leave one gold coin.

"Next I leave 1/5 of the remaining coins to my third daughter, Chiwa.

"Of course I wouldn't forget my trustworthy butler, Archer, to whom I leave one gold coin.

"To my fourth daughter, Dabria, I leave 1/5 of the remaining coins.

"Then to my staunch and upright butler, Artemis, I leave one coin.

" Finally, to my fifth daughter, Linda, I leave 1/5 of my remaining coins."

After a few moments, you hear the voice of the duchess's attorney coming from off–camera. "What about your five sons?"

To that the duchess replies, "Oh them. Who cares? Give them each 1/5 of whatever is left."

When the video ends, the duchess's butler, Richard, sniffs and says, "She never could remember my name."

At the same time, one of the sons mutters, "Sound mind and body, my foot!"

After a few minutes with a calculator, the attorney says, "Amazingly the old bird had exactly the right number of coins to make this weird behest possible."

What is the minimum number of coins the duchess could have had?

This puzzle is far too difficult to use in an interview. I've seen a couple of explanations of the solution and tried to come up with one myself, and they were more confusing than convincing.

You could try to guess the number of coins by trial and error, but even checking that a guess is correct takes some work and the correct answer isn't one of the first few guesses that you would make. It probably isn't even one of the first few thousand guesses you would make.

Figure 15–2 shows the number of the coins that each relative receives. The butler appears in the will five times so he gets five coins, just under different names.

Recipient	Amount	Coins remaining
Initial coins		3,121
Butler	1	3,120
Daughter 1	624	2,496
Butler	1	2,495
Daughter 2	499	1,996
Butler	1	1,995
Daughter 3	399	1,596
Butler	1	1,595
Daughter 4	319	1,276
Butler	1	1,275
Daughter 5	255	1,020
Each son	204	0

Figure 15–2: This table shows the disposition of the duchess's gold coins.

Although this problem is probably too hard for a job candidate to solve directly, it does make an interesting programming challenge. A program can easily use trial and error to find solutions. In fact, you could ask the candidate to allow the user to input the number of daughters and sons. For example, the program could then find a solution with seven daughters, seven sons, and coins divided into 1/7ths.

BASKET OF ORANGES

Puzzle: You have a basket of oranges and you decide to share. You give your mother half of the oranges plus an extra half orange. Then you give your father half of the remaining oranges plus an extra half orange. Finally you give your sister half of the remaining oranges plus an extra half orange. Then you realize that you didn't save any oranges for yourself.

How many oranges were originally in the basket?

There are a couple of strategies that you can use to solve this puzzle. The following sections show a backward chain of reasoning and an algebraic solution.

Backward Chain of Reasoning

It's not too hard to solve this puzzle by working backwards.

The basket ended up empty, so you gave your last oranges to your sister. You gave her half of your remaining oranges plus half an orange. That means the "half of your remaining oranges" must have been the same amount as the extra half orange. That means you gave your sister one orange in total.

Before that, you gave your father half of your remaining oranges plus half an orange, and you ended up with one orange to pass on to your sister. That means the one orange that you gave to your sister plus the bonus half orange that you gave to your father must add up to the same amount that you gave your father before the bonus. In other words, you gave your father 1.5 oranges plus half an orange for a total of two oranges. When you add in the one orange that you gave to your sister, you had three oranges before you gave any to your father.

Finally (or really initially), you gave your mother half of your oranges plus a half orange and ended up with three oranges. That means the half orange plus the three you had afterward must equal the number that you initially gave your mother. In other words, you gave her 3.5 oranges plus half an orange.

If "half of your oranges" was 3.5 oranges, then you started with seven oranges. Figure 15–2 shows how many oranges you gave to your relatives.

Recipient	# Oranges	Oranges remaining
Initial oranges		7
Mother	3.5 + 0.5 = 4	3
Father	1.5 + 0.5 = 2	1
Sister	0.5 + 0.5 = 1	0

Figure 15–2: This table shows how you gave away your oranges.

Maybe you can ask your mother for one of her oranges to fight off scurvy.

Algebraic Solution

You can also solve the problem algebraically. Let X be the initial number of oranges. Then Figure 15–3 shows the number of oranges at each step.

Recipient	# Oranges	Oranges remaining
Initial oranges		X
Mother	$\dfrac{X}{2} + \dfrac{1}{2}$	$X - \left(\dfrac{X}{2} + \dfrac{1}{2}\right)$ $= \dfrac{X}{2} - \dfrac{1}{2}$
Father	$\dfrac{1}{2} \times \left(\dfrac{X}{2} - \dfrac{1}{2}\right) + \dfrac{1}{2}$ $= \dfrac{X}{4} + \dfrac{1}{4}$	$\left(\dfrac{X}{2} - \dfrac{1}{2}\right) - \left(\dfrac{X}{4} + \dfrac{1}{4}\right)$ $= \dfrac{X}{4} - \dfrac{3}{4}$
Sister	$\dfrac{1}{2} \times \left(\dfrac{X}{4} - \dfrac{3}{4}\right) + \dfrac{1}{2}$ $= \dfrac{X}{8} + \dfrac{1}{8}$	$\left(\dfrac{X}{4} - \dfrac{3}{4}\right) - \left(\dfrac{X}{8} + \dfrac{1}{8}\right)$ $= \dfrac{X}{8} - \dfrac{7}{8}$

Figure 15–3: How you gave away your oranges.

The final number of oranges shown in Figure 15–3 is $\dfrac{X}{8} - \dfrac{7}{8}$. If you set that equal to zero and solve for X, you get 7, which agrees with the previous solution.

FRACTION REACTION

Puzzle: Which fraction is greater, $\dfrac{99^{999}+1}{99^{1000}+1}$ or $\dfrac{99^{1000}+1}{99^{1001}+1}$?

This is a somewhat complicated algebra problem.

First you might try to ignore the +1 terms because they're relatively insignificant compared to the large powers of 99. Unfortunately if you do that both fractions reduce to 1/99 so you can't tell which is greater.

You can also try plugging the fractions into a calculator. The powers of 99 are so large, however, that the +1 terms are insignificant and the calculator will probably think both fractions equal 1/99.

To solve the puzzle, you need to rearrange the values until you can find a form that makes the answer clear.

Another way to phrase the question is to ask whether the following equation is true.

$$\frac{99^{999}+1}{99^{1000}+1} > \frac{99^{1000}+1}{99^{1001}+1}$$

You can rearrange this to convert it into the following form.

$$(99^{999}+1) \times (99^{1001}+1) > (99^{1000}+1) \times (99^{1000}+1)$$

If you multiply out the products on both sides, you get the following.

$$99^{2000} + 99^{1001} + 99^{999} + 1 > 99^{2000} + 2 \times 99^{1000} + 1$$

Subtracting $99^{2000}+1$ from both sides gives you:

$$99^{1001} + 99^{999} > 2 \times 99^{1000}$$

Finally you can divide both sides by 99^{1000} to get:

$$99 + \frac{1}{99} > 2$$

Now it's easy to see that the left side is greater than the right side so the original equation is true and $\dfrac{99^{999}+1}{99^{1000}+1}$ is greater than $\dfrac{99^{1000}+1}{99^{1001}+1}$.

Follow–up: How is this puzzle relevant to programming?

This is one of those rare puzzles that is actually somewhat relevant. Sometimes when you perform numeric calculations, larger terms dominate the computer's representation of the result so the smaller terms are lost. In that case you may need to rearrange the calculation to prevent the smaller terms from being lost completely.

In this example, the powers of 99 are so large that they cannot be represented accurately even with 64–bit integers. That means you can't perform the straightforward calculation on most computers and get the right result.

ADVANCED AVERAGES

> **Puzzle:** Xavier, you, and Zander want to know the average of your salaries, but all of you want to keep your individual salaries secret. How can you calculate the average without giving away the salaries?

This puzzle is actually somewhat relevant for programmers, particularly if you're interested in cryptography and document signing.

The following sections describe four strategies that you can use to solve this problem.

Random Additions

Let's call Xavier's, yours, and Zander's salaries X, Y, and Z respectively. Then you can use the following protocol.

1. Xavier adds his salary X to a random number x. He passes the total X+x to you.
2. You add your salary Y and a random number y to the total. You pass the result X+x+Y+y along to Zander.
3. Zander adds his salary Z and a random number z to the total and passes the result X+x+Y+y+Z+z back to Xavier.
4. Now Xavier subtracts his original random number x leaving X+Y+y+Z+z. He passes the result to you.
5. You subtract your original random number y to get X+Y+Z+z, and you pass the result on to Zander.
6. Finally Zander subtracts his original random number z and announces the result, which is X+Y+Z. Now you can all divide by 3 to calculate the average.

This puzzle is as interesting for the follow–up questions as it is for the initial puzzle.

> **Follow–up:** Can you extend this algorithm for four or more people?

Sure. Just have each person add a random number and then remove it during the second round.

Follow–up: Does the algorithm work if there are only two people?

Not really. If you know the average of two salaries and you know your own salary, then you can calculate the other salary and there's no anonymity.

Follow–up: Suppose Xavier and Zander collude and tell each other the totals before and after you modify the values. Can they figure out your salary? Should you be concerned?

If Xavier and Zander share the values before and after you change them, then they know the following sums.

$$X+x$$
$$X+x+Y+y$$
$$X+Y+y+Z+z$$
$$X+Y+Z+z$$

Subtracting the first equation from the second tells them $Y+y$. Then subtracting that value from the third equation gives them $X+Z+z$. Finally subtracting that value from the fourth equation gives them Y and they have your salary.

This probably shouldn't concern you too much if Xavier and Zander really want to keep their salaries secret. If they collude to figure out your salary, then they each know their own salaries and they know yours, so they can calculate the other salary, too.

If Xavier and Zander don't care about sharing their salary information with each other, then no protocol can protect your salary because they can use their salaries plus the average to calculate your salary.

Of course either or both of them could lie about their salaries, but if your group is that untrusting then your workplace is probably some sort of Dilbertian soap opera and you might want to look for a new job.

Follow–up: Would the protocol work if only the first person included a random number?

As long as none of the other people collude, that should work. And if they do collude, you're doomed anyway.

Alternative Solution

During the first round, each person adds some fraction of his salary to the total. During the second round, each person adds the remainder of his salary to the total.

Random Pieces

Another method for calculating the average is to have each person divide his salary into three random pieces. For example, if your salary is $60,000, you could use $29,000, $17,000, and $14,000.

Next you each tell one of your three numbers to each of the other two people. You reserve the third number for yourself.

Each of you then adds the two partial numbers that he received from the others, adds on his reserved number, and announces the total. Now you can add the three totals to get a grand total and divide that by three to get the average.

> **Follow–up:** Suppose Xavier and Zander are whiners so if one of them has a salary smaller than the average, he immediately rushes to your boss to complain. What does that tell you about your salary relative to theirs?

If Xavier and Zander both rush to the boss, then you have the highest salary. If neither of them goes to see the boss, then you have the lowest salary.

The more ambiguous case is if one of them goes to the boss and the other doesn't. Suppose Xavier complains but Zander doesn't. If your salary is above the average, then you know that Xavier has the lowest salary. Conversely if your salary is below the average, then Zander has the highest salary. However, the example salaries in Figure 15–4 show that you can't tell whether your salary is in the middle of the other two.

Xavier	You	Zander	Average
$30,000	$40,000	$80,000	$50,000
$45,000	$40,000	$65,000	$50,000
$30,000	$70,000	$80,000	$60,000
$45,000	$70,000	$65,000	$60,000

Figure 15–3: Example salaries.

You have the middle salary in the first row and the lowest in the second row, but in both cases the average salary is the same. Similarly you have the middle salary in the third row and the highest salary in the fourth row, even though the average is the same in those rows.

Figure 15–3 shows that you can't be sure of the relative arrangement of the salaries.

Concluding that you can't definitively deduce the order of salaries will probably be hard for most candidates because candidates assume that interview questions always have nice, tidy answers.

Confidential Mediator

A third strategy for finding the average salary is to use a confidential mediator. For example, you could ask the Human Resources manager to calculate and tell you the average.

If you don't trust the Human Resources manager to calculate the average correctly, you could write a program to do this. It would display a prompt asking someone to enter a salary. It would then save that salary and prompt for the next salary. After everyone was done entering salaries, the program would calculate and display the average.

SUMMARY

Often you can use algebra to solve this kind of numeric puzzle. In some cases, such as in the "Duchess's Will" puzzle, the algebra can be so convoluted that it's very difficult to solve manually. Even then it's usually not hard to make a program to finds a solution through trial and error.

Before you start any long calculation, however, be sure to look for trick solutions. See if numerators and denominators cancel or if some term is multiplying by zero.

PROGRAMMING EXERCISES

1. Write a program to solve the "Flower Temples" puzzle by trial and error.
2. Write a program to solve the "Gem Shrines" puzzle by trial and error.
3. Write a program to solve "The Duchess's Will" by trial and error.
4. Write a program that implements the "Confidential Mediator" strategy for solving the "Advanced Averages" puzzle.
5. Write a program that finds all solutions to the cryptarithm SEND+MORE=MONEY.
6. Write a program that lets the user enter three strings and then solves the cryptarithm *string1+string2=string3*.

16

Artful Arrangements

These puzzles require you to find clever arrangements of objects, connect objects in patterns, or find ways to make objects move to solve problems. The solutions are generally pretty easy to remember, so candidates who have seen them before probably won't have too much trouble solving them. In a few cases you can breathe new life into a problem by adding more objects.

NINE DOTS

Puzzle: Connect the dots shown in Figure 16–1 with four or fewer straight lines without lifting your pencil off of the paper.

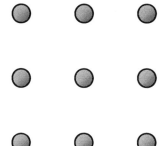

Figure 16–1: Connect the nine dots using four or fewer connected straight lines.

This is the quintessential example of an "outside the box" puzzle. In fact, Wikipedia believes that the term "outside the box" originated with this puzzle because the solution requires you to draw outside of the box defined by the nine dots. (See `en.wikipedia.org/wiki/Thinking_outside_the_box`.)

Figure 16–2 shows one possible solution.

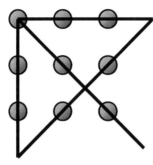

Figure 16–2: One solution to the "Nine Dots" puzzle.

Follow–up: How many different solutions are there to the "Nine Dot" puzzle?

There is only one type of solution to this puzzle and it's shown in Figure 16–2. The question then becomes, "How many different ways can you arrange the solution shown in Figure 16–2?"

Each solution begins (or ends) in one of the four corners. You can also follow each path in one of two directions depending on whether you turn left or right at the path's first corner. Figure 16–3 shows the two different versions of the solution that starts in the lower right corner.

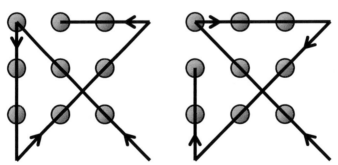

Figure 16–3: Each solution has 2 directions.

You can start in any of the four corners and you can go in two directions at each first turn, so there is a total of 4×2=8 possible solutions.

All of the solutions are rotations and reflections of each other, however, so you could say there's only one topologically unique solution with eight variations.

SIXTEEN DOTS

Puzzle: Connect the dots shown in Figure 16–4 with six or fewer straight lines without lifting your pencil off of the paper.

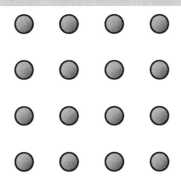

Figure 16–4: Connect the 16 dots using six or fewer connected straight lines.

Figure 16–5 shows two solutions.

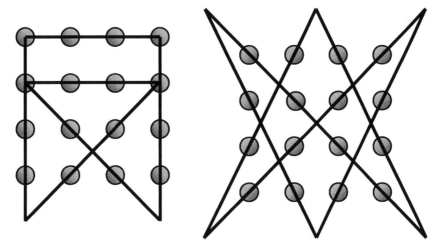

Figure 16–5: Two ways to connect 16 dots with six connected lines.

Variations: You can try to connect grids containing more dots. For example, you can connect 25, 36, or even more dots. Working through bigger arrays of dots might make an interesting group project.

THREE HOUSES AND THREE WELLS

Puzzle: Connect three houses to three wells without the pipelines crossing.

There is no way to connect each house to the three wells using three separate pipelines without the pipelines crossing. Basically the pipelines from two of the houses block the 3rd house from connecting to some of the three wells.

Figure 16–6 shows one possible solution.

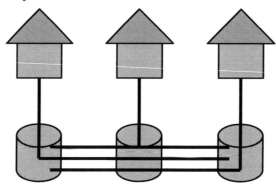

Figure 16–6: Connecting three houses to three wells without the pipelines crossing.

In this solution the pipelines don't cross, but each house really only uses a single pipeline that connects to all 3 wells.

TEN COINS

Puzzle: Arrange 10 coins so they form five straight lines containing four coins each.

If you put the coins in a grid, five lines containing four coins each would contain a total of 20 coins. You only have 10 coins, so you know that the lines must cross each other so they can share coins.

Figure 16–7 shows a solution.

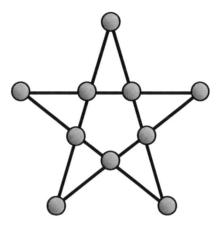

Figure 16–7: Ten coins in dive rows of four coins each.

Variation: Sometimes this puzzle tells the candidate to arrange the coins in four lines of four coins each. That may make the puzzle slightly harder because it doesn't mention the number five, which is a slight clue.

If you don't allow the previous solution because it uses 5 lines, you can just pull one of the outer coins back a bit along one of its lines until it moves off of its other line.

Variation: You can use similar puzzles where coins make other star shapes. For example, "Arrange 14 coins in seven lines of four coins each." In more complicated stars you can also add more coins where the lines intersect. For example, "Arrange 21 coins in seven lines of six coins each." These kinds of variations aren't too hard if you work up from the five–pointed star, but they can be very hard otherwise.

Variation: You can create other puzzles by drawing just about any shape with crossing straight lines and then place a coin at each point of intersection. You should stick with relatively simple shapes, however, and be prepared for candidates to find solutions other than yours.

CLEVER CAMPFIRE

Puzzle: Camp Wannamaykabuk has five cabins: Alpha Ants, Barking Rabbits, Coffee Patrol, Duct Tape Excellency, and Esteemed Deniers of Common Sense. (As you can probably guess, the kids get to name their own cabins.) Each cabin contains four campers and one counselor.

Before the campfire begins, the campers and counselors must arrange themselves into five lines of six people each. How can they do that?

Figure 16–8 shows a solution.

Figure 16–8: Arranging 25 people in five lines, each containing six people.

If you place the counselors at the corners, no campers from different cabins need to be next to each other.

(And remember, if your marshmallow catches fire, put it out by blowing on in. Don't wave it around and get it tangled in someone's hair!)

ARBORETUM

Puzzle: Professor Fuller taught geometry at a community college for many years, and that left him both extremely rich and somewhat eccentric. When he retired, he designed a modest 66,000 square foot bungalow complete with firenado Tiki torches, glow–in–the–dark toilet seats, and a sunken capybara pit. To feed the inhabitants of his indoor koala sanctuary, he wants you to plant a group of four eucalyptus trees where each tree is exactly 40 feet from the others.

Is that possible?

It's impossible to locate four objects all the same distance from each other on a flat surface, but you can do it in three–dimensions if you place the objects on the vertices of a tetrahedron. Simply create a hill that fills a tetrahedron and place the trees where the tetrahedron's vertices would be.

After Professor Fuller hears about your plan, he decides that the hill should be a tetrahedral pyramid with the trees at the vertices.

WE ROBOTS

Puzzle: Suppose two identical robots will parachute onto different positions on the real number line. Unfortunately the robots have very limited senses (there's too much electronic interference along the number line for radar) so they can only detect objects when they are within 1 unit of them.

How can you program the robots to find each other?

Note that the robots are identical so they need to both execute the same program.

If the candidate gets stuck, you can mention that the robots can leave their parachutes where they land as markers.

One solution that appeals to many programmers is to use an expanding binary search. Each robot moves one step left, then two steps right, then four steps left, then eight steps right, and so on until one of them finds a parachute. That robot then moves back and forth between the two parachutes until the other robot finds it.

That solution requires the robots to count so they can keep track of how far they should go at each step, and unfortunately we didn't say that the robots could count. Of course we didn't say they couldn't count, either, and what kind of robot can't count? Then again, what kind of robot can parachute onto the real number line but can't communicate with another robot via radio? The first variation described shortly prohibits this solution because counting isn't one of the allowed commands.

If a candidate offers this solution, ask if there is a solution that doesn't require counting.

One solution that doesn't require counting makes both robots move at one ups (units per second) to the right. If one of them finds a parachute, then that means it is the left robot and it has found the right robot's starting point. At that point it starts moving two ups to the right so it will eventually catch up with the right robot.

Variation: Some versions of the puzzle have the robots appear on the number line and then spray out oil to mark their positions instead of using parachutes. Some also allow you to use only four commands:

1. Move 1 step left
2. Move 1 step right
3. Skip the next instruction if there is oil at this position
4. Go to *label* where *label* is a line number as in a BASIC program

Follow–up: How soon will the left robot catch up to the right robot after it finds the parachute?

If the robots start N units apart, then it takes N steps for the left robot to find the right robot's parachute. During the next N seconds, the right robot will travel N additional units so it will be $2 \times N$ units from its starting position. During that same N seconds, the left robot will move $2 \times N$ units from the right robot's parachute and will catch the right robot.

That means the total elapsed time until the robots meet is $2 \times N$ seconds.

Follow–up: Suppose the robots' top speed is 10 ups. What speeds should they use to find each other as quickly as possible?

Let S be the robots' initial speed and let D be the initial distance between the robots. Then the time it takes the left robot to find the right robot's parachute is D/S.

Clearly the left robot's final speed should be as fast as possible. After it finds the right robot's parachute, there's no point in dawdling, so from now on it moves at 10 ups.

When the left robot finds the right robot's parachute, the right robot has traveled distance D from its starting point so that's how much distance the left robot needs to close. The difference between the robots' speeds is 10–S, so it takes time D/(10–S) for the left robot to close the gap.

That means the total time for the left robot to catch the right robot is $T = D/S + D/(10-S)$. Rearranging a bit gives the following.

$$T = D \times \frac{(10 - S) + S}{S \times (10 - S)} = D \times \frac{10}{10 \times S - S^2}$$

The distance D is determined by the luck of where the robots land so there's nothing you can do about it. You can minimize the fractional piece by making the denominator as large as possible. You can use calculus or whatever your favorite method is to find that maximum occurs when S=5.

That means the solution is to make the initial speed five ups and to make the left robot speed up to 10 ups when it finds the right robot's parachute. The total time until the robots meet is D×2/5 seconds.

ROBOTS ON A PLANE

> **Puzzle:** Suppose two identical robots will parachute onto different positions on the X–Y plane. Unfortunately the robots have very limited senses so they can only detect objects when they are within 1 unit of them.
>
> How can you program the robots to find each other?

In the "We Robots" puzzle, the number line had convenient notions of left and right. In two dimensions there isn't a single direction, such as right, that the robots can take to guarantee that one of the will eventually find the other's parachute. This time the robots are going to need to search around a bit, and that means they will need to count.

One solution is for each robot to start spiraling outward in a clockwise direction. It goes one unit east, one unit south, two units west, two units north, three units east, three units south, and so on until one of the robots finds the other robot's parachute.

When one of the robots finds the other's parachute, it moves back and forth on a direct line between the two parachutes. Eventually the second robot will find the first robot's parachute and also begin shuttling between the parachutes. Then the robots will meet somewhere along the path between the two parachutes.

SWAN LAKE

> **Puzzle:** In the Land of Enchanted Animals, an intelligent swan floats in the center of a perfectly circular lake. At the edge of the lake an equally intelligent wolf waits hoping to eat the swan. The wolf knows it

can't outswim the swan, but it moves four times as fast on land as the swan swims.

If the swan approaches the shore, the wolf will run over to meet it. If the swan can reach the shore without the wolf beating it there, it can escape into the forest.

What path can the swan take to escape?

This is a hard puzzle if you haven't seen it before. It's even hard to explain if you *have* seen it before.

First note that the swan can't just race for the shore because the wolf is too fast. For example, suppose the swan starts at the center of the lake and swims as fast as it can for the shore on the side of the lake opposite where the wolf is. If the lake has radius R and the swan can swim at speed S, then the swan must swim distance R in time R/S.

Meanwhile the wolf runs at speed 4×S halfway around the lake's shore. The distance is π×R, so it takes the wolf π×R/(4×S)=π/4×R/S time. The value π is less than 4, so the fraction π/4 is less than 1 and the wolf will arrive first and will await the swan with a knife, fork, and bib.

However, suppose the swan could start partway across the lake with the wolf on the opposite shore as shown in Figure 16-9. Suppose the swan is distance D from shore. Then it needs time D/S to get to shore. Meanwhile the wolf still needs time π/4×R/S to run halfway around the lake. If D is small enough, then the swan will make it shore and escape.

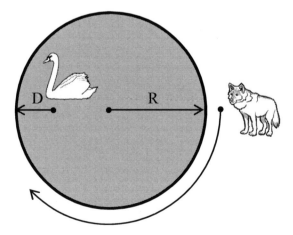

Figure 16–9: The swan's escape plan.

If the swan can swim the distance D before the wolf can run halfway around the lake, then the swan can escape.

If we set D/S<π/4×R/S, we can solve for D to get D=π/4×R. So if the distance D is less than π/4×R, then the swan can escape.

We still need a way for the swan to get into the position shown in Figure 16–9. If the swan simply moves towards the edge of the lake, the wolf will follow so he won't be on the opposite side of the lake as shown in the figure.

The trick is to notice that the swan can swim in a small circle around the middle of the lake more quickly than the wolf can run around the shore. For example, the swan can make a circle with radius one foot around the center of the lake very quickly. Meanwhile the wolf must run all the way along the shore to stay as close to the swan as possible. As long as the radius of the swan's circle is less than R/4, the wolf can't keep up.

Now consider again the distance D that the swan must swim to escape. If D is π/4×R, then the distance from that point to the center of the lake is (1–π/4)×R. The value π/4 is a bit greater than 3/4, so (1–π/4) is a bit less than 1/4. That means the point of escape is inside the limit where the swan can circle faster than the wolf. Figure 16–10 shows the new situation.

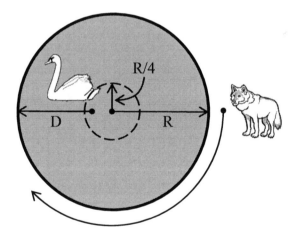

Figure 16–10: The swan's escape point is inside the limit where the swan can circle faster than the wolf.

Now we can devise a strategy for the swan. The swan should swim to a point between R/4 and (1–π/4)×R distance from the center of the lake. It should then swim in a circle around the center of the lake. The wolf will try to follow but will slowly fall behind. Eventually the wolf will be 180° behind on the opposite side of the lake. When that happens, the swan should turn toward the nearest shore and make a break for it.

An alternative solution is to spiral out from the center of the lake until the wolf is 180° behind and then dash for freedom.

Or the swan could just fly away. Those wings aren't just for show!

DOMINOES

> **Puzzle:** Suppose you have an 8×8 chessboard and a set of dominoes, each of which exactly covers two squares on the board. You can easily cover the board with the dominoes.
>
> Now suppose I remove two squares from opposite corners of the board. Can you still cover the entire board? Why or why not?

You can give it a try, but you'll probably grow frustrated (or bored) because there's no way to do this.

Opposite corners on a chessboard have the same color; either they're both black or they're both white. When you remove the opposite corners, the board is left with 30 squares of one color and 32 squares of the other.

Each domino covers one white square and one black square so, after you place 30 dominoes on the board, two squares of the same color will be left. Squares with the same color are never adjacent to each other, so you can't cover them with a single domino.

> **Follow–up:** Can you tile the chessboard if you remove all four corner squares?

This is actually quite easy. Just put three dominoes horizontally on the first and last rows. Then place four dominoes horizontally on the other rows.

> **Follow–up:** On a 7×7 chessboard, squares on opposite corners would also have the same color, but a 7×7 board wouldn't have the same number of black and white squares. In that case, could you cover a 7×7 chessboard with dominoes if you remove the opposite corners?

You still can't do it. A 7×7 chessboard would have 49 squares so you couldn't cover them in pairs.

SQUARE STICKS

Puzzle: The arrangement of sticks shown in Figure 16–11 defines 14 squares. Can you find them? Can you remove four sticks and leave only five squares? Starting from the original arrangement, can you remove six sticks and leave only three squares?

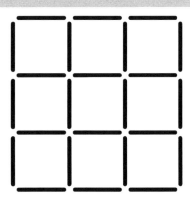

Figure 16–11: These sticks define 14 squares.

The 14 squares include nine small 1×1 squares, four medium 2×2 squares, and one large 3×3 square. For more information about counting squares, see the square counting puzzles in Chapter 13, "Creative Counting."

When you remove sticks, the idea is to not leave any "sticking out." For example, if you removed the leftmost stick on the top in Figure 16–11, then the topmost stick on the left would be sticking up. When you're done, both ends of every stick should connect to at least one other stick.

The picture on the left of Figure 16–12 shows one way you can remove four sticks to leave only five squares. The picture on the right shows how you can remove six sticks to leave only three squares.

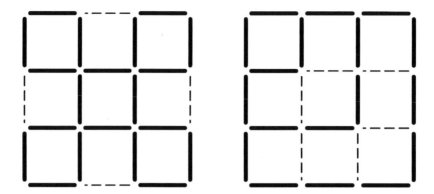

Figure 16–12: Now the sticks define five squares (left) and three squares (right).

Stick arrangement puzzles offer some test of the candidate's ability to visualize spatially, although that may not be very directly relevant for many jobs. They can lead to discussions about other arrangements, however. For example, you might try to work together to see how few sticks you can remove to make other symmetric designs.

TRIANGLE STICKS

Puzzle: The arrangement of sticks shown in Figure 16–13 defines 10 triangles. Can you find them? Starting from the original arrangement, can you remove four, five, six, or seven sticks and leave only four triangles?

Figure 16–13: These sticks define 10 triangles.

The 10 triangles include eight small triangles and two large triangles consisting of four smaller triangles each.

Figure 16–14 shows how you can remove four, five, six, or seven sticks and leave only four triangles.

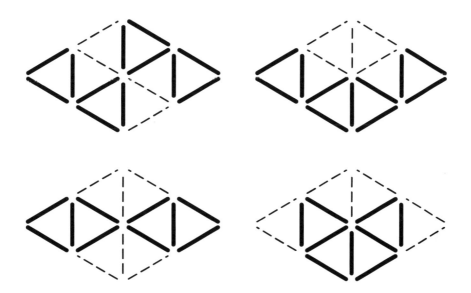

Figure 16–14: These arrangements all leave only four triangles.

You can find many similar puzzles by searching online for "stick puzzles" and "matchstick puzzles."

SUMMARY

Most of these puzzles are fairly easy if you've seen them before. The "Swan Lake" puzzle would be extremely difficult if you've never seen the solution. Even if you have seen it, working out the mathematics can be challenging.

The "dots" and "sticks" puzzles may offer the best possibilities for interview puzzles. They offer many variations and it's easy to make up your own.

PROGRAMMING EXERCISES

1. Write a graphical program that lets the user solve the "Nine Dots" problem. The program should draw the dots. Then the user should click five times to define the four connected lines that intersect the dots.
2. Repeat Exercise 1 for the "Sixteen Dots" puzzle.
3. Write a graphical program that lets the user solve the "Ten Coins" puzzle. The user should drag the coins into position and then draw lines through them.
4. Write an animated program that simulates part of the "Swan Lake" puzzle. Let the user drag the swan and wolf into positions. Then make the swan swim for the nearest shore while the wolf runs along the shore.

5. Modify the program you wrote for Exercise 4 so the swan circles around the center of the lake until the wolf falls behind. Then make the swan head for freedom while the wolf runs around the shore.

6. Modify the program you wrote for Exercise 5 so the swan escapes by spiraling out from the center of the lake.

7. Write an animated program that graphically simulates the "We Robots" puzzle.

8. Write an animated program that graphically simulates the "Robots on a Plane" puzzle.

9. Write a graphical stick removal program. The program should display sticks in an initial position. It should then let the user remove the sticks by clicking on them.

17

Outside the Box

These puzzles make you think outside the box. They can be extremely difficult because they usually don't contain any clues about the solution. They may even be designed to point you in the wrong direction. To make matters worse, the solutions to many of these problems are fairly easy to remember if you've seen them before.

HEADS OR TAILS

Puzzle: Because your last insurance premium was one day late, you've been kidnapped by a gang of tough actuaries. They seat you blindfolded in front of a table on which you can feel 10 coins.

The actuaries' leader tells you that five are showing heads and five are showing tails, although they've been worn smooth by hundreds of previous kidnap victims, so you can't feel which are which.

If you can put them in 2 piles containing the same number of heads, they'll let you go. Otherwise they'll raise your rates by 1.375%!

How can you make the piles of coins?

This is a lot easier than it sounds. Just make two piles of five coins each. Then flip all of the coins in one pile over. The trick is in seeing why this works. (And you should ask the job candidate that as a follow–up.)

To see why this works, suppose you make two piles A and B each containing five coins. Let H be the number of heads in pile A. Because pile A contains five coins, it must contain 5–H tails.

Originally there were five coins showing heads, so if pile A contains H of them, then pile B must contain the other 5–H. When you flip the coins in pile B, heads become tails and vice versa, so the 5–H heads become 5–H tails. Then because pile B contains five coins, it must now hold 5–(5–H)=H heads.

Therefore both piles contain H heads and 5–H tails.

Variations: Different versions of the puzzle use different numbers of coins, or they use different objects such as cards.

Follow–up: What conditions on the number of coins must be satisfied for the puzzle to work?

You can use any number of coins as long as there is initially the same number of heads and tails. That implies that the total number of coins is even.

INVERTED CARDS

Puzzle: The actuaries in the "Heads or Tails" puzzle aren't really such bad guys, so after they release you, they invite you to play some poker with them. (Five–card draw.) Right after one of them has dealt the cards, the lights go out.

After a few moments of confusion, the dealer says, "Okay everybody put your cards face–up in the middle of the table." He then picks up the cards and shuffles them back into the deck face–up. There were four of you playing and you each had five cards, so the deck now contains 20 cards that are face–up and 32 cards that are face–down all shuffled together.

The dealer then says, "I'll bet you a nickel that you can't divide the cards into two piles that contain the same number of face–up cards." (Actuaries don't take big chances with money so the bet is only a nickel.) How can you divide the cards into two piles containing the same number of heads–up cards in the dark and claim your just reward?

Like the "Heads or Tails" puzzle, this one is easier done than explained. Simply take the top 20 cards off of the deck, turn them over, and place them in a pile. That pile will have the same number of face–up cards as the remaining pile of 32–card pile does.

Then you can all wait around until the lights come back on to see if you're right.

As before, the trick is in seeing why this works. (And again you should ask the candidate why it works as a follow–up.)

Let F be the number of face–up cards in the pile of 20 cards that you make. There are 20 face–up cards in all, so the rest of the deck contains 20–F face–up cards.

The pile contains 20 cards and initially it contains F cards that are face–up, so it initially also contains 20–F face–down cards. When you flip the pile over, those cards become face–up cards, so the flipped pile ends up with 20–F face–up cards. That's the same as the number that the rest of the deck holds so the two piles hold the same number of face–up cards.

Variations: Different versions of the puzzle use different numbers of face–up cards, or they use different objects such as coins.

Follow–up: Would this trick still work if there were six people playing poker? (In that case there would be 30 face–up cards, which is more than half of the deck, so the real question is, "Does the trick still work if more than half of the deck is in the pile you make?")

Yes it still works as long as the new pile contains the same number of cards as are face–up.

Follow–up: What conditions must the number of face–up cards satisfy to make the trick work?

You must have between one and 51 face–up cards. The trick still sort of works for one or 52 face–up cards, but in those cases one of the "piles" of cards is empty.

Follow–up: Suppose you divide the cards as in the solution described above so you have two piles containing 20 cards and 32 cards. What happens if you flip over the pile of 32 cards instead of the pile of 20 cards?

If 20–card pile contains F face–up cards, then the 32–card pile contains 20–F face–up cards and 32–(20–F)=12+F face–down cards. When you flip them over, the face–down cards become face–up cards, so the 32–card pile now contains 12+F face–up cards. There is no value that can make F equal to 12+F so that won't work.

For a simple counter–example, suppose the top 20 cards include 10 that are face–up. Then when you flip the 32–card pile, it will contain 10 face–down cards and 22 face–up cards.

Follow–up: Can you think of any conditions where flipping the "leftover" pile would work?

That would only work if you have 26 face–up cards so you divide the deck into two piles of equal size. Then you can flip either pile. (That's basically the solution to the "Heads or Tails" puzzle.)

CRAZY CLOCKWORKS, PART 1

Puzzle: Consider the gears shown in Figure 17–1. If you turn the upper left gear clockwise, in which direction does the lower right gear turn?

Figure 17–1: Gears that are connected by their teeth, crossed belts, and uncrossed belts.

Gear problems such as this one look complicated but are really quite simple to solve. There are only two directions that the gears can turn, clockwise and counterclockwise, so you only need to keep track of which direction a particular gear is turning. To do that, you only need to know the following three rules.

1. If two gears are connected by their teeth, then direction reverses.
2. If two gears are connected by a crossed belt, then direction reverses.
3. If two gears are connected by an uncrossed belt, then direction remains the same.

Starting at the drive gear, you can use the rules to step through the sequence of gears: counterclockwise, clockwise, counterclockwise, and so forth to the final gear, which is turning clockwise.

In fact, you can use the rules to solve the puzzle even more easily. Whenever two gears are connected by their teeth or by a crossed belt, the direction changes. The order in which the changes occurs doesn't matter. All that matters is the number of times the direction reverses.

So simply count the number of times two gears are joined by their teeth or by a crossed belt, and ignore any uncrossed belts. If the number is even, then the last gear's direction is the same as the first. If the number is odd, then the last gear's direction is reversed.

In this example, the gears are connected seven times by teeth and once by a crossed belt for a total of eight times. That means the final gear will turn in the same direction as the drive gear: clockwise.

CRAZY CLOCKWORKS, PART 2

Puzzle: Consider the gears shown in Figure 17–2. If you turn the upper left gear clockwise, in which direction does the lower right gear turn?

Figure 17–2: Gears that are connected to form a loop.

This puzzle is similar to the preceding one with one exception: the gears are connected to form a loop. Before you announce an answer, use the counting trick described for the preceding puzzle to follow the entire loop. When you're done, see if the direction you calculate for the drive gear is the same as its original direction.

If the drive gear's calculated direction is the same as its known initial direction, then perform the calculation again to find the direction of the lower right gear.

In this example the gears are connected nine times by teeth and twice by crossed belts for a total of 11 times. That number is odd, so the result will reverse the direction of the gears. In this example that means if you turn the drive gear clockwise, the loop tries to turn the drive gear counterclockwise. That means these gears are jammed, pushing against each other, so they cannot turn.

The answer to the puzzle is, if you try to turn the upper left gear clockwise, the lower right gear doesn't turn.

EGG DROP

> **Puzzle:** Suppose you have 2 nearly identical dragon's eggs. They both have the same strength characteristics but one wasn't fertilized so it can't hatch. (You can think of it as a practice egg.)
>
> To make the fertile egg hatch, you need to drop it from just high enough to make it crack. If you drop it from too low, nothing happens (except you get to climb the stairs again). If you drop it from too high, you get scrambled egg.
>
> Conveniently you're standing at the base of the KK100 building in Shenzhen, China. At 1,449 feet tall, it's one of the tallest buildings in the world. It also happens to have 100 floors, and you know that the eggs will crack if you drop them from somewhere between one and 100 floors. Unfortunately the building's elevators are out today, so it's critical that you figure out how high to drop the eggs in the fewest possible attempts.
>
> What is the quickest strategy for finding out from which floor you can drop the fertile egg to make it crack?

One approach would be to drop an egg from the 1st floor. If it survives, move to the 2nd floor. Continue that way, one floor at a time, until the egg cracks. That strategy would work, but it would be fairly slow. In the worst case, if the egg only cracks when dropped from the 100th floor, you would need to drop the egg 100 times. (And climb up and down the stairs each time. That's 1+2+3+...+100=5050 flights of stairs climbed both ways! Your Fitbit friends will be impressed but you may be unable to walk for a week afterward.)

Another approach would be to drop the infertile egg from the even–numbered floors: 2, 4, 6, and so on until it cracked. Then you would drop the fertile egg from one floor lower to see if that would be high enough to crack the eggs.

With this strategy, if the infertile egg cracks on the 100th floor, you would need to drop the infertile egg 50 times and the fertile egg once (to check the 99th floor) making a total of 51 drops. That's much better than the 100 drops required by the first strategy.

A third approach would be to try every 10th floor with the infertile egg. If that egg breaks on a particular floor, you use the fertile egg to check the nine floors below that one. In this strategy, each time the infertile egg survives a drop, you add another drop to the total necessary. For example, if it breaks on the 10th, 20th, 30th, or 40th floor, you use a total of 10, 11, 12, or 13 drops. In the worst case, if the infertile egg only cracks on the 100th floor, you need 19 drops. We're getting closer to a good solution.

We can further reduce the worst case if we try to make the total number of drops the same in all cases. In other words, if we use more drops with the fertile egg, we must reduce the number of drops with the fertile egg.

To follow this approach, suppose we first drop the infertile egg from floor N. Then that egg's second drop should skip N–1 floors. Later drops would skip N–2 floors, N–3 floors, and so forth.

Then if the infertile egg breaks on one of those floors, we would use the fertile egg to check N–1 floors, N–2 floors, N–3 floors, and so forth. The total number of drops in every case would be N.

Ideally if the infertile egg only breaks on the 100th floor, then we should need only one trial with the fertile egg to verify that it doesn't break on the 99th floor.

In that case, the last floor from which we drop the infertile egg is given by the equation:

$$N + (N - 1) + (N - 2) + (N - 3) + \ldots + 1$$

We need that floor to be at least the 100th floor. If we set the preceding equation equal to 100, we can solve for N.

$$N + (N - 1) + (N - 2) + (N - 3) + \ldots + 1 = 100$$

Rearranging this a bit gives the following.

$$N + (N - 1) + (N - 2) + (N - 3) + \ldots + (N - (N - 1)) = 100$$

Or:

$$N \times N - (1 + 2 + 3 + \cdots + N - 1) = 100$$

The sum $1+2+3+...+N-1$ equals $\frac{(N-1)\times N}{2}$, so this equation becomes:

$$N^2 - \frac{(N-1) \times N}{2} =$$

$$\frac{2 \times N^2 - (N-1) \times N}{2} =$$

$$\frac{N^2 + N}{2} = 100$$

Rearranging this again gives the following quadratic equation.

$$N^2 + N - 200 = 0$$

If you use the quadratic formula to solve this for N, you get the following results.

$$N = \frac{-1 \pm \sqrt{801}}{2}$$

So N≈–14.65 or N≈13.65. If you ignore the negative root and round the other solution up to the nearest integer, N=14.

Figure 17–3 shows the number of drops needed by the eggs for various floors.

The first column in Figure 17–3 shows the drop number for the 1st, infertile egg. The second column shows the floors where you should drop the 1st egg.

The third column shows the number of drops you need to make with the 2nd, fertile egg to identify the correct floor if the infertile egg cracks on a particular floor. For example, suppose the infertile egg cracks on floor 69. Then you need to use the fertile egg to check the eight floors 61 through 68.

The fourth column shows the total number of drops that you need to make in the worst case.

1st Egg Drop #	Floor	# 2nd Egg Drops	Total Drops
1	14	13	14
2	27	12	14
3	39	11	14
4	50	10	14
5	60	9	14
6	69	8	14
7	77	7	14
8	84	6	14
9	90	5	14
10	95	4	14
11	99	3	14
12	100	0	12

Figure 17–3: This table shows the number of drops needed to find the egg cracking point.

Follow–up: What is the minimum number of drops you might need of you use this strategy?

The minimum occurs if the eggs would crack on the 1st floor. In that case, you drop the infertile egg from floor 14 and it cracks. Then you use the second, fertile egg to check floors 1 through 13, and it cracks on floor 1. In that case you use a total of only two drops.

Follow–up: Under what circumstances do you use the maximum number of drops?

You need the maximum number of drops if the second, fertile egg breaks on the floor below where the infertile egg cracked. (Not counting the 100th floor, which is a special case.) For example, if the infertile egg cracks on floor 84 and the fertile cracks on floor 83, then you use a full 14 drops.

PIECE OF CAKE, PART 1

Puzzle: Suppose you baked a rectangular cake to share with your sister, but last night your spouse snuck into the kitchen and stole a piece. It was dark so the missing piece is a rectangle taken from somewhere in the middle of the cake but its edges are not necessarily aligned with those of the cake. Figure 17–4 shows the cake.

How can you use a single cut to divide the cake into two equally–sized pieces to share with your sister?

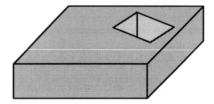

Figure 17–4: A cake that's missing a piece.

There are two solutions that work with a rectangular cake that's missing an arbitrarily positioned rectangular piece. First you can make a horizontal cut through the cake. That basically gives you two cakes with the same outline as the original cake but half as tall.

Unfortunately that also means the top half gets most of the frosting, and that could cause you to fight with your sister.

The second solution is to cut along the line connecting the cake's center and the missing piece's center as shown in Figure 17–5. The two circles mark the centers of the cake and the missing piece.

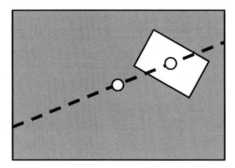

Figure 17–5: Cut along the dashed line.

Any line that passes through the center of a rectangle divides it into two equally–sized pieces. Because this line passes through the centers of both the cake and the missing piece, the two halves are as large as half of the cake minus half of the missing piece.

PIECE OF CAKE, PART 2

Puzzle: Suppose you made a round cake to serve to the eight members of your life–sized cribbage club. (You take turns being the pegs on an enormous board.) How can you use only three cuts to divide the cake into eight equal pieces?

First cut through the cake's diameter. Next make a second cut through the diameter that's perpendicular to the first cut. Finally cut through the cake horizontally. Figure 17–6 shows the cuts with dashed lines.

Figure 17–6: Cut along the dashed lines to divide the cake into 8 pieces.

Now you can have a cribbage tournament and the winners can decide whether they want the top pieces, which have the most icing.

FUNNY MONEY

Puzzle: After your life–sized cribbage club meeting, you and two others (Peg and Pone) decide to go out for dinner at your favorite Mongolian–Chinese restaurant, Khan Fusion. The check comes to $30 so you pay $10 each. (Tipping is not allowed at this restaurant.)

After you pay, the manager realizes that you were overcharged so he tells your server to refund $5. Realizing that the three of you can't spit $5 evenly, the server only returns $3 and pockets the remaining $2.

If you and your friends paid $9 each, and the server kept $2, that's a total of $29. Where did the other $1 go?

This puzzle causes confusion by adding up unrelated values. It conflates money you paid with money that was received. To solve the puzzle, you need to separate the different kinds of money.

First you can look at the money paid and received. The three of you each paid $9 for a total of $27. The restaurant received $25 and the server received $2 for a total of $27. The numbers match so no money has been lost.

For another way to look at the problem, consider who has the money at different points in time. Before you entered the restaurant, you and your friends each had $10 for a total of $30. After the meal is finished, the restaurant has $25, you and your friends have $1 each, and the server has $2. Again that adds up to $30 so no money has been lost.

BREAKFAST OF CHAMPIONS

Puzzle: Some of your friends decide to surprise you with a road trip so they appear on your doorstep at 4 AM. To help you get started quickly, they bring you a breakfast consisting of a bagel, a small container of cream cheese, a small jar of lox, a hard–boiled egg, a thermos of coffee, and a 44–ounce energy drink. What do you open first?

This kind of puzzle is specifically designed to test how well you "think outside the box." If you close your eyes and visualize exactly what you do when your friends arrive, you may realize that you need to open your front door before your friends can come in. In that case you may answer, "The front door."

If you think even more carefully, you may realize the official answer, "My eyes." (It's somewhat ironic if you have to close your eyes to visualize opening your eyes.)

Unfortunately this puzzle doesn't really ask you to visualize every step in detail so it's hard to guess the correct answer. It's also a very easy puzzle if you've seen it before.

BIRDS ON A WIRE

Puzzle: Ten birds are sitting on a telephone line. If you shoot one, how many are left?

Like the "Breakfast of Champions" puzzle, this one is supposed to test your ability to visualize a situation. Also like that puzzle, it can be hard to picture all of the details but it's extremely easy to remember the solution if you've seen the puzzle before.

The answer is, "There are no birds left because the other nine all fly away when they hear the gunshot."

PERIODICITY

Puzzle: What occurs twice in a week, once in a year, but never in a day?

This puzzle is also extremely easy if you've seen similar puzzles in the past.

This puzzle makes the most sense if someone asks you aloud. When written down the question really should be punctuated as, "What occurs twice in, 'A week,' once in, 'A year,' but never in, 'A day?'"

With the correct punctuation it's not too hard to see that the answer is, "The letter E."

LIGHT DELIGHT, PART 1

Puzzle: Suppose you're a lazy electrician. (Actually there's a saying, "A lazy electrician is a dead electrician." Or if there isn't such a saying, there should be. But for this puzzle, suppose you're a lazy electrician who hasn't fatally touched a live wire yet.) There's a room with three switches and one of them controls the bare light bulb hanging from the cracked ceiling in a nearby room.

How can you figure out which switch controls the light bulb with the fewest number of trips into the other room?

The glib answer (and what the electricians that I've known would do) is to send an apprentice into the other room, flip a switch, and shout, "How about now?"

The clever answer is to turn switches 1 and 2 on and wait for a minute or two. Then turn switch 2 off and go into the other room.

If the light is still on, then you know that switch 1 controls it.

If the light is off, touch the bulb. If you end up sucking on your burned fingers, then the light must have just been on and is now off, so switch 2 controls it.

If the light is off and cool, then switch 3 controls it.

Of course this doesn't work as well if the light has an LED bulb because they don't get very warm and don't stay warm for very long after you turn them off. If you have an LED bulb, stop being lazy and make an extra trip so you don't electrocute yourself.

LIGHT DELIGHT, PART 2

> **Puzzle:** Suppose you're a lazy electrician again. This time one room holds three switches and another room holds three light bulbs. How can you figure out which switches control which lights with the fewest number of trips into the other room?

This puzzle is relatively easy if you've seen the preceding puzzle, so it makes a good follow–up to that puzzle.

If you don't have an apprentice, turn on switches 1 and 2 and wait for a minute or two. Then turn off switch 2 and go into the other room.

The bulb that is still on is the one controlled by switch 1. The bulb that is off but still warm is controlled by switch 2. The other bulb is controlled by switch 3.

FIERY ISLAND

> **Puzzle:** Suppose you're flying a small plane in the South Pacific, looking for the island of liars and truth–tellers. Suddenly your engine splutters to a halt and you're forced to land on a small, uninhabited, brush–covered island.
>
> It's a good landing (at least you're alive and can walk), but the crash started a fire on the north end of the island. Now the wind is slowly blowing the fire south, pushing you in front of it toward the sea and the hungry sharks that always seem to show up on these occasions.

> How can you survive?

Walk up to the fire and take a burning branch. Move a hundred yards or so south and start a fire there. As the wind pushes the new fire south, follow it and stand in the burned out area. When the first fire reaches the burned out area, it will run out of fuel so it will stop.

Eventually you'll end up standing on an island covered in ashes. Hopefully someone will notice the smoke and come rescue you before you starve or die of thirst.

DR. PINCHPENNY

> **Puzzle:** Dr. Pinchpenny is scheduled to perform surgery on three people but he only has two pairs of gloves. How can he operate without any patient's blood touching any of the other patients or his hands?

First the doctor wears both pairs of gloves, one on top of the other, and he operates on patient 1.

Next he removes the outer pair, turning the gloves inside out and placing them on a sterile tray. (Because everything needs to be sterile!) He then operates on patient 2 with the inner pair of gloves.

Finally the doctor puts the pair of gloves that's on the tray back on with the clean side facing out and he operates on patient 3.

Hopefully Dr. Pinchpenny then discards the gloves instead of washing them to use them again.

BONUS APPLE

> **Puzzle:** Two fathers take their sons to the farmer's market and each of them buys an apple. When they turn away from the stall, they find that they have only three apples between them. How is that possible?

This puzzle relies on the ambiguity of words that describe relationships such as father, son, mother, and daughter. In this case, there were only three people: a boy, his father, and his grandfather. The grandfather is also a father, and the boy's father is also a son, so there are two fathers and two sons.

SPILLED MEDICINE

> **Puzzle:** You have a rare medical condition that requires you to take one each of two kinds of pills daily. You're leaving on a five–day vacation and, while you're at airport security juggling your laptop, shoes, and pocket contents, you drop the pills and the bottles break. (Note to self: Use sturdier bottles next time.) The two kinds of pills look exactly the same and are hopelessly mixed.
>
> If you go back to the pharmacy right now to get your prescriptions refilled, you'll miss your flight and have to pay a 130% flight change fee.
>
> How can you take your medicine safely so you don't have to miss your flight?

You can grind the pills and then mix the resulting powder thoroughly. Assuming you had five of each kind of pills to begin with, you can then take 1/5 of the powder each day.

Alternatively you could chop every pill into five pieces and keep each pill's pieces in a separate plastic bag. Then each day you can take 1/5 of each of the 10 pills.

GLOBE WALKER

> **Puzzle:** How many points are there on the globe where you can walk one mile south, one mile east, and one mile north and arrive where you started?

Obviously this won't work on a flat plane because you would basically be trying to follow the edges of a triangle that contains three right angles. Geometry on a sphere is weird, however, so there is a solution on the globe.

First you can start at the North Pole. You go one mile south (every direction is south from there) and then go one mile east. From that point one mile north puts you back at the North Pole. This gives you one location where you can start and an infinite number of directions that you can head to make the puzzle work.

Many people stop there and believe that there is only one place where this works.

However, this also works if you're the right distance (let's call it D_1) from the South Pole. If you start at the right distance, one mile south takes you closer to the South Pole. Then one mile east lets you make a complete circle around the South Pole so you arrive back at the point one mile south from where you started. Now one mile north puts you back where you started. There are an infinite number of such points that are distance D_1 from the South Pole, so there are an infinite number of places where this will work.

Many people think that *now* they have found all of the possible starting points, but there are more. *Many* more.

If you start another right distance (let's call this one D_2) from the South Pole, then the one mile east makes you go *two* complete laps around the South Pole. Then the one mile north puts you back where you started. There are an infinite number of points distance D_2 from the South Pole where this works.

In fact, for any positive integer N, there are an infinite number of points that are distance D_N from the South Pole where you can start and that make the one mile east take you N times around the South Pole.

In total there are an infinity of infinities of positions where you can start.

If you're trying to hire a mathematician, the candidate may be able to tell you that the total number of starting positions is the transfinite number $\aleph_1$, which is pronounced "aleph–one." If you're trying to hire anyone else, then the correct answer is, "A whole lot."

THE BEAR

> **Puzzle:** Suppose you walk one mile south, one mile east, and one mile north and arrive where you started. Then you see a bear. What color is the bear?

This is a variation of the "Globe Walker" puzzle. There are no bears in Antarctica so you can rule out the solutions near the South Pole. In that case, you must be near the North Pole and the only bears that live in that area are polar bears. Therefore the answer is, "White."

In fact polar bears have never been spotted closer than 100 miles from the North Pole, so the story doesn't quite work from a technical standpoint. You could change the puzzle to use 100 mile increments, but then you probably wouldn't want to walk that far. Then again, I wouldn't want to be walking around for any distance surrounded by polar bears.

STRANGE SIBLINGS

> **Puzzle:** Two children are born at the same hospital on the same day in the same year to the same parents, but they're not twins. How can that be?

The children aren't twins, they're triplets. (Or quadruplets, or quintuplets, or whatever.)

Another possible solution is that they were born on the same day of the week, for example a Monday, in different months of the same year. That solution relies on the ambiguity of the phrase "on the same day."

This type of puzzle relies on nit–picky little details or ambiguities in the English language. To solve this kind of puzzle if you haven't seen it before, you need to stumble across the language oddity involved.

Although these puzzles can be amusing, usually for the interviewer, they often require the candidate to make a glib, smart aleck response. The candidate usually doesn't spend much time on the puzzle and either sees the trick quickly or not at all. In either case there isn't much room for follow–up questions.

You can make these sorts of puzzles a bit more useful if you brainstorm with the candidate about other possibilities. For example, you could try to come up with parallel situations to use as riddles. Or you could try to think of alternative explanations for the same situation.

The next few puzzles follow the same sort of pattern.

OUT OF WATER

> **Puzzle:** Suppose you need to empty a bathtub and you have a teaspoon, a tablespoon, a 1/4 cup measuring cup, and a colander. What is the fastest way to empty the tub?

This type of puzzle relies on you thinking about the bigger situation and not the details. These sorts of puzzles encourage you to make a smart aleck response. In this example, the solution is to pull the plug.

Actually in this example it would be even faster to pull the plug and also use the 1/4 cup measuring cup to pour water down the sink. Or to pull the plug and start splashing water out of the tub onto the floor. Or do a cannonball into the tub, pull the plug, and then start splashing.

CALAMITOUS COFFEE

> **Puzzle:** A man orders a double skinny venti mochaccino. When it arrives, he finds a fly in it so he sends it back. The barista brings him another, but he quickly realizes that they gave him the same coffee. How did he know?

The customer had put sugar in his drink before he noticed the fly. When he got the coffee back, he could taste the sugar.

THE SHEIK'S WILL

> **Puzzle:** The Sheik heard about the Duchess's will (when he read Chapter 15). Not to be outdone, he decided to settle his own inheritance by making his two sons pass some ridiculous test. He decided that they would race to a nearby oasis and the son whose camel was slowest inherits the kingdom.
>
> Not wanting to miss the show, the sheik took a lawn chair, magazine, and pitcher of lemonade, made himself comfortable, and fired the starting gun. Startled, the two camels panicked and started racing across the desert. Soon the princes regained control and the camels started going slower and slower until they eventually lurched to a halt. The princes climbed from their saddles and sat by the side of the rode glaring at each other while the sheik laughed from a few hundred feet away.
>
> A few hours later, after finishing his magazine and lemonade, the sheik grew bored and shouted something to his sons. The princes exchanged glances, leapt onto the camels, and sped away as fast as they could.
>
> What did the sheik shout to his sons?

The sheik shouted, "Switch camels."

The will said that the son whose camel was slowest would inherit the kingdom. It didn't say anything about which prince got to oasis first.

Another solution would be for the sheik to shout, "I changed my mind! Whoever gets there first wins!" That might be more realistic but it wouldn't be as clever, so if a candidate offers that solution or something similar, you could say, "That would work, but can you think of another solution?"

STAIRMASTER

> **Puzzle:** A man living on the 20th floor of an apartment building takes the elevator to the ground floor every day on his way to work. On the way home, if it's raining or if there's someone else in the elevator, he takes the elevator all the way to the 20th floor. If it's sunny and if no one else is present, he takes the elevator to the 10th floor and then takes the stairs up to the 20th floor.
>
> What is the reason for his strange behavior?

The official answer to this puzzle is that the man is very short. He can reach the bottom floor button in the morning, but on the way home he can only reach as high as the 10th floor button. If it's raining, he has his umbrella and can use that to push the higher buttons. If someone else is in the elevator, he can ask them to push the 20th floor button.

This kind of puzzle is like a murder mystery novel where the author forgot to give you all of the clues. There's one canonical answer and it fits, but there's no reasonable way you could deduce it from the description of the situation alone.

As an interview puzzle, this story mostly tests whether you've heard the puzzle before. A more realistic puzzle along the same lines might be, "The prices and quantities look correct, and the subtotal checks out, but the grand total is off." The answer to that puzzle would be, "Let's look at the code that calculates sales tax, shipping, and handling." That kind of puzzle isn't as fun, but it's also more appropriate and less frustrating for the candidate.

One obvious drawback to the mystery story puzzle is that it's not too hard to come up with alternative explanations that work just as well as the official solution.

In the elevator story, for example, the man might be having an affair with a woman who lives on the 10th floor. He stops to see her and then later walks up the remaining flights of stairs so no one seems him getting onto the elevator at the 10th floor. If someone else is present when he first gets into the elevator, he rides to the 20th floor so no one sees him getting off at the 10th floor. Finally, the woman's husband is an avid kite fighter who flies kites in the afternoon and. If it's rainy, he doesn't fly his kite and goes home instead. In that case, the man skips his daily visit.

Fortunately there may be a way to turn the story puzzle's weakness into an advantage.

Instead of just presenting candidates with a story and then watching them flounder, you could describe the official solution. Then you could work with the candidate to see how many other explanations you can come up with together. You can take turns proposing facts that account for parts of the story while the other person looks for holes in your hypotheses.

You won't learn whether the candidate has seen that particular story before (although you could ask), but you may learn whether he's a creative thinker and more importantly whether you can work together.

FULL HOUSE

Puzzle: The Old Woman Who Lived in a Shoe went out to run some errands and left her nine children home to amuse themselves with various activities.

- Alfonse is playing *League of Legends* online.
- Beatrice is drawing cartoons.
- Charles is making a soufflé.
- Denise is watching funny videos on her smartphone.
- Edward is playing chess.
- Francine is fixing the broken refrigerator.
- Gerald is texting with his girlfriend.
- Harriette is playing fetch with the dog.

What is Ian doing?

If you think carefully about each of the children's activities, you'll notice that most of them are doing something solitary or with remote friends. The exception is Charles, who is playing chess. Because everyone else is busy, Ian must be playing chess with Charles.

As is the case with many of these "outside the box" puzzles, it's very easy to remember this puzzle's solution if you've seen it before.

SPEED RACER

Puzzle: Suppose you're competing in the Daytona 500 and you pass the car that's in second place. What position are you in now?

The tempting answer is that you're in first place. However, if you just passed the second place car, then you haven't yet passed the first place car, so you are now in second place.

> **Follow–up:** Suppose you pass the car that's in last place. What position are you in now?

This only happens if you lap the last place car. You could be in first place, but others may have also lapped the last place car. All you really know is that you're not in last place.

SUMMARY

These puzzles are designed to test creative thinking and the ability to think of unusual solutions. Usually the thing that makes them interesting is that their solutions are clever, and unfortunately that makes them both difficult to figure out and easy to remember if you've seen them before.

The solutions may seem clever to you after you're in on the joke, but they're not very amusing to a candidate who just failed to solve them.

PROGRAMMING EXERCISES

Unfortunately the nature of "outside the box" thinking makes it hard to write programming solutions for them. Unless you have some *serious* artificial intelligence skills, it's going to be hard to write programs to solve most of these problems.

1. Write a program to solve the "Egg Drop" puzzle. Make a method that takes as parameters the number of eggs you have available and the highest floor that you need to study. The method should return the maximum number of drops needed. If it has only one egg, the method must test each floor one at a time. Otherwise the method should call itself recursively to see what happens if the first egg breaks on each of the floors it's studying.

2. The straightforward solution to Exercise 1 makes the method recalculate the same partial solutions many times. For example, the program will call the method several times to calculate the number of steps needed to test the second egg when dropped from floor 5. Modify the program so it caches those values and doesn't need recalculate them.

3. Modify the program you wrote for Exercise 2 so it displays the floors from which the first egg is dropped. (The second column in Figure 17–3.)

4. Write a program that lets the user enter an integer N and then calculates how far north of the South Pole you need to be so that one walking mile east makes you take N laps around the pole and end up where you started.

Made in the USA
Middletown, DE
19 September 2017